The Year's Work in Medievalism

Edited by Gwendolyn A. Morgan

XXV
2010

WIPF & STOCK · Eugene, Oregon

The Year's Work in Medievalism
Series Editor, Gwendolyn Morgan

The Year's Work in Medievalism, volume XXV, is based upon but not restricted to the 2010 proceedings of the annual International Conference on Medievalism, organized by the Director of Conferences for the International Society for the Study of Medievalism, Gwendolyn Morgan, and, for 2009, Dr. Pam Clements. *The Year's Work in Medievalism* also publishes bibliographies, book reviews, and announcements for conferences and other events.

The 2010 volume is indexed in *The Modern Language Association International Bibliography.*

Copyright *International Society for the Study of Medievalism 2010*

ISSN 0899-3106
ISBN 978-1-60899-991-0

Wipf and Stock Publishers
199 West 8th Avenue, Suite 3
Eugene, OR 97401
www.wipfandstock.com

The Year's Work in Medievalism is an imprint of Studies in Medievalism. For the series, write Gwendolyn Morgan, Editor, *The Year's Work in Medievalism,* Department of English, Montana State University, Bozeman, MT 59717.

The Year's Work in Medievalism
Volume XXV 2010

Introduction:
Medievalism and the Popular Psyche

Gwendolyn A. Morgan

In its infancy, medievalism as a field of inquiry tended to concentrate on efforts to legitimize mainstream views—nationalistic, political, and social—by appealing to medieval precedent, just as the medievals themselves sought justification through ancient Classical authority. Arising at almost the same time, academic interest in popular culture appeared to do almost the opposite: legitimize "lowbrow" expressions and worldviews by appealing to nebulous ideas of democracy and Marxism. Collectively, this year's essays illustrate how the two have come together: how the various cross-currents of medievalism weave a single tapestry of the popular psyche. As we might expect, Umberto Eco's elucidation of the "ten little Middle Ages" offers a basic framework, providing the warp in his polarities of the "barbaric" and "romantic" re-imaginings of the period. Weaving through them are those things which we most often turn to the period to understand: sin and salvation, authority and identity, origins and purpose. In the last two decades, and complimenting such concerns, an immense popular fascination with the languages of the period—and the oral nature of its poetry—has manifested everywhere from fantasy novels, to film, to the music of the Goth subculture, as has a fearful fascination with the high medieval apocalyptic vision. In consequence, we have come to understand that, perhaps, it is now impossible to separate high art from low, the intelligentsia from the common man. Through the lens of medievalism, all are one.

One might, perhaps, consider Catholic identity least suspect of the taint of popular culture, rooted as it is in the great theological debates of the Middle Ages. To wit, Richard Utz discovers in the Church's early twentieth-century condemnation of George Tyrell a violent reaction to the "modernism" seeping into Catholic thought, a condemnation which appeals to medieval traditions, practices, and authority as "original" and somehow sanctified. However, as Utz goes on to point out, much medieval theology itself constituted a rebellion against ancient authority, where "medievalism" was, in fact, the "modernism" of that era. Later, Vatican II went on to embrace much of Tyrell's thought which, therefore, partially underlies the conservative faction of today's Catholicism. Yet in Tyrell's reasoning lies a popular and populist tenet, as true now as it was for him: that as long as man's thought, knowledge, and society evolve, the latter's institutions must embrace change, adapting and evolving themselves in order to preserve the truths and spirit that are its essence. In short, Tyrell's was a Catholicism of popular culture.

Martha Oberle, detailing the continued medieval traditions among contemporary orders of monks and friars, ultimately also finds herself commenting upon their effects on popular culture. Naturally, given that the mendicant orders were in their conception concerned with the needs of the populace—establishing and/or serving in schools and hospitals, tending to the poor, ministering to the spiritual needs of the great and common alike—they are set apart from high church policy and administration. More interesting, perhaps, are the results of their missionary work in the New World. Aside from establishing a toehold for the Catholic faith, they left their legacy in place names, architectural and furniture styles, and national iconography, most notably in the Alamo, formerly the Franciscan mission San Antonio de Valera.

Appeals to medieval precedent in affirmation of national identity similarly cannot be separated from the popular sensibility. Chelsea Gunter's examination of Paul Celan's DU SEI WIE DU shows how the poem weaves three languages—Hebrew, Modern German, Middle High German—along with direct quotations in the latter from a sermon by Meister Eckhart into a mystical interpretation of Jewish history which, in turn, defines an identity for the German Jew. Still more intricate is the process examined in William Calin's discussion of modern Breton and Occitan nationalist movements. He finds the centuries-old practice of locating one's roots in the Middle Ages has become a primary strategy for these populist factions, frequently centering on the distinctiveness of the regional dialects. Revolutionary rather than mainstream, and advocating a modern sense of brotherhood among marginalized groups, the separatists of these regions nonetheless appeal to medieval tradition to justify their claims as independent nations.

Interestingly, the heavy reliance on languages historically and currently distinct from French evident in the Occitan and Breton separatist movements appears to reflect a fascination with medieval languages in general, which permeates popular expression in the last two decades.

Sturli Gunnarsson's film *Beowulf and Grendel* (2006) actually employs language to distinguish the levels of social evolution evident in the three primary cultures in the film: Icelandic for the trolls, Cockney English for the Danes, Scottish for the Geats. More recently, Zemeckis's CGI *Beowulf* (2007/8) returns to the Anglo-Saxon language of 1000 years ago to distinguish the monsters from the humans, among other thematic purposes, and without any resort to subtitles.[1] In fantasy novels, following the early lead of J.R.R. Tolkien, authors have returned to ancient languages for dialogue and/or as the basis for invented tongues within the fiction. Jana Schulman's discussion of the blockbuster *Eragon* notes Christopher Paolini's reliance on Old Icelandic and Old Norse, as well as his retelling of ancient Germanic myth, in his fantasy epic, noting in passing that such has become a common practice with contemporary fantasy authors.

Perhaps equally interesting in Schulman's analysis of *Eragon* is her observation that the author, in adapting and retelling a number of ancient myths, actually mimics the practice of an Anglo-Saxon *scop*, the ancient English (and indeed any oral tradition[2]) poetic custom of finding artistic merit in the *how* of such retellings. Such, of course, is not so very far removed from the practices of modern film in any purported retelling of an ancient tale (*First Knight*, *The Knight's Tale*, any of the Beowulf or Arthurian renderings, and so forth). It is not, however, a new practice. Arthur Russell seeks for just such changes in the first productions of Leonard MaNally's 1874 comic opera *Robin Hood;*

or, Sherwood Forest once it crossed the Atlantic to the American stage. Songs from the original are re-assigned, others added, to cater to American tastes and imaginings of the Middle Ages, as much a part of national identity for the United States as for England. Returning to the present, Ed Risden's new stage play—printed herein for the first time—is based on the tenth-century poem *The Battle of Maldon*. Also comic, the play on one level deflates medieval heroism, while also concentrating on language and story-telling. The ancient English heroes relate the battle—but more importantly their speeches at it—to a reporter and in the presence of a (first) female secretary to Church authority. Whether intentionally or not, the frequent discussions of English grammar and other elements of oral expression in Risden's play elucidate the evolution of the language itself, as well as oral poetic expression. Immediately preceding it in this volume is my own imitative translation of the original poem,[3] offered for purposes of comparison to elements therein. Nonetheless, the collection originally including it also indicative of the contemporary taste for experiencing ancient English poems, first evident in the overwhelmingly positive acceptance of Seamus Heaney's rendering of *Beowulf*, just over a decade ago.

T. S. Miller's analysis of the Beowulf tradition in contemporary popular music, evident in the professional names adopted by performers, songs involving incidents and characters from the Anglo-Saxon epic, and thematic albums, elucidates yet another aspect of contemporary obsession with not only medieval epic but language and oral tradition. Of particular note is the prominence of monsters—Grendel, his Mother, the dragon—as sympathetic and even heroic characters in the genre. Such is, indeed, indicative of the radical demand for recognition of marginalized groups, but also seems to reflect a morbid, at times nihilistic, obsession with sin, salvation, and the apocalypse as depicted in medieval texts. Monsters are thus frequently sympathetic, despite their monstrosity. Aspen Hougen finds the same to be true in her analysis of the fictional vampire's devolution from object of divine punishment to hapless victim of disease. While the process certainly reflects modern understanding of blood-borne disease as well concern for various pandemics (cholera, AIDS, etc.), it nonetheless does not entirely allay the association of plague with ill moral health. Also in common with Miller, Hougen locates the (sometimes vengeful) claims of social outsiders in the contemporary fascination with the sympathetic vampire. Nonetheless, both the Beowulfian monsters and the vampire, whether defiantly so or not, retain their association with immoral behavior, whether as cause or result of their monstrosity and, as Hougen also notes, the medieval understanding of terrible disease as a consequence of moral choice persists in many sectors of society, not only with AIDS but others such as cirrhosis and cancer.

The equation of disease to immorality also resurfaces in the monsters of Post-Apocalyptic science fiction, according to Peter Johnsson. In this genre, they regain their full medieval association with evil and punishment from God, frequently dividing survivors of global holocaust along lines of good and evil, sin and virtue, with redemption the goal of the non-monstrous. Indeed, apocalypse is almost always attributable to the sins of modern society—technological, moral, or social—and retains strong associations with supernatural retribution. The most persistent imagery such fantasies employ, Johnsson finds, echoes medieval depictions—particularly those of Dante—of Purgatory. The same is true of William Morris's Froissartian poems, according to Gerald Nachtwey. Creating narratives around incidents reported in the Chronicles of Jean Friossart, Morris illuminates the evil hidden within the medieval period so romanticized by his pre-Raphaelite associates and contemporaries. The silence which results from the inability to deal with such inhumanity is also the silence of his own era regarding their similar collective moral guilt. Morris's poems result in frozen images reminiscent of Dante, accusatory in their silent horror. A century later, the melding of medieval and modern image continues as a critique of social ills, evident in Sanders and Birks' recent updating of Dante's *Inferno*, examined by Karl Fugelso. Their illustrations are at once reflective of their medieval predecessors, suiting punishment to sin, and directly referential of the ills of contemporary American culture: consumerism, pollution, technological immorality, inhumanity to man.

When one considers the medievalism of contemporary popular culture as a whole, several things become evident. First, we must dismiss intellectual elitism, if the average movie fan of CGI *Beowulf* is expected to grasp the basics of exchanges in Anglo-Saxon (also expected of Peter Jackson's *Lord of the Rings* audience); if the *New York Times* best-seller list includes an imitative translation of *Beowulf*; if popular stage and popular music depend upon a familiarity with ancient English epic. Second, while sin and salvation, and their relation to the global apocalypse, have changed their garb, they retain their medieval equation, and the popular concern with redemption from evil has not diminished. Third, while we continue, as Eco suggests, to seek our proverbial childhoods and our *raison d'être* in the Middle Ages, we have become inclusionist despite our guise of separatism. Ten years ago, eminent medievalist Tom Shippey wrote of the dangers of medievalism; I should like to compliment that with the assertion of the salvation offered by medievalism, as evinced by the essays in this collection, and by the sophisticated popular view they collectively indicate. We academic medievalists have long desired recognition of the importance of our field. It has arrived, in the most potent of all social forces, popular opinion and popular world view. Let us embrace it, bask in it, and encourage it as we remain cognizant of its "dangers."

MONTANA STATE UNIVERSITY

NOTES

1   I have examined the use of language and dialect in Gunnarsson's film at length in my article "Beowulf and the Middle Ages in Film," *The Year's Work in Medievalism: 2009* , ed. Amy Kauffman, Eugene, OR: Wipf and Stock, 2010. In the same essay, the

use of Anglo-Saxon—along with the rather startling assumption that the CGI *Beowulf*'s audience needs no interpretation of it—is also discussed in detail.

2   One need only return to Albert's landmark study *The Singer of Tales* (Cambridge: Harvard UP, 1960) for confirmation of this universal characteristic of oral poetry.

3   Originally published in Gwendolyn A. Morgan, *Anglo-Saxon Poems in Imitative Translation*, Lewiston: Edwin Mellen, 2001.

Pi(o)us Medievalism vs. Catholic Modernism: The Case of George Tyrell

Richard Utz

In Lent of 1908, Desiré Mercier, Cardinal Archbishop of Malines and Primate of Belgium, wrote a Pastoral Letter to his diocesan flock on the subject of modernism. Although he assured his people that Belgium was mostly free from this contemporary threat, he informed them that there were representatives of modernist thought in the Catholic Church. Intriguingly, Mercier mentioned only one single such representative who had "best divined its spirit" and was "more deeply imbued with it than any other," an "English priest" by the name of "Tyrell."[1] It is difficult to surmise how Mercier's original audience reacted to a Pastoral Letter about a supposedly grave general threat for Catholicism when it could only be substantiated by the opinions of one completely unknown English priest. What his audience would have needed is at least a modicum of contextualization.

The immediate context

Two years prior, the Anglo-Irish Father George Tyrell had been expelled from the Society of Jesus. After getting in trouble with local and Roman censors because of his critical views, Tyrell had realized the unsustainability of his position in the Catholic Church, exploring, according to historian Gabriel Daly, the possibility of leaving the Jesuit Order "in a manner that would satisfy the requirements of canon law and his own sense of honour."[2] After the publication of some excerpts from Tyrell's privately circulated "Letter to a University Professor" in the *Corriere de la Sera*, he was dismissed from the Society of Jesus in February 1906 on the specific request of Pope Pius X. As a suspended priest, Tyrell's problem was now to find a bishop who would accept him in his diocese, and he found such a temporary 'home' at the English convent of Bruges in Belgium. Mother Mary Stanislaus, the convent's prioress, requested that Archbishop Mercier intervene on behalf of Tyrell with Rome. Mercier inquired with Cardinal Ferrata, Prefect of the Congregation of Bishops and Religious, and consequently offered Tyrell to remain in his diocese as long as he would "pledge himself formally not to publish anything on religious matters nor engage in epistolary correspondence" without the approval of the cardinal's designee.[3] Tyrell considered these conditions unacceptable and moved on to Storrington in Sussex.

In September 1907, after Pope Pius X promulgated his conservative encyclical, *Pascendi Dominici Gregis* ("Feeding the Lord's Flock"), Tyrell, upon invitation to respond to the Encyclical by the *Giornale d'Italia* and *The (London) Times*, expressed his criticism openly and unhesitatingly. One month later, the bishop of Southwark, Peter Amigo, informed him that the Holy See had decided to deprive him of the sacraments due to his published opposition to the Encyclical. Only shortly thereafter, Cardinal Mercier embarked on a series of anti-modernist activities, culminating in an anti-modernist speech at the University of Louvain and the 1908 Lenten Pastoral, which condemned Tyrell.[4] Tyrell, in turn, wrote to Mercier, announcing that he would respond to the gratuitous mention of his name in a small volume and asking permission to reprint Mercier's Pastoral Letter to provide context. Mercier agreed, and Tyrell produced his response within six weeks. The book he wrote, *Medievalism. A Reply to Cardinal Mercier* (1908), became quite widely known, perhaps mainly because it recommended replacing the centralized authoritarianism of late nineteenth- and early twentieth-century Roman Catholicism with an almost democratic, certainly more consultative conception of the church.

What is most fascinating to scholars of medievalism about this episode in twentieth-century church history is Tyrell's confrontation of Pope Pius X's Roman medievalism with his own Catholic modernism. The term "Modernist," Tyrell states in chapter XVI of his treatise,

> has been used in a sufficient variety of senses to cause a considerable amount of confusion. If not invented, it has, at least, been established by the Encyclical *Pascendi* as the prejudicial designation of a party in the Roman Catholic Church. But already it is accepted as the designation of liberal Christians of all sorts, and bids fair to supplant the older term "liberal," which, as standing for a political as well as a religious principle, is somewhat less exact. "Modernist" as opposed to "modern" means the insistence on modernity as a principle. It means the acknowledgement on the part of religion of the rights of modern thought; of the need of effecting a synthesis, not between the old and new indiscriminately, but between what, after due criticism, is found to be valid in the old and the new. Its opposite is Medievalism, which, as a fact, is only the synthesis effected between the Christian faith and the culture of the late Middle Ages, but which erroneously supposes itself to be of apostolic antiquity; which denies that the work of synthesis is necessary and must endure as long as man's intellectual, moral, and social evolution endures; which therefore makes the medieval expression of Catholicism its primitive and final expression. (pp. 132-33)

Tyrell then condenses the opposition of both terms even more:

> Medievalism is an absolute, Modernism a relative term. The former will always stand for the same ideas and institutions; the meaning of the latter slides on with the times. If we must have a sect-name, we might have a worse than one that stands for life and movement as against stagnation and death [...]. (p. 133)

It is clear from this section that Tyrell's book was more than a specific response to Cardinal Mercier's specific mention of his name in his Lenten Pastoral. Since Mercier had made him the poster child of modernist tendencies within the Catholic Church, Tyrell retaliated as the spokesperson for the numerous

Catholic thinkers who were opposed to the medievalist turn Rome had taken since the mid-nineteenth century.

The broader context

The *Catholic Encyclopedia* (1904-1912), a project that began four years before and was completed five years after Tyrell's treatise was published, provides an authoritative contemporary source for the broader context of the controversy. In its entry on "modernism," the *Encyclopedia* summarizes Pope Pius X's encyclical *Pascendi* and, consequently, condemns Catholic modernists' views as heretical. Aiming at a "radical transformation of human thought in relation to God, man, the world, and life, here and hereafter, which was prepared by Humanism and eighteenth-century philosophy, and solemnly promulgated at the French Revolution," modernism's goals were a

> spirit of complete emancipation, tending to weaken ecclesiastical
> authority; the emancipation of science, which must traverse every field of
> investigation without fear of conflict with the Church; the emancipation
> of the State, which should never be hampered by religious authority; the
> emancipation of the private conscience whose inspirations must not be
> overridden by papal definitions or anathemas; the emancipation of the
> universal conscience, with which the Church should be ever in agreement;
> A spirit of movement and change, with an inclination to a sweeping form
> of evolution such as abhors anything fixed and stationary; A spirit of
> reconciliation among all men through the feelings of the heart. Many and
> varied also are the modernist dreams of an understanding between the
> different Christian religions, nay, even between religion and a species of
> atheism, and all on a basis of agreement that must be superior to mere
> doctrinal differences.[5]

In many ways, Rome's far-reaching attack against a vague "Modernism" within its own ranks was little more than the creation of a mythical negative model for the church's response toward various aspects of the modern world. Powerless against an ever-accelerating modernity, Rome decided to bring to bear Draconian measures against its own dissidents, thereby revitalizing the Catholic will to resist modernity on its own terms. This process can be said to begin in 1863, when Pope Pius IX condemned the existence in Germany of a movement, consisting of exactly one scholar by the name of Ignaz von Döllinger, who had attacked the sterile scholasticism of historical scholarship in the Latin countries. Rome's ensuing clericalism, papal pretence to unrestrained control over all scholarship, and affirmation of scholasticism as the language of that control, were all part, in the words of Thomas O'Meara, of a "militant and successful neoscholasticism" that brought "energy and formal clarity to Catholic theology; it also brought limitations, controversy, and intolerance."[6] Pius X's encyclical *Pascendi* as well as the suppression of Tyrell's views were only two examples of Rome's long-term ecclesiological strategy, which also included

Pope Leo XIII's 1879 encyclical letter *Aeterni Patris*. That Encyclical made not just scholasticism in general, but Thomism in particular, the compulsory philosophico-theological foundation for the entire church.[7]

Pi(o)us Medievalism vs. Catholic Modernism

This is not the place to speak of the wide-ranging reception of Tyrell's treatise. While Tyrell passed away only two years after the publication of *Medievalism*, his voice gave hope and inspiration to numerous Catholic thinkers who did not dare speak their minds in the McCarthyite atmosphere dominating their contemporary church.[8] However, the methodological brilliance of Rome's radical return to medieval scholasticism as well as Tyrell's outraged resistance against that return deserves some consideration.

In its most abstract simplification, the controversy is grounded in two mutually exclusive perceptions of temporality. Ever since the Protestant Reformation, Roman Catholicism had been under pressure to defend its most precious tenets, all of which were developed during the 1000 years that commonly circumscribe the medieval period. Continually assailed and forced to assimilate revolutionary scientific findings that would debunk the medieval view of humanity, nature, and the universe, Catholicism found itself at a decisive disadvantage against Protestantism which, as a post-medieval and even anti-medieval development, was able to incorporate, if not embrace, most early modern and modern inventions, discoveries, and mentalités. If early sixteenth-century artists, writers, and thinkers had no trouble bridging, let's say, the more than 1900-year-long temporal gap between Alexander the Great's victory over the Persians at Issus in 333 and their own time, the perception of historical distance had undergone a remarkable process of temporalization by the second half of the eighteenth and early nineteenth century.[9] Enlightenment philosophers and the French Revolution left no doubt that the long Middle Ages that had supported the particular symbiosis between monarchs and Roman Catholicism had come to an end, that the medieval past and the modern present had become two utterly non-contiguous points in history separated by an unbridgeable chasm of time. Immanuel Kant's denial of the capacity of human reason to come to know God or affirm his existence through sensory perception can be seen as only the best-known philosophical representation of that temporal distance.

The application of some of the new historico-critical methodologies in philosophy, history, archaeology, philology, anthropology, and sociology to the subject of theology destabilized foundational traditional beliefs, such as the inerrancy of scripture and many other, mostly external norms and obligations to a point where Rome decided to consolidate its position by denying any and all temporal distance between the church's medieval origins and its modern present. Once this strategy had been implemented, any Catholic who, like Tyrell, would publicly promote an organic growth and development of faith over time, seek to express traditional truths in new ways, and remain open to modern society and contemporary intellectual speculation was collectively branded a modernist and disciplined and silenced. Small wonder, then, that any uses of the term "medievalism" in the *Catholic Encyclopedia* of 1917 would focus on pro-medieval implications: Thus, Renaissance Humanists like Giambattista Vico and Lorenzo Valla are said to have made scholastic logic "the object of their merciless attack against medievalism;" the famous architect and archaeologist Augustus Welby Northmore Pugin is praised for having "fought for the Christian inspiration of medievalism as against the cold paganism of the classic style." And German literary romanticism's "predilection for medievalism" is credited with promoting a religious revival that "gave to the romantic movement a pronounced Catholic tendency" and rescued art from the "sway" of enlightenment rationalism.[10]

George Tyrell, whom Rome turned into one of the scapegoats for an entire movement of so-called "modernists" in the Catholic Church, chose to define medievalism as a term encompassing everything retrograde and reactionary. Similar to several other writers and thinkers who, trained in modern historical categories, recognized the temporal character of historical responses to the Christian faith, Rome's return to the Middle Ages meant to him that his church's response to the religious problems of the modern age were now little more than the reiteration of Christian truths formulated and systematized in the thirteenth century. Thus, they were without argued connection and re-evaluation for contemporary Christianity. As Oliver Rafferty explains, Tyrell

> believed that in some respects the idea of eternal punishment for sins sat uneasily with the idea of a God who took the suffering and sins of humanity upon himself so that we might be saved. He thought that in some respects the Church's teaching on hell was both cruel and unjust. But perhaps the boldest statement of all was his assertion that a certain 'temperate agnosticism' about the prescriptions of Catholicism in matters such as hell was an essential prerequisite for intelligent faith.[11]

Tyrell's desire for an intelligent faith, one that would adapt to the cultural environment in which Christians practiced it, would be acknowledged fifty years after his death by the Second Vatican Council, which cut many an umbilical cord between medieval ritual and twentieth-century society, but also ushered in a more welcoming attitude toward historical criticism and the application of modern scientific criticism to Biblical exegesis.[12]

In 1907, Tyrell's particular brand of intelligent modern Catholicism was unacceptable and suffered, after his death, the final insult of Pi(o)us medievalism. Since Tyrell could not be buried according to Catholic rites, some of his friends arranged for him to be buried in the Anglican churchyard at Storrington, Sussex, ironically in a spot almost exactly halfway between the Catholic and Anglican churches. The French priest, and former Jesuit, Abbe Henri Bremond read some prayers and gave a funeral address. Thus, in the words of Oliver Rafferty, was laid to rest one of the most intriguing thinkers the Church in this country has produced in modern times. The issues he dealt with are still germane to our own age and time, and will be for every age. Tyrrell was ultimately concerned with the question of how to make Christianity meaningful in a scientific age, of how to recast the formulation of Christian belief in a manner that made sense to the 'modern' world. The idea of adaptability has, in another context, been well summarised by [Cardinal] Newman in a maxim that could serve as a motto for life as a whole: 'to live is to change, and to be perfect is to have changed often'.

WESTERN MICHIGAN UNIVERSITY

NOTES

1   Gabriel Daly translated Cardinal Mercier's "Foreword" in George Tyrell, *Medievalism. A Reply to Cardinal Mercier* (Tunbridge Wells, Kent: Burns & Oates, 1994), p. 8.
2   Daly, "Foreword," p. 8.
3   M. D. Petre, *Autobiography and Life of George Tyrell* (London: Edward Arnold, 1912), volume 2, p. 504.
4   Daly, "Foreword," p. 12.
5   *The Catholic Encyclopedia* (1917); online: http://newadvent.org/cathen/10415a. htm; accessed January 12, 2010.
6   Thomas F. O'Meara, *Church and Culture: German Catholic Theology, 1860-1914* (Notre Dame, IN: U of Notre Dame P, 1991), p. 25.
7   Gabriel Daly, "Theological and Philosophical Modernism," in Darrell Jodock, ed., *Catholicism Contending with Modernity: Roman Catholic Modernism and Anti-Modernism in Historical Context* (Cambridge: Cambridge University Press, 2000), pp. 88-112, here pp. 102-103, explains: "In an unprecedented act – Rome normally kept out of disputes between the schools – Leo wrote to the General of the Franciscans informing him that the Order was not free to follow St. Bonaventure and Scotus, if it meant departing from the mind of St. Thomas."
8   For an excellent contextualization of the controversy, see David Wells, "The Pope as Antichrist: The Substance of George Tyrrell's Polemic," *Harvard Theological Review* 65/2 (1972), 271-83.
9   For a discussion of the fundamental change in the perception of time and the past during the early modern era, see Reinhart Kosellek, *Futures Past: On the Semantics of Historical Time* (New York: Columbia UP, 2004), pp. 9-10. For the impact of this change for the study of medievalism, see Richard Utz, "*Medievalitas Fugit*: Medievalism and Temporality," *Studies in Medievalism* 18 (2009), 32-43.
10   See the entries on "Gothic architecture," "Pugin," "German literature," and "logic" in the online version of the *Catholic Encyclopedia* at http://newadvent.org/cathen/.
11   "George Tyrell and Catholic Modernism," online: http://www.thinkingfaith.org/articles/20090706_1.htm.
12   On this issue see Bruce Holsinger's summary description in *The Premodern Condition: Medievalism and the Making of Theory* (Chicago: U of Chicago P, 2005) p. 160.

The Legacy of Medieval Mendicant Orders

Martha Oberle

A long time ago, one particular, well-known, and oft reviled late medieval politico directed his aides to take the body of his royal, and dead, relative to Whitefriars; the trains on one route of today's London Underground stop at Blackfriars. Black, white—who were these friars and what are they to us? The short answer is that the varying orders drew their names from the style of their habits: Blackfriars are the Dominicans; Whitefriars are the Carmelites, and gray, the Franciscans. Missing from the sartorial designations are the Augustinians, who are the fourth of the mendicant orders, and the Benedictines, whose everyday name recognition springs not from dress but from the fine brandy made in the Order's monasteries. To be precise, the Benedictines are monks, cloistered or cenobitic, whereas the other four are friars, living in community in convents, usually in the towns.

The basic history of each of the Mendicant Orders offers some insight into the functions of those orders in the medieval world and in our own time. The two-fold mission of Francis' (1182-1226) followers was to alleviate the suffering and burdens of the poor or marginalized as well as to preach repentance (Dickinson 88-9). Saints Bernardine of Siena and James of the Marches come to the minds of students of the early Renaissance, and Leonardo Boff and Liberation Theology to modern minds.

Dominic's (1170-1221) first instruction, from the Pope, was to preach and to teach, a mission which has become the defining mark of his followers. Preaching is done through word and through deed ("The Fundamental Constitutions"). One cannot, or should not, preach what he does not know (Knowles, *Evolution*, 231; Dickinson 90); the study following from that maxim has given us the thinking of Albertus Magnus and the great Thomas, as well as the continuing tradition of Dominican schooling and scholarship. That scholarship currently includes, in the light of new findings, a re-examination of the documents of Scripture.

The Carmelites began as hermits on Mount Carmel, but driven out by the strife over the Holy land, moved to Europe and to England. Their governance, the Rule of Albert, modified by Innocent IV, allows a shift from eremitical life to a ministry simultaneously contemplative and pastoral. Brought to England by Richard de Grey, a returning Crusader, landholder and member of the lesser gentry, the Carmelites first establish themselves at Aylesford in 1242 (Carmelites.org; the friars.org/UKhistory). Abiding by the final mandate of their Rule, "See that common sense is the guide of the virtues" (Welch 181; *Albert's Way* 21), these friars went wherever their abilities, the needs of the people, and the opportunity to minister came together (Lawrence 267). Gradually, they gravitated to the University towns and moved into the middle and upper levels of society, to the point that they became preferred priests and confessors in the court of John of Gaunt (Knowles, *Evolution;* House of White Friars). In such a context, that Shakespeare should send the corpse of Henry VI (1421-71; 1422-61 & 1470-71) to Whitefriars makes perfect sense.

But as is so frequently the case with Shakespeare, there is a bit more to the picture. Initially, according to Shakespeare (*Richard III*, I, ii, 225) the bearers of Henry's body had been headed to Chertsey, the Benedictine abbey some 16 miles from London. In fact, according to a number of Chronicles, Henry's body was to go to St. Paul's, then to Blackfriars, and from Blackfriars to Chertsey (Myers 317-19). Did Shakespeare's pen slip? Were the editors of the First Folio asleep, or does something other obtain? Shakespeare cannot be accused of revisionist history because he was not an historian but a dramatist. In fact, there was a Whitefriars in the heart of London, and again in fact, Henry IV (1367-1413: 1399-1413), first of the Lancastrian kings, did have a Carmelite confessor. David Knowles writes, "During the reign of the first three Edwards, the Order of Preachers are acting, by dispensation, as household chaplains to the great, and for some 200 years without a break, the post of royal confessor was given to the friars. From the reign of Henry III to Richard II, they were sole confessors to the kings although the House of Gaunt favored the Carmelites, who held the office through the reign of Henry IV. At Stephen Partington's death [1417], Henry V returned to the Order of Preachers" (Knowles, *Religious Houses* 167). What Shakespeare has really written, then, is a bit of medievalism: he has brought a fact of the late Middle Ages, Henry IV's preference for the Carmelites, forward to the late 16th century in order, in high literary style, to bring the House of Lancaster full circle. Whitefriars counseled the ascendant Henry IV; Whitefriars will receive the corpse of the fallen Henry VI. From 1585 to the present, and with or without the appreciation of the audience, productions of Richard III have repeated Shakespeare's literary device.

We left Henry VI in Chertsey Abbey, but eventually Yorkist Richard III had his predecessor's body removed from the custody of the monks of Chertsey and re-interred in the safety of Windsor Castle (Wagner). However, that safety did not apply to Chertsey which, with many other abbeys and monasteries, fell prey to destruction by Henry VIII. Paradoxically, the number (about 800), the extent, and the variety of the ruins—Jervaux, Rivaux, Walsingham, Whitby destroyed, others plundered and left to fall into disrepair, and still others sold and converted to secular use—stand today in silent testament to the monastic power and influence Henry sought to demolish. Wordsworth, Turner, and Ellis Peters bring the images of Tintern, Bolton, and Shrewsbury Abbeys into our schools and homes, and the National Trust/British Heritage ensure the abbeys with their history, their architecture, and the stories of their defenders—some of whom were simply hanged and a few of whom were hanged, drawn and quartered at the time of the Dissolution—make their way to travel brochures and must-see lists.

Until the reign of Henry Tudor, however, the monks and friars constituted a continuing part of the political, economic, educational, and religious fabric of English society for centuries. Medieval kings might come and go—and they did—but the same cannot be said of the monks and friars.

The Benedictines were the first of the monastic groups to make their way to England. The Peterborough Chronicle, E-text, (*passim*) tells of their survival through the invasions of Angles, Jutes, Danes, Norse, and Normans. The Chronicle records the back and forth, the reciprocal relations between the monasteries and the kings. Monks became bishops and ambassadors; kings became monks. Prayer and ritual were certainly part of this exchange, but so also had to be a clear understanding of rule and administration. Abbots were in charge of monasteries, and the monastery has to be understood as holding and managing or overseeing vast acreage, farm land, mills, towns, and people(Jocelyn *passim*; Gerald *passim*). The monks let the fields, collected the rents, marketed the goods, and flourished, often to the point of great wealth. As the abbey grew, so usually did the town attached. In our modern world, Lego, the toy-maker, replicates that story: presently available are the directions and pieces necessary to re-create or re-construct, a "medieval market village."

The Chronicle of Jocelyn of Brakelond sets out the plan and functions of the parts and of the members of the monastic enclosure. The monasteries were destined to be self-sustaining, and the various monks had duties appropriate to the keeping of that endeavor. Jocelyn describes them: the cellarer ran the monastery's manor and all its holdings; the sacrist took care of the Church and other conventual buildings; the almoner's charge was the charity of the house; the chamberlain attended to the monks' clothes, and the guest master welcomed travelers. In short order, we will see a variant of this system of organization in the New World. Jocelin also notes that duties were assigned by the Abbot (88-99; Dickinson 98-103). Greenway and Sayers observe, "The abbot is God's tool and representative....The sixth century Rule of St. Benedict...describes the abbot as 'holding the place of Christ' in the monastery....For his... flock the abbot is responsible and answerable to God" (xxii, Wolter 661; Madden 84). As we shall soon see, Timothy Radcliffe OP, speaking in our own day, makes the same point.

The Dominicans (Blackfriars) came to England in 1221 (Dickinson 91). Passing by the ecclesiastical center, Canterbury, and the political hub, London, these men, the heirs of Albertus Magnus, Thomas Aquinas, and Meister Eckhart, made straight for Oxford where they lived in the section called Jewry, east of St. Aldate's, which still stands, and close to Christ Church ("First Priory"; Knowles, *Evolution* 661). According to Bede Jarrett, the first foundation was significant and speaks to the heart of the Dominican idea. "These friars arrived....They became part of the University, so much so that three served as Chancellor of Oxford, and one of these three also held that post at Cambridge." ("Second Priory"). Henry VIII forced the Oxford convent closed on August 31, 1538, of which destruction Dr. John London of Thomas Cromwell's staff writes, "There I defaced the church windows and the cells of the dorter...." ("Second Priory"). A hundred years later, Anthony Wood writes "not so much as one stone...give[s] testimony to the world that so famous a place as the college of the Dominicans at Oxon was there once standing" ("Second Priory").

Founded in 1223, Blackfriars in London cared for and defended the marginalized. From among those Dominicans in 1255 came the defenders of the

Jews accused of murdering Hugh of Lincoln, the matter of Chaucer's *Prioress'*
Tale. Today, the Dominicans of Oxford, Blackfriars in St. Giles, are once again
part of the University, and among their many pastoral ministries one is to the
disadvantaged children of a nearby suburb.

Coming to England under the leadership of Annelius of Pisa, the Franciscans
(Greyfriars) settled first, in dire poverty, at Canterbury (*A Concise History;*
"Franciscans Come"). However, the appeal and the effects of their ministry
were so great that within three years they had convents in Oxford and in
London. Entering into the intellectual fray at Oxford, as Bonaventure, Duns
Scotus, and Ockham had at Paris, they came to offer to that University and
to the rest of the world some of the best minds of the later Middle Ages:
Alexander of Hales, Robert Rufus, Roger Bacon (Southern 294-5; Sayles 377;
A Concise History). R.W. Southern notes the passion of the friars, Franciscan
and Dominican alike (298).

The Franciscan pastoral ministry ranged from the poorest of the poor—
and like some of the folk to whom they ministered, some of the first English
Franciscans picked scrap baskets for food—to those in very high places. Henry
VIII was among their English followers (Sayles 366-67; *A Concise History*).
However, the Franciscan position and Henry's ideas collided, and by Elizabeth's
reign the English Franciscan Province had removed to Douai (*Concise History*).
In the meanwhile, the Franciscans in Spain had come to the New World.

We have noted the relevance of the monks and friars in their own time:
spirituality, education, care for the poor, redressing of injustice, and holding
for their beliefs even in the face of exile or death. Such a fate is not restricted
to early modern times. The ever-developing disciplines of Philosophy and
Theology have come to include the works and writing of Edith Stein and Titus
Brandsma , Carmelites both, whose lives were lost at Auschwitz and Dachau,
respectively.

Perhaps the most efficient way to demonstrate the relevance of the monks
and friars in our own day is simply to point out that if we wished to close down
who knows how many elementary and secondary schools, innumerable clinics,
and several dozen colleges and universities in the United States, all we have
to do is send the monks and friars elsewhere. But doing so did not, and does
not, put them out of business. Coming with the Spaniards to South America,
the Franciscans moved across the Rio Grande and established themselves
in five missions in what is now San Antonio. The missions are Concepcion,
San Jose, San Antonio de Espada, San Juan Capistrano, and San Antonio
de Valera, which became a garrison and is far better known as the Alamo
(wwwlsjunction.com; www.tms.org). To this day, Texans regard—and insist all
visitors respect—the grounds of that chapel and fort as holy ground, not only
from the spiritual perspective but also as the dearly bought birthplace of the
Republic of Texas. By now,"Remember the Alamo" has become a watchword
of American patriotism and culture.

A second of those missions is widely known for an engineering feat that
calls to mind both Antiquity and the Middle Ages: San Antonio de Espada's

dam *cum* aqueduct is one of a kind, a built-backward dam of brush turned into cement by the lime salts in the waters of the San Antonio River (www.tms. org; www.uiw.edu/sanantonio; www.waymarking.com; wikipedia.org). The ditch carried the water pooled by the dam to the mission's fields, and working irrigation came to Texas. Four of the missions—Concepcion, San Juan, San Jose, and Espada—are active parishes (www.lsjunction.com) and now belong to the National Park System, the governmental entity whose function is to preserve for future generations the keystones of this country's cultural heritage and natural wonders. The fifth, the Alamo, belongs to the Daughters of Texas. Like the medieval Franciscan houses, all perform a teaching role.

Even as the settlers in the North were making their way through the Cumberland Gap, the Franciscans in the south central part of the country were making their way west and north, up the California coast to San Francisco. The route they established, the Camino Real, still exists and runs very much as it did in missionary days except that travel is now by car, truck, or motorcycle at speeds the friars could only dream of. That highway, which bears California historical markers all along its way, is Route 101, the major north-south thoroughfare along the California coast (California Missions). As they moved up the Coast, the Franciscans, instead of moving from town to town as they had in medieval Europe, founded missions, 24 in all, now memorialized not only by the windows in the Basilica of San Francisco (known as Mission Delores) but also in the very names of the cities of California: San Diego, Santa Cruz, San Jose, San Luis Obispo, San Miguel, and San Juan Capistrano, to mention a few. The furnishings of those missions were simple; they had to be, for travel was not easy and materials had to be used for survival. The simplicity and lovely proportion of that furniture can be seen not only in the museum of San Juan Bautista but also in many homes across the land, in pieces known by their design: Mission Style.

As they had in Texas, the friars brought with them the knowledge necessary to construct systems of irrigation, one of which, an aqueduct tapping the nearby river and leading to a reservoir, can easily be seen at Mission San Antonio near Jolon, California (Mission San Antonio's Visitor's Map). That mission now sits on eighty or so acres which, after the vast lands of the missions were secularized, eventually became part of the Hearst estate and is now surrounded by the property of the United States Army (Mission San Antonio De Padua Home Page). Thanks to that arrangement, a visitor can see not only the surviving buildings and foundations of the monastery structures but also sense the activity, size, and solitude of a mission. Just as Jocelin and Gerald had described centuries before, the fields of San Antonio were planted and harvested; livestock was raised and still is on the nearby ranches; orchards were planted, pruned and picked; people lived, learned, died, and were buried. The Church, the dorter, and the Indian cemetery are intact (Visitor's Map to Mission San Antonio). In sum, the organization of the medieval monastery served as pattern for the missions of Texas and California.

That Church music is an accomplishment of the Middle Ages is a given. That notes and scales are painted on the walls of Mission San Antonio as a teaching device indicates clearly that music had to have been part of the life of the Mission San Antonio community.

Although secularization took over the mission lands, the friars' agricultural contributions—for Jocelin and Gerald let the reader know that monasteries are farms—are very much with us. Mission San Juan Bautista keeps a Mission olive press in its museum. In 1769, Fra Junipero Serra was the first to bring wine grapes to California (www.bellavistaranch.net) and wine grapes first came to the Napa Valley with the founders of the Sonoma Mission in 1823 (www. bellavistaranch.net).

As for architecture, the missions resemble one another in their cloisters, bell towers, arches, red tile roofs, and design of the façade, elements handed down over the centuries and brought from Spain. That façade, as symbol of welcome and hospitality, is replicated in a number of La Quinta Inns, whose corporate home is Texas. Less obvious in terms of design and architecture is the tradition of the stone mason, those who work on buildings such as the National Cathedral in Washington and whose tools and tactics are much the same as they were for the men who, under the aegis of the monks and friars, worked on the churches of the medieval monasteries and the great medieval cathedrals (*Washington Post* ,C6, May 2,2010*)*.

In representations in every medium, the friars are pictured traveling in their cowled habits, with staff in hand. We know a form of that habit as the very popular outer gear, the hoodie.

Despite changes in time and place, coming down through the ages is a constant, the virtually unchanged Rules. Five great Rules guide the orders: the Rule of St. Benedict, the Rule of St. Augustine, the Rule of Dominic, the Rule of Francis, and the Rule of Albert. All offer guidelines for life in a monastery or convent under the supervision of a superior. To that superior, whether abbot or prior, the monks and friars owe obedience, not necessarily unquestioning, but necessarily total. Timothy Radcliffe writes, "When we accept a brother into the Order, we express our confidence that he will be capable of taking his place in the government of his community and province and help us to arrive at and implement fruitful decisions" (83). Radcliffe continues, "From the beginning we have arrived at these decisions democratically, by debate leading to voting. But what makes this process properly Dominican is that we are not seeking merely to discover what is the will of the majority but what are the needs of the mission….The test of good government is whether it is at the service of the mission"(85).

And what of Abbot or Prior? Radcliffe writes, "When you make profession you put your hands into the hands of your superior and you promise obedience" (199). He continues with an analogy to the natural world: the religious life as an ecosystem which enables the unusual and strange to flourish. "To be a religious is to choose a strange form of life…a good superior is an ecologist who helps his brethren build the necessary environments in which they may thrive" (229). Both abbot and novice thus have made a pledge of faith, and such an understanding is far from new in the secular world. Geoffrey of Monmouth states that before Arthur set off to single-handed combat, he had required that his knights not interfere, no matter the consequences. When Arthur falls, the knights are tempted to move to his rescue but before they can break their word, the King rises and slays his opponent (*History* 224.). The word Geoffrey uses is fedus, faith (Griscum, ed. *History*, 449); the agreement is a covenant. Quite different, according to Geoffrey, is the action of Modred, who struck bargains to gain allies in usurping Arthur's crown and state (Griscum, ed. *History* 496-7). Such action is a quid pro quo, a contract. As Geoffrey continues, he makes an implicit distinction between Arthur and his nephew: Arthur is killed by a blow struck in time of truce, a time of word given and then broken. The action is a type of quid pro quo: Modred breaks his word; he gets the crown. He gets, not necessarily something for the common good, but certainly something for himself.

In contrast, the abbot's actions are directed to the common good, the welfare of the priory. Responsibility, the ability to respond, rather than accountability, the ability to count, together with covenant rather than quid pro quo, lie at the heart of monastic government. In today's world, the prevailing modus operandi is often a version of the Deep Throat mentality: the way to determine cause and course of an action is to follow the money, quid pro quo.

But a certain well-know modern politico saw things a bit differently. Having determined a course of action and set out both the general and particular reasons for that action, one fraught with risk and uncertainty, Thomas Jefferson concludes, "For the support of this Declaration with a firm reliance on the protection of Divine Providence, we mutually pledge to each other our lives, our Fortunes and our Sacred Honor." Perhaps we are well advised to heed history, medieval and national, as we consider our actions and determine our course.

FREDERICK COMMUNITY COLLEGE

WORKS CITED

Albert's Way: The First North American Congress on the Carmelite Rule. Ed. Michael Mulhall, O. Carm. Rome: Institutum Carmelitarum. Barrington, IL: Province of the Most Pure Heart of Mary, 1989.

Benedictine Abbey of St. Peter, Chertsey. http://stpeterschertsey.f2s.com/StPeters/abbey/index.

California Missions. Santa Barbara: Map Link, 2000.

Dickinson, J.C. *Monastic Life in Medieval England*. London: Adam & Charles Black, 1961.

Dominicans in Oxford. "First Priory," "Second Priory," "Third Priory." Oxford: Blackfriars in St. Giles, nd.

Dominican Spirituality. Oxford: Blackfriars in St. Giles, nd.

Espada Acquia. http//enwikipedia.org/wiki/Espada_Acequia

Franciscans (of) Province of England. "A Concise History of the Friars in Britain 1224" http://www.friar.org/about-us/heritage.html

Friars—Aylesford. http:www.the friars.org.uk/history.htm

Friaries—Carmelite Friars. http:www.british-history.ac.uk/report.aspx?compid=39936

Friaries—The House of White Friars. http:www.british-history.ac.uk/report. aspx?compid=40198

Fundamental Constitutions of the Order of Friars Preachers. Oxford: Blackfriars in St. Giles,nd.

Geoffrey of Monmouth. *The History of the Kings of Britain.* Trans. and Ed. Lewis Thorpe. New York: Viking, 1987.

Geoffrey of Monmouth. *Historia Regum Brittaniae.* Ed. Acton Griscum. New York: Longmans, Green & Co., 1929.

Gerald of Wales. *The Journey through Wales. The Description of Wales.* London: Penguin, 1978.

Glimpses of Christian History. "Franciscans Come to England." http://www. christianhistorytimeline.com/DAILYF/22003/09/daily-09-10-2003.shtml

House of Benedictine Monks Abbey of Chertsey. http://www.british-history.ac.uk/report. aspx?compid=37813

Jocelin of Brakelond. *Chronicles of the Abbey of Bury St. Edmunds.* Trans. Diana Greenway and Jane Sayers. Oxford: UP, 1989.

Knowles, David. *The Evolution of Medieval Thought.* New York: Vintage Books, 1962.

Knowles, David. *The Religious Orders in England.* Cambridge: Cambridge UP, 1959.

Lawrence, C.H. *Medieval Monasticism.* 2nd ed. New York: Longmans, 1989.

Lives of the Brethren of the Order of Preachers 1206-59. Trans. Placid Conway, OP. Ed. Bede Jarret, OP. London: Burns Oates and Washburne, 1924.

Madden, Richard, O.C.D. *Men in Sandals.* Milwaukee: Bruce Publishing, 1954.

Mission Espada Aqueduct. http://www.waymarking.com

Myers, A.R. and David Charles Douglas. *English Historical Documents.* London: Routledge, 1995.

Nigg, Walter. *Warriors of God.* New York: Alfred A. Knopf, 1959.

Peterborough Chronicle. Trans. Harry A. Rositzke. New York: Columbia UP, 1951.

Radcliffe, Timothy OP. *Sing a New Song.* Dublin: Dominican Publications, 1999.

Sayles, G.O. *The Medieval Foundations of England.* New York: A.S. Barnes, 1961.

Shakespeare, William. *Richard III.* The Pelican text Revised. Baltimore: Penguin, 1969.

Southern, R.W. *Western Society and the Church in The Middle Ages.* London: Penguin, 1990.

"The San Antonio River and its Seven Acequias." *Journal of the Life and Culture of San Antonio.* http://www.uiw.edu/sanantonio/sevenacquias.html

"The Five Spanish Missions of Old San Antonio". http://www.lsjunction.com/facts/ missions.htm

" TMS 2006 Annual Meeting and Exhibition". http://www.tms.org/Meetings/Annual-06/ AM06tours.html

War of the Roses: King Henry VI of England. httpp://www.luminarium.org/encyclopedia/ henry6.htm

Welch, John, O.Carm. *The Carmelite Way.* New York: Paulist Press, 1996.

Wheeler, Lucy. *Chertsey Abbey.* Wells, Gardner et al, Ltd. 1905. Institute of Medieval Studies, Toronto: Internet Archives.

Wolter, Maurice, O.S.B. *The Principles of Monasticism.* Trans. Bernard A. Sause, O.S.B. St. Louis: B. Herder. 1962.

"DU SEI WIE DU, immer":
Mysticism and Messianism in the poetry of Paul Celan[1]

Chelsea Gunter

DU SEI WIE DU, immer.	YOU BE LIKE YOU, ever.
Stant up Jherosalem inde	*Ryse up Jerosalem and*
erheyff dich	*rowse thyselfe*
Auch wer das Band zerschnitt zu dir hin,	The very one who slashed the bond unto you,
inde wirt	*and becum*
erluchtet	*yllumyned*
knüpfte es neu, in der Gehugnis,	knotted it new, in memorance,
Schlammbrocken schluckt ich, im Turm,	spills of mire I swallowed, inside the tower,
Sprache, Finster-Lisene,	speech, dark-buttress,
kumi	*kumi*
ori.	*ori.*

Of the various poems from Paul Celan's oeuvre that can be argued to echo the sermons of Meister Eckhart, it is only DU SEI WIE DU[2] that directly quotes the fourteenth-century mystic, and in his own language—Middle High German. The poem's inclusion of Hebrew and Modern German, as well as reference to Jerusalem, positions it within a specific historical context—that which prompted Adorno to write "Nach Auschwitz, ein Gedicht zu schreiben ist barbarisch." That Celan lifts directly from the sermon of a medieval mystic in a poem so placed suggests that mysticism—specifically mystical utterance—is central to his poetic enterprise as a German Jew. Moreover, Celan's incorporation of Eckhart in this poem, and his adoption of some of the rhetorical devices common to Eckhart's mystical tracts, point to a messianic interpretation of history characteristic of the criticism of Walter Benjamin. It is Benjamin's concept of origin, as that which is recognizable as a restoration, which is most useful for illuminating the movement of Celan's poem and the poet's ultimate revision of language as medium.

Mystical experience is, in a useful definition by Ninian Smart, "an interior or introvertive quest, culminating in certain interior experiences which are not described in terms of sense experience."[3] In other words, mystical experience cannot be described by everyday language. Rather than silence, though, mystics may use two methods to overcome the limitations of communicating experience—paradox and negation[4]—both of which Celan employs in DU SEI. In adopting these strategies, and in quoting directly Eckhart's imperatives to

"Ryse up Jerosalem / [...] / and becum yllumyned" in a poem that so clearly thematizes language, DU SEI is a summons for the undifferentiated nature of mystical speech. The achievement of such undifferentiated speech would be to make the medieval German and Hebrew pasts contemporary, thereby bridging the chasm between the unspeakable of the Holocaust, the past, and the present. In Celan's words, the poem expresses a desire for a mode of discourse that could communicate across the "thousand darknesses of death-bringing speech,"[5] forming a coherent historical reality where languages with such disparate political and cultural valences as Modern and Middle High German, and Hebrew, become equal. However, whether the poem insists on the reality of this possibility remains ambiguous; the imperative of Eckhart's text and the Hebrew of Isaiah—"kumi / ori"—demonstrate that the desire for undifferentiated speech is just that—a desire.

The motivation for Celan's ambiguous endorsement of metaphysical modes of speech becomes clearer when we read this poem in light of the discourse in and around Benjamin's "Task of the Translator." Paul Celan wrote DU SEI WIE DU from Jerusalem, in 1969, on his first journey there, a year before his suicide. In rendering present the languages that this poem does, Celan aligns himself with the fate of Jerusalem and sees in the city the messianic fulfillment of a particular historical trajectory. In the same way, DU SEI is fulfilled by the quoted "kumi / ori," or "arise / shine"—lines from the same passage of the Bible as those concerning the sermon of Eckhart's which Celan quotes: Isaiah 60:1. The poem, three languages in eleven lines, thus moves back, from Celan's German to Eckhart's to the Hebrew from which it derives, ending in words the poet had originally written in Hebrew script. In a movement towards origin, written from the imminent locale of that origin, Celan here highlights the generative, rhythm-shaping task of origin, and his uncertainty of the capacity for mystical language to engender religious enlightenment is a result of the incompleteness, the unfulfilled nature of this origin. In highlighting the way that origin sets the pace for the future, Celan inscribes, as Richard Wolin describes the work of Benjamin, an aesthetics of redemption.[6] As Benjamin writes, origin is a "springing forth that emerges out of a coming-to-be and passing away," which does not reach its messianic fulfillment and is always seeking after that which it will never achieve.[7] Writing DU SEI from Jerusalem imminent, the origin and inspiration for the Biblical passage he quotes, Celan causes the city to lose the mystical aspect of Eckhart's Jerusalem, and its fulfillment for Celan could only be anticipated.

While Celan's text is not a translation—his incorporation of Hebrew and Middle High German more an instance of *bricolage*—it shares in additional thematic concerns that appear in Benjamin's "Task of the Translator." In its desire for undifferentiated communication, DU SEI points towards translation's gesture to pure language as formulated by Benjamin. As Sam Weber, in *Benjamin's –abilities*, explains of the critic's essay, languages "relate not to human needs, which is to say to meanings as messages, but to what Benjamin calls 'pure language' [which] emerges out of the interplay of [...] their 'way (or mode) of signifying."[8] Ideal translations thus point to the mode of symbolization itself. This relation between languages—in Celan bricolage, in Benjamin translation—moves away from the original by "lead[ing] in the direction of other words and other meanings, exposing a complex and multidimensional network of signification."[9] This is what we may say Benjamin, via Weber's excursus, means by pure language: the way of meaning. And it is this for which Celan's urge toward undifferentiated speech ultimately calls, as Eckhart in his sermon had called for, too. This is the messianic teleology of DU SEI—the fulfillment of pure language itself.

Celan's task, like Benjamin's, so clearly touches upon a past. In its macaronic quality, diffusing the valence that each of the languages of DU SEI alone may have, it too, as Weber argues of Benjamin, redefines media. The lines "the very one who slashed the bond unto you" and "you be like you" we can construe as reimagining the interval between physical place that defines medium. Here, again, it is medium of poetry and translation, it is language, that Celan wishes his poem to fulfill: "kumi / ori." In its content and mode of expression, DU SEI WIE DU reenacts the movement towards origin and the redefinition of medium that is central to Benjamin's work; Celan's incorporation of Eckhart into this poem represents a sort of medievalism that is indistinguishable from messianism, a medievalism that is restoration, and it is perhaps no coincidence that Celan, like Benjamin, composed this work while meditating on the continuing legacy of German history.

INDEPENDENT SCHOLAR

NOTES

1   An earlier version of this essay was published in the Fall 2008 "Perception" edition of the New York University student journal *Anamesa*.
2   This is John Felstiner's translation. Felstiner translates Eckhart using the English of John Wycliffe's 1382 Bible from the Vulgate for the passage from Isaiah.
3   Smart, Ninian. "Interpretation and Mystical Experience," *Religious Studies* 1 (1965): 75.
4   Jones, Richard Hubert. "A Philosophical Analysis of Mystical Utterances." *Philosophy East and West*. 29.3 (1979): 255-274.
5   "Deathbringing" as a single word is Felstiner's innovation. Celan, Paul. "Der Meridian: Rede anlässlich der Verleihung des Georg-Büchner-Preises (1961)". *Selected Poems and Prose of Paul Celan*. Trans. John Felstiner. New York: W. W. Norton, 2001. 401-413.
6   Wolin, Richard. *Walter Benjamin: An Aesthetic of Redemption*. Berkeley: U of California P, 1994.
7   Weber, Samuel. *Benjamin's -abilities*. Cambridge: Harvard U P, 2008. 88.
8   Ibid. 90.
9   Ibid, 92.

Postcolonialism and Medievalism:
How French Regional Cultures/Literatures Reshape Their Past and Present

William Calin

In a recent issue of *The Year's Work in Medievalism* I discussed one facet of postcolonialism – Orientalism – and the Middle Ages, arguing that an early form of Orientalism formed an essential element in *chanson de geste* and courtly romance, that early medieval narrative was grounded in that latent Orientalism, and consequently that Orientalism and the reaching for Empire are intimately bound to the rise of the novel, taken in the broader sense of the term, the novel in the twelfth century and not the eighteenth, as proposed by Edward W. Said.[1]

This essay will scrutinize postcolonialism and medievalism from a different perspective: the impact of the Middle Ages on postcolonialism in French regional cultures today. I shall refer primarily to literature written in Occitan, the language in the South of France which used to be called Provençal, and in Breton, the Celtic language spoken in Brittany.[2]

We find many currents in postcolonial theory. As to be expected, scholars question how we should define the "post-" in postcolonial, whether it should be read as coming after, contesting, supplanting, or related to. Scholars differ also concerning the ideological grounding of the field. One stance, which I find especially pernicious, can be identified as a form of reductionist political correctness.[3] The perpetrators excoriate the British and French colonial cultures and practices in their totality, including even the English and French languages. They also excoriate or simply ignore first-class native writers – here I am thinking of the Haitian poet Etzer Vilaire – who, abandoning the local, sought instead the global, the universal, and became English and French in their *oeuvre*. Equally unfortunate, of course, are those Anglicists who work on the postcolonial in the English literature of South Asia without having learned a word of Hindi, Bengali, or Urdu.

This said, to French nationalists who would argue that the notion of the French colonizing other French within the borders of the Republic is manifestly absurd, the reply states that inner or internal colonialism is an idea broached by the Breton and Occitan modernists, especially since the 1960s. Robert Lafont's political essays in French develop the notion of an Occitan nation colonized by a foreign power from Paris.[4]

As early as 1967 he devotes a chapter to "Le colonialisme intérieur" (Internal Colonialism) (*Révolution régionaliste*) (*Regionalist Revolution*) 140-83). He writes:

> Plusieurs fois la comparaison des régions sous-développées avec des
> régions colonisées s'est imposé à nous. . . Mais pour nous, cette expression,
> non pas de *colonialisme* tout court, mais de colonialisme *intérieur*
> n'est ni une bannièrede révolte, ni un moyen d'attirer l'attention par le

scandale. Il est l'expression la plus commode que nous ayons trouvée à la réflexion pour définir un certain nombre de processus économiques dont le sous-développement régional est l'enveloppe perceptible. (*Révolution régionaliste* 140-41)

[Several times the comparison of underdeveloped regions with colonized regions forced itself on us. . . But for us, this expression, not just of *colonialism*, but of *interior* colonialism is neither a banner of revolt, nor a means to attract attention by scandal. It is the most convenient expression that we have found upon reflection to define a certain number of economic processes of which regional underdevelopment is the visible packaging.]

These processes include industrial dispossession and colonizing investment, the primacy of extractive industry over industries of transformation, and the dispossession of touristic resources. Lafont raises also the question of cultural – or, rather, of human – stereotyping:

Le Français de l'ethnie dominatrice et le Français breton ou occitan (dans la mesure, immense, où *ce dernier* aliénait son être dans la tyrannie nationaliste) ont ainsi pensé que la Bretagne était *par nature humaine* un pays de sots en costumes folkloriques et le peuple méridional un peuple de doux fainéants. (*Révolution régionaliste* 206-07)

[The domineering ethnic French person and the Breton or Occitan French person (to the extent – immense – that this latter alienated his very self in the nationalist tyranny) thought thus that Brittany was *by human nature* a country of fools in traditional costumes and the Southern people, a people of gentle idlers.]

In *Sur la France* (On France) Lafont goes farther in his historical analysis of the myth of the French nation inside its natural borders, the borders due in fact to the imperialist conquest of other peoples, who are degraded by the loss of their traditions and identities, all this embodied in the alienation from their languages now treated as mere local patois. Jean Larzac then denounced Lafont for not going far enough, for not condemning all of French history (including the Revolution of 1789) and for not recognizing that all colonization is external and that it leads always to destroying the soul, to cultural genocide. He does this in a two-volume study entitled *Descolonisar l'istòria occitana* (Decolonizing Occitan History), which replies to Lafont's *Sur la France* and which borrows from the title of Lafont's *Décoloniser en France* (Decolonizing in France).[5]

In Brittany Morvan Lebesque, in his powerful and brilliantly rhetorical book *Comment peut-on être Breton?* (*How Can One be Breton?*), titles one chapter "Des colonisés, mes frères!" (Colonized, my brothers!).[6] In it he unveils some of the inner workings of the colonial center in its relationship to the outer, Breton colony:

La querelle. . . est uniquement entre des Bretons conscients et une certaine structure héritée des pouvoirs de contrainte qui transmue la différence en antagonisme, l'unité en nivellement, l'universalisme en impérialisme....en affirmant qu'aucun gouvernement n'a le droit de monopoliser un service public ou que la répression d'une langue est en tout état de cause un acte de colonialisme, le démocrate et moi remontons à un principe que notre interlocuteur ignore: il vit dans le relatif, nous dans la Loi. Ici commence l'exil. (*Comment peut-on* 135, 153)

[The quarrel...is only between mindful Bretons and a structure inherited from the powers of coercion that transformed difference into antagonism, unity into leveling, universalism into imperialism....by affirming that no government has the right to monopolize a public service or that suppression of a language is in and of itself an act of colonialism, the democrat and I go back to a principle of which our interlocutor is ignorant: he lives in the relative, we in the Law. Here begins exile.]

Fañch Morvannou, in *Le Breton: La jeunesse d'une vieille langue* (*Breton: The Youth of an Old Language*), entitles two chapters "En feuilletant le florilège colonial" (Leafing through the Colonial Anthology) and "La source du discours colonial" (The Source of Colonial Discourse).[7] And scholars at the University of Rennes include Brittany in a collection of articles on one of the major concepts in postcolonial theory: *métissage* (hybridity).[8]

Finally, and perhaps most importantly, the various poetic anthologies which grew out of the militancy of 1968 – *Défense de cracher par terre et de parler breton* (*No Spitting and No Speaking Breton*), *Breizh hisiv* (*Brittany Today*), and, the title is significant, *Occitanie 1970: Les poètes de la décolonisation* (*Occitania 1970: The Poets of Decolonization*) – scream support for the Third World and national liberation, in the Third World and also at home.[9] Here a few examples:

Arab, va breur karet. . .
Nann, sell ouzin
Nann, m'hen tou did,
N'on ket gall evid eur gwenneg...
Pa welan va foblad reuzeudig,
Laosk, pilpous hag estren dezi heh-unan,
Em eus hoant bout arab.[10]

[Arab, my beloved brother, no, look at me; no, I swear to you, I am not French one little bit (not for a penny). When I see my people are wretched, lax, hypocritical, and alien to themselves, I want to be an Arab.]

Denig, denig,
na leñv ket war eskern da bobl
strewet tro-war-dro d'ar bed:
sentet he deus d'he mestr;
pobl kredus
pobl kreñv he gwan war un dro

poble harluet
er brioiù estren
hag en he bro.[11]

[Little man, little man, do not wail over the bones of your people scattered
around the world; they obeyed their master; gullible people, strong and
weak people, exiled people in foreign lands and in their own country.]

Batejan los enfants que sabon pas parlar
Extremoncian los vièlhs qu'an pas de connoissença
E fan votar los morts
E dison als occitans
"Podètz pas far mesprètz
de tant de sègles viscuts ensemble"
coma lo vèrme dins la frucha
lo capital e lo trabalh
lo cabucèl e sa nevròsi
"Avèm una istòria comuna."[12]

[They baptize children who can't speak. They give extreme unction to old
people who are unconscious. They have dead people voting. And they say
to the Occitanians: "You must not despise so many centuries lived together"
like the worm in the fruit, capital and labor, mind and its neurosis. "We
share a common history."]

Cantatz, Kurdas, cantatz
en devalant la còsta
i a pas res per manjar
cantatz
i a pas cap de cigalas
cantatz alavetz
que las vacas son mòrtas
que lo dròlle es mòrt que viviá l'an passat
e lo nenin se mòr.[13]

[Sing, Kurds, sing while hurtling down the slope. Is there nothing to eat?
Sing! Is there not even a cricket? Then sing that the cows are dead, that the
boy is dead who, last year, was alive, and that the baby is dying.]

Roinas roïnadas
Dels estatjants de l'ombra
Cloriosas roïnas de la misèria
De mon país.
De mon país torísticat,
De mon país tot mespresat,
De mon país folklorizat,
Qu'avètz roïnat,

Vos, d'amont-naut.[14]

[Ruined ruins of the dwellers of the dark, glorious ruins of the misery of my
country, of my touristised country, of my totally despised country, of my
folklorised country, which you devastated, you, from up there.]

What does this have to do with medievalism? One feature of the modernism
and the more militant postmodernism in the regional literatures is their quest
for cultural roots and cultural identity in history, in the past. Here the Middle
Ages occupies a place of honor just as it does for some African writers who
evoke the memory of ancient empires – in Ghana, in Mali – to bolster their
postcolonial identities.

With the French regions, there are two approaches. The first is largely
cultural, a reshaping or renewal of medieval themes and actual works of
medieval literature. Per Jakez Helias's play *An Isild a-heul* (*The Other Isolt*)
treats the Tristan and Isolt story from the Breton perspective.[15] The heroine is
Isolt of the White Hands, Isolt of Brittany, the princess whom Tristan weds in
exile – Tristan's wife whom he never touches. The villain, so to speak, in the
Old French *Roman de Tristan* (Thomas of Britain's version), who is responsible
for her husband's death, here becomes a magnificent creature, a young girl who,
conversant with the story, wills to be worthy of Tristan and Isolt of Ireland, to
emulate them in passion and in sacrifice. She slays her husband in order to
free him, to bring him deliverance:

Re vraz kalon a oa dezañ evid ar bed-mañ. Hirvoudi a ree da veza bahet
ennañ. . . . Nag eñ hepti, nag hi heptañ. Med eun dra a zo asur, Kaerden:
warnon-me e fizie d'e zieubi. Kalon awalh 'm-eus bet d'henn ober. (*Isild*
133)

[He (Tristan) had too great a heart for this world. He lamented that it was
too much for him to be contained in it. . . Neither he without her nor she
without him. But one thing is certain, Kaerden: he trusted me to free him. I
had the courage for that deed.]

She will make a place for herself in their romance just as, symbolically, Helias
makes a place for himself and Brittany in the French Tristan tradition. And he
does in a Celtic language, one the medieval characters would have spoken
or understood.

Robert Lafont's play *La Loba* (*The She-Wolf*) develops the central episode
in the brief fictional *vida* of the troubadour Peire Vidal.[16] According to the
vida, Peire so loved the countess Loba that he called himself lo Lops (the
wolf) and dressed in wolf pelts. Although the play does treat his wolfitude,
the main action concerns tragic *fin' amor* (courtly love) centering on Loba,
her husband, and her lover (the real one, not the troubadour), with, happily,
all three perishing at the end, rather like Tristan and his two Isolts. The three
tear each other apart, devour each other, slay each other – rendered beasts
by desire, jealousy, and the thirst for vengeance. Hence, Ugon's rage at the
thought of Loba and Rogier all night in her chamber:

E d'aquela pòrta silenciosa qu'ausas pas butar, tota una nuech de tèmps!.
. . Femna, Loba, ai que mon revenge, ieu, pèr m'escaufar lo còr a l'auba!
(*Loba* 12)
[And that silent door that I dare not push open, all night long! Woman,
Wolf, at dawn I have only vengeance to warm my heart!]

Hence, Loba's demand to Rogier: You want me to leave with you? Here is my
condition:

Partirai amb tu se tuas Ugon. Se lo tuas pas, d'eu totjorn me sovendrai, e lo
souvenir totjorn serà entre nosautres. (*Loba* 144)

[I will leave with you if you kill Ugon. If you don't kill him, I will remember
him always, and the memory will stand between us always.]

As I see it, Lafont writes a Racinian tragedy grounded in medieval Occitan *fin'
amor*, *fin' amor* being the forerunner, the ancestor, of the passion in Racine. He
can *do* Racine and in the *Ursprache*, Occitan. A wag – actually a distinguished
professor – once commented to me that Lafont had the ambition to write all
the books over the centuries that, since the Middle Ages, Occitan did not have
but should have had, and that, unfortunately, he almost succeeded.

Maodez Glanndour is, in my opinion, the greatest of the Breton poets; his
masterpiece may well be the long poem *Imram* (*Sea Trek*).[17] The poem recounts
the Speaker's spiritual quest, conceived as a maritime voyage in the tradition
of heroes of Celtic myth: Bran the Blessed and Saint Brendan especially. The
Speaker sails to the Isle of Sin, the Isle of Women, and the Isle of Nature. On
the first island the Ogre of War devours hordes of people, crushing, nibbling,
and gnawing at them. When he sleeps, his rats fill up on the remains:

Douar milliget, ur Ramz a zo roue warnout,
Ar Roñfl hudur, loudour,
Gourvezet teurek en e vougev goude re-gorfad
War bern eskern an dud en deus debret.
Hag e-pad ma roc'h o mestr e ra fest ar razhed.
                              (*Imram* 148)

[Accursed land, you have as king a Giant, the loathsome, filthy Ogre, lying
bloated in his cave after having stuffed his belly, on the heap of bones
of the people he has eaten. And while their master snores the rats have a
banquet.]

The "pleasures" of all three islands prove to be illusory; the Speaker learns to
probe the night of his soul and to turn to God. He learns to love Christ on the
Cross, loves him for his thorns, wounds, and vinegar. He loves Christ in his
great beauty and, a second Juan de la Cruz, begs to be ravished by him:

O deus! Mall am eus d'az kwelout,
Daoulagad ouzh daoulagad
Kalon ouzh kalon,

Diharz da viken, Hollgened!
Ennon e vi, ennout e vin da viken,
Soubet ez frond, o sunañ da zouster,
Evel ar wenanenn en kalon ar vleunienn.

(Imram 160)

[Oh come! I long to behold you, eye to eye, heart to heart, totally, for
ever more, All-beauty! You will be in me, I will be in you, forever, bathing
in your fragrance, sucking your sweetness, like bees in the heart of the
flower.]

Here is valorized Celtic passion, Celtic spirituality, and Celtic darkness, in
contrast to Latin (French) reason, materialism, and enlightenment. Glanndour's
exaltation of a *bretonnité* to be set off against Frenchness takes roughly the
same form as that of the African and Caribbean poets of *Négritude* in their
resistance to European values. Max-Philippe Delavouët composed five volumes
of a vast lyrico-epic panorama entitled *Pouèmo* (*Poem*).[18] The Speaker is a poetic
persona entitled the Prince. In an archetypal Provence in an archetypically
mythical past, the Prince undertakes quests, encounters dead cities, hermits,
buffoons, and his alter ego, the other prince. Above all, he encounters the
Eternal Feminine, an archetypal lady-princess-queen-goddess. As one princess
addresses the Prince:

Te dise moun soulèu, as pèr iéu d'àutri noum.
Siés la lanço de sang que coungreio la vido,
e siés l'ancro pintado au cor di gounfaloun,
e siés lou founs lauroun ount l'aigo nous convido
quouro nautre nous dessecan
e, parié, se durcis la terro dóu trescamp.

(Pouèmo: 88)

[I call you my sun, you have for me other names. You are the blood lance
which begets life, and you are the anchor painted at the heart of gonfalons,
and you are the depths where water invites us when we wither and the
earth of the heath hardens.]

Unlike the three preceding writers, Delavouët does not rework or revalorize
a famous literary text from the Middle Ages. The term "Middle Ages" never
appears in *Pouèmo*. The events, such as they are – this is a poem of incantation
and celebration, not one of telling a story – can be thought of as having
occurred at any time between 496 and 1789, that is, between the Fall of the
Roman Empire and the French Revolution. The spirit, the time, the ambiance
are meant to be medieval – we would say, not medieval but medievalish or
medievalistic or neomedieval. Thus does the Middle Ages slowly but surely
annex preceding and subsequent historical periods in the popular imaginary.
In the American popular imaginary there is the Bible, then the Middle Ages,
and then us, although we go back to, say, 1776.

The other approach is one of militancy, with writers evoking moments of oppression and resistance. One example would be Lafont's *La Croisade* (*The Crusade*), a play which treats the Albigensian Crusade against Catharism.[19] One of his characters is the Anonymous Monk who wrote *La Cançon de la Crosada*, known as *La Chanson de la Croisade Albigeoise* (*The Song of the Albigensian Crusade*), basically a chronicle written in Occitan and from the Occitan perspective. A Breton example would be *Gurvan ar Marc'hez estranjour* (*Gurvan the Foreign/Stranger Knight*) by Tanguy Malmanche, a play in the Symbolist tradition, under the influence of Maeterlinck.[20] For all its dream-like, archetypal distance from the concrete, the plot tells of a courageous Breton warrior who defeats Gifrez, the evil and lecherous commander of a Frankish army which had invaded and now occupies the land of Brittany.

What conclusions can be drawn? And, for example, why are there significantly fewer political texts than cultural texts situated in the Middle Ages? The major writers, in reclaiming their cultural history, created cultural myths in order to do so. One of these is that in a pre-conquest time Brittany and Occitania were culturally and politically alive, with everyone, from the duke or the count down to the lowliest peasant, happy and fulfilled; the courts were more genteel; women had more rights; and decisions were made in a more democratic manner – all this "more" than at any time under French domination. When was this mythical portion of history? The Middle Ages, of course, when else? The Middle Ages, the time par excellence prior to the modern world. The Middle Ages would have been quintessentially Breton and Occitan because the South did enjoy a rich cultural flowering back then – the troubadours – and the Bretons could imagine a rich cultural flowering because the characters in Arthurian romance have Celtic names and the literary genre, in French, is called *roman breton*. Welsh did enjoy a rich cultural flowering back then, and one myth, impossible from a linguistic perspective, states that, up until the thirteenth century, Welsh and Breton were the same language.[21] This mythical medievalness of the provinces is then set off against a no less mythical classicism, the presumed hallmark of the French in Paris. Thus, the Middle Ages are evoked in terms of nostalgia, of wish-fulfillment, overtly in Delavouët yet, to some extent, in all the writers I have cited. Politics, confrontation, rebellion – these motifs will be cultivated in texts treating a later historical frame (except for Toulouse), the history of the province incorporated into the kingdom or, from their perspective, of the nation subject to foreign conquest and colonization. So, when Paol Keineg and Robert Lafont write plays of rebellion, of regional uprising against Paris, they situate their narratives in the seventeenth century.[22] Finally, when the great modernists were criticized, and they were, for not being sufficiently Breton or Occitan – attacked either for renouncing old regional identity and old local color or for failing to embody the direct struggle of national liberation (the same sort of critique directed against some African and Caribbean writers, not to speak of French Canada), the response was immediate. Here I quote Roparz Hemon, the creator of the Skol Walarn and the father of the modernist renascence in Brittany:

[S'ils] savaient combien cette littérature a peu le souci de "faire breton," s'ils savaient combien au contraire, elle recherche l'universel et répugne à toute emprise du terroir....Qu'ils l'accusent de n'être pas bretonne, d'être anti-bretonne. Elle n'en a cure. Elle est écrite en breton![23]

[(If they knew to what an extent this literature couldn't care less about "looking Breton," if they knew how much on the contrary, it seeks the universal and is adverse to any local/rural ascendancy. . . Let them blame it for not being Breton, of being anti-Breton. It doesn't care. It is written in Breton!]

It is true, these writers suffer less from the language question than do their opposite numbers in Africa or the Caribbean; they write directly in the language, their language. Indeed, some of them are native French speakers who, in their teens or twenties, chose to become Breton or Occitan. Perhaps because of their having chosen to write in the "native dialect," they don't have to denounce France and the French, crudely and vociferously. Their tactic is to strive for the universal, to embrace modernism and the international style the same as if they were born and raised in Paris or Lyon. The message can be presented softly, obliquely, as I have indicated.

I believe that the postcolonial approach, for that matter the reality of postcolonialism, will help illuminate the phenomenon of medievalism in the Breton and Occitan revival cultures. Secondly, the medievalism cultivated by the great writers in the modernist style forms part and parcel of their perception of postcolonialism and their subsequent reaction against the dominant, purportedly classical culture emanating from Paris. We find in the literature the cultivation of medieval themes and historical events, especially in the theater. This is part of their quest for origins, for a political past of independence and a literary past of glory. Last but not least, medievalism can offer a practical and methodological aid to scholars in postcolonial studies who explore the sense of the past in the cultures, the subjects, of their work. If they only knew...

UNIVERSITY OF FLORIDA

NOTES

1   William Calin, "Is Orientalism Medievalism? Or, Edward Said, Are You a Saracen?" *Year's Work in Medievalism* 22 (2008): 63-68; Edward W. Said, *Culture and Imperialism* (New York: Knopf, 1993).
2   Some material will be taken from my book, *Minority Literatures and Modernism: Scots, Breton, and Occitan, 1920-1990* (Toronto: University of Toronto Press, 2000).
3   This position was critiqued as far back as 1993 in *Post/Colonial Conditions: Exiles, Migrations, and Nomadisms*, ed. Françoise Lyonnet and Ronnie Scharfman, a two-volume issue of *Yale French Studies* 82-83. Yet many in the field continue to adhere to it.
4   Robert Lafont, *La Révolution régionaliste* (Paris: Gallimard, 1967); *Sur la France* (Paris: Gallimard, 1968); *Clefs pour l'Occitanie* (Paris: Seghers, 1971); *Décoloniser en*

France: Les régions face à l'Europe (Paris: Gallimard, 1971); *La Revendication occitane* (Paris: Flammarion, 1974); *Autonomie: De la région à l'autogestion* (Paris: Gallimard, 1976).

5   Joan [Jean] Larzac, *Descolonisar l'istòria occitana*, 2 vols. (Toulouse: Institut d'Études Occitanes, 1977-80).

6   Morvan Lebesque, *Comment peut-on être Breton? Essai sur la démocratie française* (Paris: Seuil, 1970), 127-57.

7   Fañch Morvannou, *Le Breton: La jeunesse d'une vieille langue* (Lannion: Presses Populaires de Bretagne, 1980).

8   *Métissage du texte: Bretagne, Maghreb, Québec*, ed. Bernard Hüe (Rennes: Presses Universitaires de Rennes, 1993).

9   *Défense de cracher par terre et de parler breton: Poèmes de combat (1950-1970)*, ed. Yann-Ber Piriou (Paris: Oswald, 1971); *Breizh hisiv: Anthologie de la chanson en Bretagne* (Paris: Oswald, 1976); *Occitanie 1970: Les poètes de la décolonisation*, ed. Marie Rouanet (Paris: Oswald, 1971).

10   Erwan Evenou, "Plouk" (Hick/Hayseed), in *Défense* 104-06.

11   Youenn Gwernig, "Harlu" (Exile), in *Défense* 132.

12   Joan Larzac, "L'ora" (The time when it happened), in *Décolonisation* 44.

13   Alan Ward, "Chantez Kurdes!" in *Décolonisation* 148.

14   Joan-Batista [Jean-Baptiste] Seguin, "Sirventes," in *Décolonisation* 172.

15   Per Jakez Helias, *An Isild a-heul* (Brest: Brud Nevez, 1983).

16   Robert Lafont, *La Loba, ò la frucha di tres aubas: Peça de tres actes* (Avignon: Aubanel, 1959).

17   Maodez Glanndour, *Imram*, in his *Komzoù bev* (Brest: Al Liamm, 1985), 143-90.

18   Mas-Felipe [Max-Philippe] Delavouët, *Pouèmo*, vols. 1-3 (Paris: Corti, 1971-77), vols. 4-5 (Saint-Remy de Provence: C.R.E.M., 1983-91).

19   Robert Lafont, *La Croisade* (Aix-en-Provence, Édisud, 1983).

20   Tangi [Tanguy] Malmanche, *Gurvan ar Marc'hez estranjour: Mister* (1923) (Brest: Al Liamm, 1975).

21   One example is *Le Brasier des ancêtres: Poèmes populaires de la Bretagne*, ed. Jean-Pierre Foucher and Loeiz Ar Floc'h, 2 vols. (Paris: Union Générale d'Éditions, 1977), «Introduction,» 9-22. Note that, prior to the thirteenth century, Breton was separated from both Cornish and Welsh by the Channel for at least seven centuries.

22   Paol Keineg, *Le Printemps des Bonnets Rouges: Théâtre* (Paris: Oswald, 1972); Robert Lafont,*Lei Cascavèus* (Toulon: Centre Dramatique Occitan de Provence, 1977).

23   Cited by Yann-Ber Piriou in his "Preface" to *Défense de cracher*, 7-46, esp. 29-30.

Retelling Old Tales:
Germanic Myth and Language in Christopher Paolini's *Eragon*

Jana K. Schulman

Christopher Paolini was fifteen when he wrote the book *Eragon*. From interviews with various people as well as reviews published in various venues, from teenreads.com to the *New York Times Book Review*, it is clear that Paolini read widely, both translations of medieval literature and fantasy. Hs mother home schooled him and encouraged his love of reading. His acknowledged influences include J.R.R. Tolkien's *Lord of the Rings*, Seamus Heaney's translation of *Beowulf, Le Morte D'Artur*, Norse sagas, and Anne McCaffrey's *Dragon Riders of Pern* series.

Mike Jones noted in his review of the book that,

> "*Eragon* is an impressive debut from a young writer, an epic fantasy tale that evokes Tolkien and Lloyd Alexander, among others. The trappings are nothing new: dragons, elves, dwarves, a rebellion against an Empire, a young man from a poor background with a powerful destiny, grandiose battles and mighty magics. Where Paolini shines is in making it all sound fresh, told with a certain enthusiasm and respect for the material that makes it perfectly okay to go back to the basics" (30).

On the other hand, Liz Rosenberg is a little more even handed, noting both its strengths and weaknesses. "It is a familiar plot, but originality has never been one of the fantasy genre's strengths." Specifically mentioning writers like Ursula K. Le Guin and Anne McCaffrey who use "exquisite prose," and Tolkien and J. K. Rowling who "create reverberating plots that twist and dive," Rozenberg notes that Paolini is not there yet: "He often slips into clichéd descriptions: 'his tanned skin rippled with lean muscles'—or B-movie dialogue: 'Boy!' roared Brom. 'You demand answers with an insolence rarely seen." Another weakness is that Paolini's plot "stumbles and jerks along, with gaps in logic and characters dropped, then suddenly remembered, or new ones invented at the last minute." Yet Rozenberg sees in Paolini "great talent" and describes him having an acute sense of place; she closes her review with the following words: "Like countless other readers, I am waiting to see what happens next, with wonder, with admiration and with hope" (34).

In various interviews, Paolini explains where and how he got the idea for his ancient language: "I've always been fascinated with the sources of most modern fantasy that lie in Teutonic, Scandinavian, and Old Norse history" (Interview by Anonymous). "The ancient language I based on Old Norse, mainly the words and the sounds, and then I went my own way with the grammar and structure. I had a lot of fun with that" (Interview by Trudy Wyss). As someone who speaks modern Icelandic and teaches Old Norse, I found it fascinating to examine the language that Paolini "created," although I use that word loosely.

Many of the words that one finds in *Eragon* are Germanic, mostly Old Norse. Paolini has created his ancient language in a variety of ways. Some words he takes directly from Old Norse and forms sentences with them. In fact, of some forty-three nouns in *Eragon*, fifteen are from Old Norse; three are from other Germanic languages; and three are from Old Irish. Some he modifies by replacing a consonant or prefixing a letter. For instance, an Old Norse word meaning *death* is 'andlat;' Paolini has replaced the **d** with a **g**, forming 'anglat.' An Old Norse word meaning *hallowed* or *holy* is 'helgr;' Paolini has prefixed an **s-** to the word, resulting in 'shelgr'. Some he takes and simply changes or expands the meaning. The Old Norse word *sei>r* means 'spell,' 'charm,' or 'incantation;' in *Eragon*, it refers to a witch, someone who might cast a charm or spell.

Others words Paolini forms based on the language's word formation system. Both Old Norse and Old English use compound words to add to the language, both lexically and artistically. Here, one can argue that Paolini does more than just borrow words. While there are quite a few synonyms for bird and dragon in both Old Norse and Old English, Paolini has rejected these and formed compound words, two of which appear to combine Old English and Old Norse. His word for bird is *fethrblaka*. In Old Norse, the word for feather is *fij>r*, in Old English, *fei>er*. Paolini has replaced the eth with a –th—a standard change made when transcribing Old English and Old Norse—and dropped the **e**, but the first part of the compound is the Old English word. The second part is an Old Norse verb that means to flap. Hence a bird is a feather-flapper. A dragon is a scale-flapper. Instead of using *draca*, a word for dragon found in *Beowulf* and other texts, Paolini opts to develop a compound: *skulblaka*. The first part of this compound is a bit unclear. There is an Old Norse word, *skel*, that means 'shell' and an Old English one, *sciell*, that means 'scale.' Paolini has a tendency to change a root vowel and since he indicates that he consulted an etymological dictionary, either one of these words are a possibility. Paolini's compounds demonstrate his most creative use of languages.

Another difference between Paolini's ancient language and Old Norse is the structure. Old Norse is a fully inflected language, which means that each word shows its function in the sentence by its ending. Paolini follows English word order and with few exceptions does not decline the words, using them in a fixed form. For example, this sentence in the ancient language, "Ai varden abr du Shur'tuglar gata vanta" (A warden of the Riders lacks passage), does not show an awareness of cases. In the Old Norse, the word *gata*, which is in the accusative or object case here, would be *götu*. Also, the demonstrative, *du* or 'the', in Old Norse must agree in case, gender, and number with the noun it modifies. Since Shur'tuglar is plural, so too should be the demonstrative. In this instance, Paolini's choices make sense; his readers know English more than they know Old Norse and are familiar with the sentence structure of English. One can argue that Eragon benefits from an ancient language in a familiar structure; it is both foreign yet, in translation, comprehensible.

Paolini's creation of an ancient language from a dead language is one way that he incorporates the past into his present work. Another way of incorporating is in the act of retelling, a time honored means of entertaining in the Middle Ages. While some may criticize *Eragon* for its debt to Tolkien, Anne McCaffrey, and the Star Wars movies, Paolini's blending and retelling of older stories would have been acceptable and understandable in the Middle Ages, where poetic talent was recognized in how the *scop* or poet chose the language with which to tell that tale and made a traditional tale new.

Telling tales serves several purposes in *Eragon*; the people telling the tale may spread rumors, as in the case of the two traders who tell the people in Carvahall that the Varden have allied with the Urgals (40-41). A tale may provide information, and sometimes confirm a legend, as in when Solembum the werecat speaks to Eragon. Solembum tells Eragon that he is a werecat: "'there aren't many of us left, but I think even a farm boy should have heard of us.' 'I didn't know you were real,' said Eragon, fascinated. A werecat! He was indeed fortunate. They were always flitting around the edges of stories, keeping to themselves and occasionally giving advice. If the legends were true, they had magical powers, lived longer than humans, and usually knew more than they told" (292). In this example, Paolini has deftly woven together a legend that Eragon has heard, perhaps as a child's tale, with the new reality that confronts Eragon: he is communicating telepathically with a cat. Here we see a legend within a tale within the story itself. A question may initiate a tale that confirms someone else's legend, as we see when Murtagh asks Eragon, shortly after Brom's death, "'Is your Brom *the* Brom? The one who helped steal a dragon egg from the king, chased it across the Empire, and killed Morzan in a duel? I heard you say his name, and I read the inscription you put on his grave, but I must know for certain. Was that he?'" (405). Although Eragon himself had not known Brom's history at the beginning of their journey, he had learned from Brom as Brom taught him to fight; not only did Brom pronounce him an expert swordsman, but he also taught him the language necessary for the practice of magic, and to practice magic safely. Murtagh's question forces Eragon to realize not only what he has learned from a legend, a former Rider responsible for rescuing one of the other three remaining dragon eggs, but also what he has lost.

In addition to acknowledging the power of the storyteller, of legends, within his own tale, Christopher Paolini also incorporates motifs and sometimes names from other sources and tales. When Brom gives Eragon a sword, not only does Paolini describe the sword at length—it has a gold pommel and a ruby in the hilt; it is decorated with silver wire, and "burnished until it gleamed like starlight" (148-49)—but he also presents the sword's history. "'This was once a Rider's blade,' said Brom gravely. 'When a Rider finished his training, the elves would present him with a sword....The sword is named Zar'roc'" (149-50). In *Beowulf* and many other epic literatures, swords have histories and names. Unferth, a member of King Hrothgar's court in the poem *Beowulf*, loans Beowulf his sword:

> The brehon handed him a hilted weapon,
> A rare and ancient sword named Hrunting.
> The iron blade with its ill-boding patterns
> Had been tempered in blood. It had never failed
> The hand of anyone who hefted it in battle,
> Anyone who had fought and faced the worst
> In the gap of danger. This was not the first time
> It had been called to perform heroic feats (Heaney, ll. 1457-1464).

In echoing the motif of the epic sword, Paolini links his story with many epics of the past.

Another way *Eragon* connects with ancient tales is by interweaving other heroic themes. Anglo-Saxon heroic poetry, like *Beowulf* and the *Battle of Maldon*, provide their audiences with a perspective on heroic behavior, on what it means, at some level, to be a hero. Eragon debates this with himself and Saphira at various times in the book. At the same time, though, these poems explore what happens when the hero's life changes; in other words, what happens when a warrior is in exile, away from his king or lord, his land, and his friends. Exile poetry presents this other side in poems as diverse as "The Seafarer" and "The Wanderer." In this latter poem, the narrator reminds us that he is "wretched with care, removed from [his] homeland, far from dear kinsmen" (Donaldson, 112). Paolini evokes the theme of exile, with all the emotion it brings, when Eragon, getting ready to leave his home, insists to himself, "This cannot, will not, be a permanent exile" (162).

In addition to motifs and themes, Paolini also does not hesitate to borrow Germanic names from other tales. Some critics have noted the similarity between the name Eragon and Aragorn, the reluctant king in Tolkien's *Lord of the Rings*. Paolini himself explained that he named Angela the herbalist after his sister. In *Beowulf*, Hrothgar is the king of the Danes who, when we first meet him, rules a Denmark ravaged by the depredations of Grendel. The latter attacks Heorot, the great hall, famed far and wide, that Hrothgar built. In *Eragon*, the king of the dwarves is named Hrothgar. Given that Hrothgar in *Eragon* lives in and is charged to protect a great hall, one could argue that the poem *Beowulf* may have influenced Paolini here.

The interactions between King Hrothgar and Eragon have much in common with those between King Hrothgar and Beowulf. To bring Eragon to Hrothgar requires several intermediaries. One dwarf gives him the initial summons and brings him to Orik, another dwarf. Orik guides Eragon to meet Hrothgar. When Beowulf arrives in Denmark, he is first challenged by the coastguard who sends him on to Heorot, where he is greeted by Hrothgar's herald, Wulfgar. It is Wulfgar who, after eliciting further information from Beowulf, presents Beowulf to the king, first verbally and then in person. Unlike the poem *Beowulf*, though, which provides little to no description of its characters, *Eragon* does. Paolini paints a vivid portrait of Hrothgar, whom Eragon sees when he enters the throne room:

A gold helm lined with rubies and diamonds rested on Hrothgar's head in place of a crown. His visage was grim, weathered, and hewn of many years' experience. Beneath a craggy brow glinted deep set eyes, flinty and piercing. Over his powerful chest rippled a shirt of mail. His white beard was tucked under his belt, and in his lap he held a mighty war hammer with the symbol of Orik's clan embossed on its head (646).

Paolini's descriptions of Hrothgar and Orik, who is described as short and stocky, with a long-braided beard, wearing chain mail, and carrying an axe, invoke Tolkien's descriptions of dwarves in *The Hobbit*. Unlike Paolini who provides composite descriptions, however, Tolkien doles out only tidbits of information about his dwarves. The first dwarf who comes to Bilbo Baggins' door, we learn, is Dwalin: "It was a dwarf with a blue beard tucked into a golden belt, and very bright eyes under his dark green hood" (20). As the story progresses, we learn dwarves are musicians, singers, workers in gold and other metals, makers of beautiful things; that they live underground where they tunnel and mine; they are famous as smiths and can make a fire almost anywhere (20-44).

Tolkien drew his dwarven lore from various Icelandic sources, which provide, like him, bits and pieces of information about dwarves. The two most useful sources are Snorri Sturluson's *Prose Edda* and the *Poetic Edda*. The stories in the *Prose Edda* tell us that dwarves are master smiths; they have fashioned amazing items for the gods: a ship named Skidbladnir constructed with the greatest ingenuity, a fetter named Gleipnir made of magical elements, a spear named Gangnir for Odin, a golden boar, and Thor's hammer, Mjollir. They made swords that once drawn must kill before they are sheathed. The poems in the *Poetic Edda* allow us to tease out certain motifs: dwarves dwell in stones or underground or in golden dwellings, and often deceive human beings. They make amazing and magical jewelry, such as the magic ring, Draupnir, which produces eight gold rings every ninth night, and the *Brisinga men*, the necklace of the Brisings obtained by Freyja after she slept with four dwarves, one dwarf each night for four nights, a necklace so well known that it is mentioned in several Eddic poems and in *Beowulf*. Middle High German texts, such as the *Ruodlieb* and the *Nibelungenlied*, confirm that dwarves are bearded, long-lived, strong, skilled in healing, and wise. Another text, *König Laurin*, pits the hero Dietrich von Bern against a dwarf king named Laurin, who lives in a hollow mountain where gold and silver and precious objects adorn the entire inside of the mountain (Battles, 52-53, 58).

Eragon is filled with echoes of these stories' dwarves and their work. Farthen Dur is a volcanic crater discovered by a certain Korgan, father of the dwarf race, while he tunneled for gold. "And in the center stands our greatest achievement: Tronjheim, the city-mountain built from the purest marble" (581), filled with gold and silver, items of beauty, and tunnels. King Hrothgar carries a hammer; according to the *Poetic Edda*, the dwarves forged Thor's hammer, and it need not be surprising that a dwarf would carry a hammer.

Whether Paolini read the *Poetic Edda* is unclear, but he himself has said that he read Old Norse sagas. While he has not listed the ones he has read, two come to mind, based on what is taught in schools and what is available easily in translation: *Njal's Saga* and *Laxdœla Saga*. He may also have read the *Saga of the Volsungs*, especially since he is interested in Wagner's Ring Cycle. I mention these texts because all three of them demonstrate the importance of dreams and visions as well as the fact that the audience, along with the teller of the tale, believed in ghosts, prophecies, dreams, hallucinations, fetches (guardian spirits) and portents (Introduction, *Njal's Saga*, 17). Eragon asks Brom if it is possible "to conjure up an image of something you cannot see" (283). Brom answers the question, explaining the difficulties involved, and then tells Eragon the necessary phrase in the Ancient Language. The words are *draumr kópa*—two Old Norse words, the noun 'dream' and the verb 'to stare'—translated in *Eragon* as 'dream stare.' This phrase allows someone to scry, "to see images in pieces of crystal, water, etc., which reveal the future or secrets of the past or present" (OED/*Eragon*, 284-85). The act of scrying as well as the frequency of dreams connect *Eragon* to these earlier texts.

Because *Eragon* is a fantasy as opposed to an Old Norse saga, the hero himself is able to scry. He first sees an unknown woman in his dream, but later attempts to scry her and/or her whereabouts. She is injured and in a cell when he first sees her in a dream. When he attempts to gather more information by scrying, she looks at him. Later, he dreams of her again and it is clear that her situation is dire and getting progressively worse. At this time, Eragon does not know that this is the elf who sent Saphira's egg to Carvahall, but he is drawn to her and senses that he must save her for reasons that are not clear. Like the seers and dreamers in *Njal's Saga*, Eragon receives information through dreams, but cannot always interpret it.

One example from *Njal's Saga* can demonstrate the power of these visions, some seen asleep, others while awake. A minor character sees, "a ring of fire with a man on a grey horse inside the circle, riding furiously....Hildiglum heard him roaring out:

'I ride a horse
with icy mane,
forelock dripping,
evil bringing.
Fire at each end,
And poison in the middle,
Flosi's plans
Are like this flying firebrand—
Flosi's plans
Are like this flying firebrand.'"

Hildiglum consults a neighbor who interprets the vision, saying, "You have seen the witch-ride, and that is always a portent of disaster" (260-61). Here, the disaster foretold is Flosi's burning in and killing of Njal and all of his family—an act that affects the entire community.

In his essay, *Dreams in the Sagas*, Lars Lönnroth notes that

> "one obvious function of saga dreams is to anticipate future events, for a dream in a saga, usually reported by the dreamer to a confidant, is always a concealed warning to the dreamer, a warning that the proper confidant will be able to interpret correctly: the meaning of the dream is always that this or that—usually something horrible—is going to happen to the dreamer, his kinsmen, or the neighborhood where he lives" (455-56).

When Eragon dreams of the elf Ayra, all he knows is that he feels called to rescue her. Yet one can interpret his dreams of her and her impending death akin to the way Hildiglum's neighbor did: what he sees, if not remedied, will result in disaster for the one in the dream, the Varden, and the greater community desirous of overthrowing Galbatorix.

Christopher Paolini's *Eragon* reveals the author's fascination with Scandinavian mythology and the Old Norse language. The medieval Icelandic *Prose Edda* and the *Poetic Edda*, filled with stories of dwarves, swords, and the stuff of fantasy, may have provided Paolini with direct access to these myths. If they did not, then his reading of *The Hobbit*, in particular, and the *Lord of the Rings*, could have illuminated a fantasy world, ripe for modification. Tolkien, let us not forget, was the Rawlinson and Bosworth Professor of Anglo-Saxon at Oxford University and many themes, images, and motifs from Old Norse and Anglo-Saxon texts abound in his abovementioned works. The Anglo-Saxon poem *Beowulf* probably provided the name Hrothgar for Paolini, as well as information about the significance of named swords, although it is true that many epics and sagas reveal the importance of a named, inherited sword for the hero—as such a sword, significant in its own right, also links the hero to a heroic past. Paolini's incorporation of dreams and other supernatural elements into *Eragon* further links his fantasy tale to Icelandic literature and mythology.

In addition to Paolini's reading of medieval and other primary sources, he also read fantasy works whose authors may have drawn some of their ideas from medieval texts. Paolini does not name Robert Jordan's *Wheel of Time* series, but Jordan clearly was familiar with Germanic mythology; his characters practice *seidr* or *seidin*—both words that mean magic and that are derived from the Old Norse word *seir*. While the authors Paolini does name are, with the exception of Tolkien, not so easily connected with a Germanic/Icelandic mythos, they do connect him not only to the fantasy genre but also to what those authors read and incorporated, processed and retold.

By incorporating elements of other stories, both medieval and modern, into his own work, Paolini situates himself thoroughly into the fantasy genre. With Old Norse as the basis for his Ancient Language, he further confirms his interest in Old Icelandic literature and emulates Tolkien. It is important to note, though, that Paolini, unlike Tolkien, does not so much create an entirely new language as adapt preexisting ones (Old Norse, Old Irish, and Anglo-Saxon); the way he does this reveals his creativity and/or, perhaps, his youth or inexperience (is it creative to stick to Modern English word order when the language adapted is a fully inflected one or a sign of grammatical inexperience?).

Paolini retells traditional tales with motifs and words borrowed, changed, and incorporated into *Eragon*. In doing so, he can be said to follow in the footsteps of many a *scop* of the Middle Ages. The stories were well known; it was what a teller of tales did with that story or its elements that determined his success, an audience's enthusiastic response. Based on the numbers of fan sites devoted to Paolini's work as well as the number of copies sold, he has succeeded. While some may pan him because of his very lack of originality, others, as audience members might have done during the Middle Ages, have praised him for his—decidedly uneven—but creative work.

WESTERN MICHIGAN UNIVERSITY

WORKS CITED

Battles, Paul. "Dwarfs in Germanic Literature: Deutsche Mythologie or Grimm's Myths?" *The Shadow-Walkers: Jacob Grimm's Mythology of the Monstrous*. Ed. Tom Shippey. Tempe, AZ; Turnhout, Belgium: Arizona Center for Medieval and Renaissance Studies; Brepols, 2005. 29-82. Print.

Beowulf. A New Verse Translation. Trans. Seamus Heaney. New York: W.W. Norton & Company, 2001. Print.

Clark Hall, J.R. *A Concise Anglo-Saxon Dictionary*. 4th ed. Toronto: University of Toronto Press, 1960. Print.

Cleasby, Richard and Gudbrand Vigfusson. *An Icelandic-English Dictionary*. Second edition with a supplement by William Craigie. 1957. Oxford: Oxford University Press, 1982. Print.

Jones, Mike. Rev. of *Eragon* by Christopher Paolini. *Chronicle* 25.11 (December 2003): 30. 28 April 2010. Web.

Laxdœla Saga. Trans. Magnus Magnusson and Hermann Pálsson. London: Penguin Books, 1969. Print.

Lonnöth, Lars "Dreams in the Sagas." *Scandinavian Studies* 74.4 (Winter 2002): 455-64. Print.

Njal's Saga. Trans. Magnus Magnusson and Hermann Pálsson. London: Penguin Books, 1960. Print.

Paolini, Christopher. *Eragon*. New York: Random House, 2006. Print.

Paolini, Christopher. Interview by Anonymous. Random House, 2003. Web. 28 April 2010. <http://www.bookbrowse.cpm/author interviews/full/index.cfm/author number/934/Christopher-Paolini>.

Paolini, Christopher. Interview by Trudy Wyss. Borders Book Stores, 2003. Web. 2 May 2010 <http://www.borders.com/online/store/ArticleView_paolini>.

Poetic Edda. Trans. Carolyne Larrington. Oxford: Oxford University Press, 1996. Print.

Rosenberg, Liz. "The Egg and Him." *New York Times Book Review*, 108 (November 16, 2003): 34, col 2. 28 April 2010. Web.

"Scry." Def. 2. *The Oxford English Dictionary*.

Sturluson, Snorri. *Edda*. Trans. Anthony Faulkes. London: J.M. Dent & Sons Ltd, 1987. Print.

Tolkien, J.R.R. *The Hobbit*. New York: Ballantine Books, 1984. Print.

"The Wanderer." Trans. E. T. Donaldson. *Norton Anthology of English Literature*. 8th ed. Ed. Stephen Greenblatt et al. New York: W. W. Norton & Company, 2006. 111-13. Print.

From English Stage to American Page:
The Transatlantic Dissemination of Leonard MacNally's
Robin Hood; or, Sherwood Forest

Arthur Russell

Leonard MacNally's *Robin Hood; or, Sherwood Forest* first premiered at the Theatre Royal Covent Garden on April 17, 1784. In its first season *Robin Hood* was performed thirteen times and took in over £2,000, placing it among the most successful staged works of that year.[1] MacNally's three-act comic opera was performed a total of 64 times at Covent Garden, and 32 times as a two-act afterpiece.[2] In subsequent years the opera was also popularly performed at Drury Lane, Theatre Royal (Bath), Dublin, Annapolis, New York, Philadelphia, Charleston (SC), and Baltimore.[3] A collection of songs from *Robin Hood* were first printed and sold at Covent Garden in April 1784, and in October 1784 John Almon completed the first publication of the entire libretto. Over the next few decades MacNally's comic opera was printed in over a dozen editions by printers in London, Dublin, Philadelphia, and New York. Of MacNally's nine plays, *Robin Hood* was the best received both on stage and in print. The dissemination of the printed text from the England to America follows the transatlantic migration of the stage productions—where the play was acted, the text was printed.

Robin Hood in England

The textual history for *Robin Hood; or, Sherwood Forest* begins with the stage. Examination of MacNally's papers and Almon's 1784 edition reveals that the opera underwent significant changes between the first and second performance seasons and prior to its first full publication. In her examination of the libretti and vocal scores, Linda Troost catalogs the opera's major changes. Troost's research shows that MacNally rewrote the second of three acts, cut erroneous characters, and contracted the composer William Shield to set six new songs to music.[4] MacNally appears to have taken these drastic editorial measures with hopes of counteracting some rather scathing criticisms of his work. Following *Robin Hood*'s debut (April 17, 1784), *The London Magazine* published the following review:

> The author of this opera has done nothing but write the dialogue, which
> is every where scanty, and compile the ballads, which are selected from
> Milton, Goldsmith, Shirley, Bate, Johnson's collection, Irish ballads, &c. &c.
> There is not that structure of fable in it which we usually call plot; the story
> is simple, and the termination such as the audience are led to expect.[5]

After receiving this critical lashing, MacNally completed and staged a revised version of his libretto on October 12, 1784: "The opera of Robin Hood was this evening represented in an altered state....The second act is almost newly written, and the language of the whole opera amended and pointed with great neatness."[6]

Despite *London Magazine*'s scathing review, *Robin Hood; or, Sherwood Forest* enjoyed a profitable first season. MacNally, whose previous works had been notoriously unsuccessful, naturally hoped to capitalize upon his newfound popularity. The first printing of the opera includes a letter from MacNally to Shield in which MacNally confesses his anxiety over being forgotten:

> Gil Blas advised a friend who had written for the stage with success, to publish his works, observing that as he imposed upon the public by the representation of bad pieces, he ought to open their eyes in gratitude for the reception they had met. This Opera, I fear, like the works of the Spanish dramatist, tho' applauded on the stage, may fall under censure in the closet, where it must appear divested of that aid it received from your excellent musical compositions.[7]

Whether or not this letter is wholly authentic, or a self-fashioning creative preface, it concerns more than MacNally's anxiety: it also reveals his entrepreneurial understanding of print culture. In 1773, MacNally moved from Dublin to London with hopes of studying law. *The Annual Biography and Obituary, for the Year 1821* tells of MacNally's early career as a writer working himself through school: "His means of subsistence entirely arose out of his pen; for, by his various talents, he superintended several magazines; and, at length, became editor of the Public Ledger."[8] MacNally's obituary exhibits his knowledge of print culture and its potential for income for publishable writers. In print, MacNally's opera would fully realize its author's inventive aspirations, both artistically and financially. With the success of *Robin Hood* on stage, achieving publication was relatively effortless. The revised of libretto performed on October 12 was picked up and printed by John Almon shortly thereafter. On October 30, 1784, the *Public Advertiser* reports: "This day is Published by J. Almon ROBIN HOOD."[9] Prior to Almon's publication, only songbooks for *Robin Hood* were available to theater goers; now, to MacNally's satisfaction, the entire libretto was for sale.[10]

John Almon is best known as a politically radical champion of the free press, unrivaled as the chief opposition bookseller of the late eighteenth century.[11] Almon's career was consumed by writing, publishing, printing, and selling articles, pamphlets, and books both for and about political opposition parties in England. After the death of his first wife, Elizabeth Jackson, Almon married the widow of William Parker in September, 1784. This marriage proved to be advantageous, as the late Mr. Parker was the owner and printer of the *General Advertiser*, and Almon began business at 183 Fleet Street.[12] He must have acquired MacNally's libretto sometime between late September and his October 30 advertisement of the printing. Almon was the primary printer of *Robin Hood; or, Sherwood Forest*, publishing five editions between 1784 and 1787, and later editions for booksellers W. Lowndes in 1789 and G. Goulding in 1798.[13]

During the 1786-87 theatre season a new songbook was printed for MacNally: "ADDITIONAL SONGS | IN THE OPERA OF | ROBIN HOOD."[14] It is unclear whether Almon had a hand in the printing of the songbook, or if was printed by the theatre. The additional songs are printed as part of the libretto in his 1789 edition for W. Lowndes. Almon had access to the songs either because he had printed the songbook or because he was later granted them for the Lowndes edition; the evidence is inconclusive. In addition to the libretto and subsequent songbooks, John Bland printed the musical compositions of William Shield, to which *Robin Hood* owed much of its success, in 1785.

Transatlantic *Robin Hood*

The earliest surviving American text related to MacNally's *Robin Hood* is a songbook printed by M. Carey in 1794: *Songs in the Comic Opera of Robin Hood*. The songbook was made available during performances at The New Theatre in Philadelphia and could be purchased for ten cents. The first and only complete American edition of the play was printed by David Longworth at the Dramatic Repository, Shakespeare Gallery (New York) in 1808.[15] Longworth began work there in 1802, publishing small playbooks for both actors and theatergoers. In 1807, Longworth began printing the drama series, *The English and American Stage*, which would total forty volumes. Longworth was also the first American printer to specialize in drama. From 1802 through 1821, Longworth printed 429 editions of 347 plays.[16]

The title page of Longworth's *Robin Hood* mentions a 1786 edition of the play upon which his 1808 text is based. It also provides the essential information needed to trace the probable dissemination of MacNally's opera, both on stage and in print, from England to America. It reads:

ROBIN HOOD; | OR, | SHERWOOD FOREST: | A COMIC OPERA, | IN TWO ACTS. | [decorative rule] | By LEONARD MAC NALLY, Esq. | [decorative rule] | WITH ALL THE ADDITIONAL SONGS. | AS PERFORMED AT THE THEATRE, NEW YORK. | (from Hodgkinson's prompt-book.) | [first published 1786] | [double rule] | NEW YORK: | PUBLISHED BY D. LONGWORTH, | At the Dramatic Repository, | Shakespeare Gallery. | [decorative rule] | 1808

Hodgkinson's 1786 promptbook does not survive, but it is most likely a version of John Almon's 1786 edition.

The 1786 London edition and 1808 New York editions have only a handful of differences, mainly punctuation preferences. Despite Longworth's claim to include all additional songs, the 1808 edition possesses only one song is not found in Almon's. Longworth's claim to include additional songs may reflect the frequent striking of songs from stage performances in New York or other American theatres, as songs were often cut or augmented depending on the health and talent of the cast.[17] What is most interesting about Longworth's claim, however, is that there were at least six additional songs printed in London after 1786 and one additional song printed in the Philadelphia songbook (1784). Of the these seven printed songs, only one is reprinted by Longworth, "The

Juice of Sparkling Wine."[18] Longworth's American edition is clearly not from Hodgkinson's "promptbook"; rather, it is most likely from Hodgkinson's copy of Almon's 1786 edition.

The importation of *Robin Hood* follows the transient career of the actor John Hodgkinson. In 1790, John Hodgkinson moved from Exeter to join the Bath-Bristol players and soon thereafter, he became one of the leading actors of the troupe. *Robin Hood* was often played at the Theatre Royal, Bath from 1785 until 1805. In Hodgkinson's brief stint at Bath, the company performed *Robin Hood* twice, one performance each season.[19] After refusing several offers from London theaters, Hodgkinson wrote Lewis Hallam and John Henry in New York in December 1791, hoping that he might secure a position for himself and his second wife, actress Frances Brett, in America. In June 1792, Mr. Henry came to Bath to recruit Hodgkinson. After reaching an agreement for both he and his wife, Hodgkinson came stateside in 1793.[20]

Robin Hood was first performed on the American stage in Annapolis on January 24, 1794, nearly one year after Hodgkinson moved to Philadelphia.[21] At that time, during the construction of the New Theater, Annapolis was the temporary home of the Philadelphia theater troupe. And, while there is no record of his involvement in this particular production, Hodgkinson was certainly behind the opera's import: where Hodgkinson went, MacNally's opera followed. After spending only a few months with the Philadelphia troupe, Hodgkinson moved to New York. The New York theater company debuted *Robin Hood* on April 30,1794, with Hodgkinson playing the role of Ruttekin.[22] As part of the Old American Company, Hodgkinson was also connected to, acted with, and sometimes owned and managed theaters in Boston and Charleston. MacNally's libretto only made it to the stages of companies associated with Hodgkinson, and having brought Leonard MacNally's *Robin Hood; or, Sherwood Forest* to the American stage, Hodgkinson, in turn, also brought it into American print.

Textual Variants and Unexpected Continuities

The printed texts of MacNally's libretto remained relatively uniform to Almon's 1784 edition in both Britain and America.[23] The few major variances among the printed texts all concern the inclusion, induction, or subtraction of songs. These changes not only reflect the evolution of the stage production, but also illustrate how the successes of the stage production shaped the contents of the printed text. *Robin Hood*'s author, actors, and printers all demonstrate a willingness to cater to consumer's tastes. By the time the 1789 W. Lowndes edition was printed, three songs were cut: "Holy Land," "Oh, Love," and "The Archers are Mad;" one song was reassigned: "Nut Brown Ale;" and four songs were added: "Charming Clorinda," "Generous Wine," "The Morn, Who Night Adorning," and "Bright Sol." Most of these changes are simple substitutions that scarcely affect the integrity of work or its meaning. The major alterations are limited to the moral redressing of the Friar. One might have expected more revisions by American directors and printers, as the piece is one of the earliest

Robin Hood texts in the post-Revolution era. The version of the medieval folk-hero American audiences will come to love—the rebel champion of justice—is nothing like the gentrified Robin Hood found in MacNally's opera.

The Friar's outlandish behavior and suggestive immorality appears to have been somewhat problematic for audiences, if not MacNally himself, as he is the site of the opera's major revisions. *Robin Hood* features a scene in which the Friar and Little John engage in a bow contest. After receiving a thorough lashing, John instructs a fellow bowmen to "let him [the Friar] have liquor to moisten the clay, for I see his ruby nose, he is a wet soul with a dry liver."[24] Thus far, the libretti of the 1784 and 1787 editions are the same, but hereafter they vary considerably. The 1784 text has the Friar responding to John's command most favorably: "Go on, my lad, remember your orders—let me have liquor."[25] The Friar continues with a rather humorous song, "Holy Land," in which he sings of his many adventures:

> I am just arrived from the Holy Land,
> Over the bush and under the briar;
> And I drink till I neither can sit, walk, or stand,
>
> . . . .
> If on my way I meet a bonny lass,
> Over the bush and under the briar;
> Then a blessing I give—snug on the grass—
> For I am a jolly old Friar.[26]

The scene then ends with the bowman and Friar's exit and John's pithy remark: "a goodly psalm-singer: yet his notes would sound better in a tavern than a cathedral."[27] Here, MacNally follows the medieval tradition of lampooning friars, as the Friar's song is a confession of his own debauchery. How audiences might have received this is uncertain, but the alterations of this scene in the 1787 edition may provide some insight.

Following John's instructions to give the Friar a drink, the 1787 edition includes a new stage direction: "exit John."[28] The Friar's former lines are canceled and replaced by an anonymous archer's: "I warrant we'll plenty of liquor to 'moisten our clay.'"[29] The Friar's song, "Holy Land," is then replaced by "Nut Brown Ale," which is also sung by the Archer:

> O give me stout brown ale—
> Ale that the plowman's heart up keeps,
> And equals it to tyrant thrones;
> And wipes the eye that ever weeps;
> And lulls in sweet and dainty sleeps
> Th' o'er wearied bone—
> Old brown ale
> Nut brown ale
> Stout brown ale[30]

Little John, without the aid of any stage direction, returns to deliver the same cutting line. This once pithy line, however, now falls flat. To imply that a yeoman's behavior is more appropriate to the tavern than to a catherdral seems to be a statement of the obvious, rather than a good joke.

In the 1784 edition, "Nut Brown Ale" is song by the Friar in reply to Robin Hood's invitation to drink "Ale-ale-ale." [31] Having been reassigned to the anonymous archer, the song is replaced in this scene with a new composition, "Generous Wine," in the 1787 edition. Here, the second of the tavern scenes is wholly revised. Rather than eagerly chanting for ale, the Friar instead politely asks for wine. Robin responds with "Generous Wine," a song celebrating the wonders of wine in a pastoral mode. Why MacNally decided to change the moral nature of the Friar is unclear. Perhaps the emendations were in response to changing audience tastes, as the end of the Restoration period witnessed a rise in the Catholic faith in England.[32] In America, the textual history does not reveal a problem with the lampooning of an immoral religious figure. The 1808 New York edition partially revives the drunken Friar by returning to him his original tavern psalm, "Nut Brown Ale."

The liberal alterations to the Friar by the author and subsequent printers exhibit a willingness revise and present a more palatable version of the opera. The revisions seem to only address moral and not the expected thematic concerns, namely the lack of any "Robin Hood business."[33] In the abovementioned letter to William Shield, MacNally goes on to acknowledge the rich literary tradition upon which his opera is based:

> The three principle ideas which combine the subject are not original, but borrowed from ballads of *Robin Hood*, the *Nutbrown Maid*, and the *Hermit of the Dale*....It was my first intention to have taken all the songs from old ballads; those I selected are, I trust, not ill chosen, or unacceptable to the piece. Robin Hood and his merry Archers have often been upon the Stage. The *Biographia Dramatica* gives an account of six pieces in which this celebrated outlaw was the hero, exclusive of the *Sad Shepherd* by Ben Johnson; but it does not appear that any of them met with success.[34]

MacNally's opera, then, is little more than collage of "borrowed" Robin Hood materials, a literary patchwork of medieval ballads and Early Modern plays. Recent scholarship has shown that MacNally's likely ballad source is Thomas Evans's 1777 collection, *Old Ballads, Historical and Narrative*.[35] In his landmark anthology, Evans reproduced twenty-seven Robin Hood ballads, many of which had not been before printed. Stephen Knight argues that, "while Thomas Evans's collection appears to have made MacNally aware of the ballads, there is little sign that they are used for more than a few names."[36] Knight's criticism of this Restoration-era Robin is founded on the notable absence of the "bandit action" characteristic the medieval source material.[37]   To be sure, the outlaw's contests, tricks, guises, and adventures are all left wanting. The libretto is preoccupied with estranged lovers whose reconciliation drives the plot. And, in the opera's anticlimactic conclusion, Robin Hood is justified not by his rebel might, but through a compliant marriage. MacNally suppresses the "bandit action" of medieval folklore to assert a more gentlemanly hero. In the first act, Little John explains the circumstances behind Robin's outlawry: "[Robin] was betrothed to the fair Clorinda…on the very eve of marriage he was ordered from the court… in that instant the noble Huntington became an object of the King's displeasure." Cast as the exiled "noble Huntington," MacNally's Robin Hood is a direct lift from Anthony Munday's sixteenth-century play, *The Downfall of Robert Earl of Huntington*. Of all the available Robin Hoods to choose from, MacNally offers audiences Munday's flat Robert Earl of Huntington in the bandit's stead.

MacNally's characterization of Robin Hood is a fitting choice for his English audience, who had grown accustomed this kind of disenfranchised noble outlaw. But, apart from his temporary trouble with the king, this version of Robin Hood seems the least attractive of the ready-made Robins waiting to be adopted by Revolutionary-minded audiences in America. *Robin Hood; or, Sherwood Forrest* is among earliest known Robin Hood narratives to be performed and published in America; and the import of the gentrified, even loyalist leaning, Robin Hood defies all expectations. After all, in the years following the Revolution, American medievalists were busy reviving the fallen heroes of the Peasant's Revolt as the ideological forerunners of the newly liberated nation; and these hagiographic accounts of Wat Tyler and Jack Straw are certainly akin to the Robin Hood of the late medieval ballad tradition.[38] Regardless of contemporary expectations, *Robin Hood* is witness to the continued popularity of medievally themed works and their significance to the study of transatlantic literatures. The popular reception of *Robin Hood* in both England and America, on stage and in print, highlights the critical relevance of the two countries' shared medieval heritage and underscores the cultural ties binding the two nations together.

WESTERN MICHIGAN UNIVERSITY

NOTES

1   Charles Beecher Hogan, *The London Stage 1660-1800, A Calendar of Plays, Entertainments and Afterpieces*, Part 5: 1776-1800, vol. 2 (Carbondale, Illinois: S. Illinois UP), 638, 696-711.
2   In its forth season (87-88) Robin Hood was performed 29 times (Hogan 1002); in its first three seasons the play had been performed a total of 26 times (Hogan 638, 732, 823). Anticipating success in the 87-88 season, a song book was to be sold to the theatre that included six new songs (Hogan 1014). On 28 December, 1789 MacNally's comic opera was cut down into two acts for the first time, without MacNally's knowledge: "MacNally brought [Arthur Murphy] to Covent-garden Theatre to see [Robin Hood]; when, to the surprise of the author…the opera was that night performed as an afterpiece . . . cut down into two acts" (John O'Keeffe, *Recollections of the Life of John O'Keeffe, written by Himself*. London [1826] 45).

3   Alfred Loewenburg, *Annals of Opera: 1597-1940*, vol. I, 2nd ed., (Geneva, 1955): 1.409-10.

4   Linda V. Troost, "Robin Hood Musicals in Eighteenth-Century London," *Robin Hood in Popular Culture: Violence, Transgression, and Justice*, ed. Thomas Hahn. (Cambridge: D.S. Brewer, 2000), 256.

5   *The London Magazine*, April 1784, 325.

6   *The London Magazine*, October 1784, 315.

7   Leonard Macnally, *Robin Hood; or, Sherwood Forest* (London: Almon, 1784), v.

8   Anon., *The Annual Biography and Obituary, for the Year 1821* (London: Longman, 1821), 311.

9   Hogan, *London Stage*, 696.

10   That same year J. Exshaw also printed the opera in Dublin It is unclear whether Exshaw's printing was authorized, a possibility since MacNally was a native of Dublin. *Robin Hood; or, Sherwood Forest* had debuted in Dublin on December 30, 1784. The Exshaw edition is practically identical to the Almon, save minor punctuation variations. Either Exshaw's edition was authorized to coincide with the opera's debut, or it is was pirated. *Robin Hood* was reprinted in Dublin in 1788 by Sleater, Chamberlaine and etc., but this imprint has not been reviewed. To further complicate the matter, Troost notes a 1783 Dublin edition; however, there is no record of this edition, save her own. Troost's dates should be confirmed or amended as they could shed new light on the publication history and the dissemination of the text between Dublin and London.

11   Deborah D. Rogers, "John Almon," *Dictionary of Literary Biography*, vol. 154 (Detroit: Gale, 1986), 3-8.

12   Ibid.

13   The texts of Almon's editions do not vary considerably. The first edition (1784) and second edition (1786) are identical and subsequent printings contain "alterations and additions as it is now performed" which concern, primarily, changes in the songs. The printing for Lowndes contains differences in punctuation, inclusion of new songs, and the reassigning of old songs, which most likely reflect changes in the stage production. I have not reviewed the Goulding edition.

14   Hogan, *London Stage*, 1014. In a copy of the first edition housed in the special collections at Ohio State University, there is, tipped in after the page 1, a copy of the songbook. The songbook contains six "additional" songs printed on four sheets, eight pages.

15   The National Catalog records an 1803 printing by Longman, yet the date is questionable; this impression has not been reviewed. The only known copy of the 1803 printing is at Harvard. Longworth began work at the Repository in 1802, making the date possible.

16   Theodora Mills, *American Literary Publishing Houses*, ed. Peter Dzwonkoski, vol. 49 of *Dictionary of Literary Biography* (Detroit: Gale, 1986), 227.

17   Longworth's two-act title page is also a reflection of the stage performance, as the printed text actually includes MacNally's original three-act libretto.

18   "The Juice of Sparkling Wine" was previously printed in the aforementioned 1787-8 Covent Garden songbook.

19   Arnold Hale ed.,*Theatre Royal, Bath: The Orchard Street Calendar 1750-1805* (Dublin: Kingsman P, 1977), 132, 137.

20   Philip H. Highfill, *A Biographical Dictionary of Actors, Actresses, Musicians, Dancers, Managers and Other Stage Personnel in London: 1660-1800*, vol. 7 (Carbondale, IL: S. Illinois UP, 1982), 350-51.

21   George O. Seilhamer, *History of the American Theatre from 1774-1797 vol. 3.* (New York: Harper, 1896), 150.

22   Seilhamer, *History of the American Theatre*, 81, 91. The New York premier was part of a benefit for "Mrs. Hodgkinson" (81), who also played the part of Clarinda that evening (91).

23   Most of textual variances tend to reflect each publisher's preferences in punctuation and style. Almon's London printings capitalize formal titles like "Earl," "Lady," "Friar," and even that of "Tinker," whereas Exshaw's Dublin edition does not. Further variances include Exshaw's preference for colons in place of Almon's use of semicolons. The text of the New York edition is also, if not more so, true to Almon's. The only prominent variance of the New York libretto is Longworth's substitution of "knave" for "sirrah."

24   Leonard Macnally, *Robin Hood; or, Sherwood Forest* (London:Almon, 1784), 11.

25   Macnally, *Robin Hood* (1784), 11.

26   Ibid., 11-12

27   Ibid., 12.

28   Leonard Macnally, *Robin Hood; or, Sherwood Forest,* 5th ed., (London: Almon, 1787), 10.

29   Macnally, *Robin Hood* (1787), 10.

30   Ibid.

31   Macnally, *Robin Hood* (1784), 37.

32   MacNally was himself a descendent of devote Catholic believers from Ireland; see *The Annual Biography and Obituary, for the Year 1821*, (London: Longman, 1821), 310.

33   Troost, "Robin Hood Musicals," 256.

34   MacNally, *Robin Hood* (1784), vi-vii.

35   See Stephen Knight, *Robin Hood: A Mythic Biography*, (Ithaca, NY: Cornell UP, 2003), 92; and Troost, "Robin Hood Musicals," 256.

36   Knight, *Robin Hood Biography*, 92.

37   Ibid.

38   See Roger Wood, "'The History is Concisely This': Thomas Paine's Account of the Peasant's Revolt," in *Medievalism in North America*, ed. Kathleen Verduin, *Studies in Medievalism VI* (Cambridge: D.S. Brewer, 1994), 2-20.

The Battle of Maldon in Imitative Translation[1]

Gwendolyn A. Morgan

...........was broken
He bade the bold warriors abandon horses,
force them far off, and forth march on,
consider their sword-play and sovereignty.
Then Offa's kinsman, earlier learning
that his leader would not allow cowardice,
freed from his hands and let fly his valued
hawk to the holt, and to the battle hied.
(Thus a man would know that never would this one
weaken at the war.) Then his weapons he seized.
Also would Eadric his earl serve well,
fight for his old friend, and so went forth bearing
spear to the slaughter. His spirits were high
all the while he with his hands might still hold
board and broadsword, proving his boast
that he for his friend would fight boldly.
Then great Byrhtnoth did incite his brave men,
encouraged and called, showed his kinsmen
how they should stand and keep their stead,
and bade them hold their shields bravely in their hands,
fast in their fists, and never fear.
When he had his folk fairly arrayed,
he remained with the men who were most dear to him,
where his friends of the field he knew most faithful.
There stood on the strand, stoutly calling,
the Vikings' herald. It hot words
of pride he imparted the pirates'
errand to the earl where he stood by the ocean:
"I am sent to thee by the surly seamen,
ordered to say to you that you must send now
booty under truce; for it is better for you
that this war you should win with tribute
than we such a bloody battle fight:
no need to spill life if you speed in this.
We will for such treasure make a truce.
If you will grant this, you who are greatest here,
that you your people's price will buy,
concede to the seamen and suffer their terms—
give gold meekly and gain peace from us—
we will with that treasure return to our ships

and fare on the flood, and you will keep your freedom."
Byrhtnoth answered, his board aloft
and spear shaking, spoke these words,
angry and awful, and thus answered him:
"Hear this, pirate, what these folk say?
They will for your tribute tender spears,
evil ash-points and ancient swords,
such gear of war as will gain you nothing.
Vikings' vassal, this vaunt return:
tell your people this more fearsome boast,
that here stands an honored earl with his throng,
of a mind to hold this homeland,
soil of Aethelred, my honored sire,
his folk and farms. Fall you shall,
heathens, in heaps. It is harsh, I think,
that you with our gold should go to your ships
still unfought, since you this far
into our homeland have come.
You shall not so timidly our treasure gain;
first ash-spear and edge must urge us,
with grim gashes, ere we give tribute."
He bade them bear shields, bravely advance
till they on the estuary all stood firm.
Because of the water the war could not begin;
there came a flooding flow after ebbing—
the looming waters locked. Too long it seemed to them
before they could together clash their spears.
Beside Panta's stream the press now stood,
the East Saxons' shafts and the ship's force.
Not one of them could do another harm
but those earls who, through arrows' flight, earned death.
The flood went out; the seamen stood eager,
pirates in force, praying for battle.
The heroes' leader bade them to hold the bridge.
A war-hard warrior who was called Wulfstan,
bravest of his band and bred of Ceola,
did the foremost man with his Frankish spear strike
when he boldly stepped on the bridge.
There stood with Wulfstan fearless warriors,
Aelfere and Maccus, men most daring,
who would not at the ford flee the battle,
but they fought hard with their foes' band
while they their weapons wielded strongly.
When men understood and earnestly learned
that those bridge wardens fought bitterly,

they began to lie then, those loathed guests,
asking to be allowed to land in safety,
to lead through the flood's ford their foot-soldiers.
Then the earl began, being overly proud,
to allow too much land to those loathed men.
He began calling then over the cold water,
Byrhtelm's best son, (and brave ones listened):
"Now your way is cleared, come quickly to us and
grapple with these guards. God only knows
who this war-field shall win today."
The sea-wolves waded through water in plenty,
those wild warriors, west over Panta.
Over sheer water, shouldering weapons,
the loathed men landed, lifting their shields.
Then against their foes fearlessly stood
Byrthnoth with bold men; he bade them with shields
to work the war-hedge, and the warriors held
fast against the fiends. Then the fight neared,
and rewards of war-play, and wyrd brought that time
when those fated men would fall.
Then a wail arose. Ravens whirled and
eagles were eager for flesh. Earth heard the cries.
They loosed from their fists flint-hard spears.
Well-sharpened shafts flew.
Bows became busy; boards took spears.
Bitter was the battle-rush. Brave men fell.
On either hand earls lay dead.
Wulfmar was wounded, his war-rest chosen,
Byrhtnoth's kinsman. By cunning sword
his sister's son was sorely hewn.
Then the sea-wolves were rewarded in kind.
I heard that Edward an earl slew
sorely with his sword, swinging so fast
that he fell at his feet, the fated warrior.
For this his chief gave him great thanks,
his master, when he had a moment.
Thus, standing firmly, the stout-hearted
friends in the fray fondly wondered
who, with his shaft, should first
from the lost men take life,
warriors with weapons. Woe fell on earth.
They stood steadfast. Byrhtnoth instructed them,
said that each should think only of war,
who would on the Danes bring doom.
Men went to war eagerly, weapons upheld,

shields as their shelters, one shoulder to the next.
On rushed the earnest earl at his foe,
each to the other intending evil.
A seaman then sent forth a southern lance
that woefully wounded the warriors' lord.
He shoved it with his shield so that the shaft burst
and the spear split, and it sprang away.
The earl was grimly angry. With his ash-spear he stung
the haughty heathen who had wounded him.
Wise was the war-lord; he let his weapon go
through the man's throat, threw it so hard
that he tore the loathed one's life away.
Then he was again so gravely stabbed
that the bright armor burst; hurt in the breast he was,
through the locked rings, riven in his heart
by poisoned point. The earl was proud.
He laughed, the merry man, gave his Maker thanks
for the day's works which the dear Lord gave him.
Then some Dane let go a dart from his hand
flying with such force that it went fully
through the earl, Aethelred's man.
By his side stood a youth still not grown
who camped with his kin— he quickly
pulled from the proud lord the bloody point.
Wulfstan's son, Wulfmar the young,
let it go so hard it flew back again.
The lance drove in, and on the earth lay
he who had wounded the war-lord.
The daring warrior went to the dead—
he would that bold one's bracelets fetch,
his rings and armor and rich sword.
Then Byrhtnoth brought his blade from the sheath,
broad and bright-edged, and on that breast smote.
He was quickly parried by some pirate
who thus the earl's arm destroyed and
gave to the ground that gold-hilted sword.
He could not hold onto the hard blade
nor wield weapons. Yet these words he spoke,
the hoary hero, to hale warriors,
bade them keep on, bold comrades.
He could no longer stand firm on his feet.
He looked to heaven:
"I thank Thee, thane's Lord,
for all the joys I had on this earth.
Now have I, mild Maker, much need

that You to my ghost grant goodness,
so that my soul be sent to Thee
into Thy heart, Lord of hosts,
and depart with peace. I am praying to Thee
that the hell-foe not harm it."
Then he was hewed down by heathen soldiers
and both the bold ones that had stood by him,
Aelfnoth and Wulmar, both lay dead,
who alongside their lords had sold their lives.
Then they fled from the fight, those who feared it.
Then Odda's son slunk off first:
Godric left the battle and abandoned the brave one
who had given him many horses.
He leapt on the stallion belonging to his lord,
riding on the saddle where he had no right,
and his brothers with him both ran:
Godric and Godwig gave no battle
but wended from the war and sought the woods,
fled to that fastness to save their flesh.
So did many more than was meet
if they had his kindness at all recalled
and the good he tendered to his troops.
So had Offa one day earlier said
in the communal place where he held council
that there were proud claims crowed by many
who, once in danger, would not endure.
Now there had fallen the folks' leader,
Aethelred's earl. They all saw,
mighty warriors, that their master lay.
Still there poured forth proud fighter,
men yet unafraid eagerly hurried,
wishing for either one or the other:
to lose their lives or see their lord avenged.
So they exhorted Aelfric's son,
a warrior of few winters, to give them words.
Aelfwine thus boasted in brave speech:
"Remember that many times over the mead we spoke,
when we on our benches boasted out loud,
heroes in the hall, about hard combat.
Now let us prove those proud claims.
I will my honors even thus assert:
in Mercia I was of mighty family—
my grandfather was the great Ealhelm,
a wise ruler of worldly renown.
I shall not be reproached by princes of any folk

that I from this war wished to flee,
to seek my native land now my lord has fallen
and gone to his grave. That is my greatest sorrow—
he was both my kin and my brave leader."
Then he went forth, wanting revenge,
and with his spear sprang at another
foe in the field so that he lay dead,
wasted with that weapon. Then to the warriors he called,
comrades and kin, that they come forward.
Offa then spoke, ash-spear aloft:
"Now you, Aelfwine, have reminded all
brave ones of their boasts, as our bold leader lies,
the earl on the earth. Duty orders
that each of us exhort the other
warriors to war, as long as we our weapons may
yet have and hold— hardened mace,
good spear, and gilt sword. Godric has,
Odda's evil son, betrayed us all.
Many of us held that, when he took to horse,
on that strong stallion, that it was our stalwart lord.
Whence here on the war-field warriors split
and broke the shield-wall. Shame on his action
which here put so many men to flight!"
Leofsunu then spoke, his linden upheld,
shield to serve him, and said to the warriors,
"This do I swear: that I hence will not
flee a foot's length, but will go forward,
wreaking havoc on our foes for my ring-giver.
Never will Sturmere's steadfast men
whip me with their words, now my wine-lord is dead,
that I, lordless, left for home,
wended from the war. I shall seize my weapons,
ash and iron." He strode angrily
and fought fearlessly, despising flight.
Dunnere then spoke, drawing his spear,
old comrade, to all called out,
bade the brave ones avenge Byrhtnoth:
"Never may he linger who longs for revenge
on the foes of the field, nor fear for his life."
Then they marched forward, defying danger.
The stalwart started a strong offensive,
grasping spears grimly, to God swore
that they would work vengeance for their wine-lord
and their enemies evilly slay.
Even their hostage began to help them then;

he was a Northumbrian of hardy kin,
Ecglaf's son, he was Aescferth by name.
He winced not a bit at the war-play,
but sent flying forth fearsome arrows.
Sometimes he hit a shield, sometimes shot a warrior,
every once in a while he wounded someone,
as long as he could wield his weapons.
Ever in the front stood Edward the tall,
bold in battle. Boastfully he vowed
that he would not flee a footstep of ground
back from the battle when his better lay dead.
He broke the board-wall and with the brave ones fought
until he his silver-giver on the seamen
viciously avenged, ere the Vikings slew him.
So did Aetheric, honorable man,
worthy and willing, war earnestly.
Sibryht's brother besides many others
cleaved curved shields, comrades in arms
burst shields' borders, and burnished mail sang
terror-songs in plenty. Then in battle slew
Offa a pirate, and the earth received him.
There too Gadd's kinsman sought the ground.
Soon in awful combat Offa had fallen;
but he fulfilled his vow to his dear lord first,
his earlier boast to his brave ring-giver,
that they should both ride to the burg and
come home whole or here meet death
on the war-field, wounded fatally.
He lay honorably beside his lord.
Then shields were shattered. Pirates surged forth,
made war-mad. Many spears pierced
doomed soul-dwellings. Onward Wistan drove,
Thurstan's son, slaying enemies.
He was in the throng, the bane of three foes
before Wigelin's son killed him in the slaughter.
There was fierce battle. Standing fast,
war-proud warriors felt the weight of swords and
fell, weary from wounds. Woe fell on the earth.
Oswald and Eadwald all the while,
both those brothers, boldly exhorted
their dear kinsmen, encouraged
them to endure dire hardships,
unwavering in weapons' use.
Byrhtwold shouted, shield in hand,
(he was a loyal thane), his lance quickened;

in high spirit he spoke to his men:
"Courage will be keener, hearts the clearer,
spirit the surer, as our number shrinks.
Here lies our better, lifeless now,
our cherished comrade. Ever cursed be
he who now from this war-play wishes to go.
I am old of life. I will not leave
but by the side of my silver-giver,
by my dearest lord, I wish to lie."
And so Aethelgar's son they all encouraged,
Godric, to grim war. Oft the let go a pointed
war-spear to whirl on the seawolves.
So he in the force firmest continued,
cutting and crushing, until he succumbed to death.
Godric was never one who war forbore…

MONTANA STATE UNIVERSITY

NOTE

1   This translation originally appeared in Gwendolyn Morgan, *Anglo-Saxon Poems in Imitative Translation: The Harp and the Cross,* Lewiston: Edwin Mellen, 2001.

The Battle of Maldon:
A One-act Play for Readers' Theater

Edward. L. Risden

<u>Characters</u>
Ellen Ræd, reporter for the *Anglo-Saxon Chronicle*
Godric, an English soldier
Ælflæd, wife of Byrhtnoð, Earl of Essex
Mæðhild, secretary of Bishop Wulfstan
Byrhtnoð, Earl of Essex
Leofsunu, an English soldier
Ivar, the Vikings' messenger
Anlaf, leader of the Vikings
Byrhtwold, an English soldier

The first and third scenes take place in a Studio; the second scene occurs at Ely, not far from Maldon, a village in Essex on the east coast of England.

Scene 1

Ellen

Good evening gentlemen, ladies, and freemen. You slaves, if you have your master's permission, welcome; if not, get back to work! I hope all our audience heard the report from the year 937, which included the exciting account of the Battle of Brunanburh. In case you missed it, we won!

This is Ellen Ræd reporting for *The Anglo-Saxon Chronicle* on the year 991. But first a word from our sponsors, the Roman Catholic Church of Norfolk and Edwin's Wheelwrights. Got family members backsliding to heathendom? See the friendly, hard-working priests in Norfolk: we'll get the fire of faith back in them or back under them, one way or the other! Bogged down? Queued up? At Edwin's Wheelwrights we'll get you off your heels and on some wheels. Six convenient locations in Sussex and Essex, and for you Aristotelian moderates, opening soon in Middlesex!

Now for the news. In this year 991 Danish pirates, denied protection money by regional authorities, continued their depredations along the east coast, harrying around Ipswich. A stout band of English soldiery confronted them at the River Pant estuary, opposite Northey Island near Maldon. There, in a pitched battle, Ealdorman Byrhtnoð was killed by the raiders and his forces discomfited. A short time later the local bishop, the honorable Sigeric, paid the raiders the 10,000 pounds they had demanded. Can't expect every year to go like 937.

Now we go to site of the Cathedral at Ely where a tapestry, commissioned by Ælflæd, Byrhtnoð's grieving widow, depicts the entire battle in living color! Update: I've just received a report that the widow actually wove the tapestry herself. Always trust *The Anglo-Saxon Chronicle* for our up-to-decade investigative reporting. At Ely our roving reporter covered not only the tapestry story, but also a local re-enactment of the so-called "Battle of Maldon" based on Ælflæd's work, performed last year by the Ely guilds. Following, you will hear that re-enactment. While the first part of the original text has been lost, our exciting story begins: "And so he commanded the lads that they lead their horses hence, far afield, and return again, that each should direct his thoughts to his hands and high deeds."

Scene 2

Godric

I saw that the Earl would tolerate no slackness, so I released the hawk from my wrist, let it fly to the woods, prepared for battle. No sport that day but the swinging of swords.

Ælflæd

You fled that day, Godric! The poem says so: "Godwine and Godwig, and their brother Godric, no heart for fighting, fled for the forest."

Godric

Not me! That was Odda's Godric. I'm the other Godric. I "hewed and hacked, till dead I dropped." Please make sure you get it right in the tapestry, Lady Ælflæd.

Ælflæd

Good, I'll just record it all here: "Godwine, Godwig, and their *other* brother Godric."

Godric

No, no, Godric Æþelgar's son! I fought to the bitter end. Spear after spear I slung, lo! deadly darts among the dastardly Vikings.

Ælflæd

Just let me get it down correctly: "slung low," right. "Dastardly likings." Must be sure I get it all exactly.

Godric

Oh, gods. Listen, please. I slung the spears high, *high*, strung spears thick as stalks in a sheaf, rained them down on the skulls of the invaders, hewed and hacked till the battle cranked down upon me.

Ælflæd

Yes, I'm getting it. "High strung, thick stalk, cranky at the battle," was it? And what was that you said about "gods"?

Godric

Madam, can't you get a proper secretary to help you with the record?

Ælflæd

Good idea, that, and yes, I think I can. Wulfstan's secretary arrived today to deliver a message from the Bishop.

Godric

Thank Thor! I mean, thank God! No backsliders here. Can we call him in?

Ælflæd

Whom?

Godric

Wulfstan's secretary.

Ælflæd

Her.

Godric

Who?

Ælflæd

Whom.

Godric

What?

Ælflæd

Whom! Get your pronouns right. You're an Englishman!

Godric

I'm befuddled.

Ælflæd

You're who? I thought you said you're Godric the Englishman. Now, will we need that secretary or not?

Godric

I am Godric the Englishman, and, yes, I do want the secretary.

Ælflæd

Right, then, Godric, high strung and cranky: be sure to get that down. Here she is.

Godric

Who?

Ælflæd

Bishop Wulfstan's secretary: Mæðhild is her name.

Godric

A female secretary? *Rather!* Everyone knows that's a man's job, secretarial work.

Mæðhild

Not so, sir: new employment initiatives and equal opportunity. The woman secretary is the wave of the future. We have stronger verbal skills, and we're more sensitive to nuance of feeling and have greater dexteity, so we can copy speech more quickly and accurately.

Godric

It'll never catch on. You want a man for such duties: more attentive and trustworthy. All the old wives' tales say so.

Mæðhild

One wants.

Godric

Wants who?

Mæðhild

You do seem to have trouble with your pronouns, sir. But why would you trust old wives for their tales, yet not your professional women for their work?

Godric

Truly, I trust few people with words and fewer with tapestries. But I hear you came to deliver a message from the Bishop. Should you do that first?

Mæðhild

I should. I await only the presence of the Earl as well as his lady's to deliver it.

Byrhtnoð

Deliver then, young woman. The Earl himself greets you.

Mæðhild

Good day, sir. Ahem. Quote: "Bishop Wulfstan commands Ealdorman Byrhtnoð of Essex and his Lady be greeted both lovingly and respectfully. Lo, the end is near, at least of the world as we know it, unless we find a means to resist these Godless Vikings. "Settlers," they like to call themselves—*bosh*, I tell you. Mere pirates in our garden of earthly delights. Too many Christian Englishmen have failed in their duty to defend our island. Too much profit motive, too little courage. We must remember the bravery of our forefathers and, in God's name, resist these cowardly heathen invaders. And don't say they're not *cowards*: they're cowards if I say they're cowards." The Bishop's always good at anticipating interruptions. Quote: "So have your people screw their courage to the sticking place." End paragraph. Sorry: I don't know what the *sticking place* is. Maybe some poet can figure it out.

Godric

Forefathers, heathen invaders . . . But our forefathers weren't Christians. They *were* heathen invaders.

Ælflæd and Byrhtnoð (together)

Hush!

Godric

Sorry. I'm just saying.

Mæðhild

Ahem! Quote: "The signs of the prophets appear! Unless we heed God's warning and defend God's people, believe it, the end is near. Mere alms are not enough"—oh, off the record, I forgot that the Bishop also asks you to send more money for alms to the poor. Ahem. Quote: "The English must prepare from coast to coast to drive off the heathen invaders in God's name. We know we can count on you, brave and faithful . . . blank, place name here . . . Byrhtnoð, to do your part. In the name of the Father, and the Son, and the Holy Ghost, Amen." End quote. That's all! Sign here, please, for confirmation of receipt. The Earl signs here, and the Lady here, thanks. Dual responsibility laws in Essex, you know. Thank you!

Byrhtnoð

So I should understand that you're acting as Bishop Wulfstan's secretary?

Mæðhild

Yes, sir.

Byrhtnoð

Isn't that rather odd, a female secretary?

Godric

Don't ask, sir. We've been through all that.

Byrhtnoð

Ah, modern times and all that. Next thing you know they'll want to nurse injuries and teach small children, too. Can't be helped, I suppose. But surely you didn't travel alone?

Mæðhild

No, sir! I came by United Parsonage Service, UPS. It's the newest thing, faster and cheaper than government courier, just so the message isn't too long or the messenger too big: they have size restrictions. You'll recognize them by their short, brown tunics and brown horses. All over the kingdom these days.

Ælflæd

Mæðhild, do you have time to help us record a story for my tapestry before you go?

Mæðhild

Just let me check the sundial in the garden, please. Yes, ma'am, if we can hurry.

Byrhtnoð

Not too much *hurrying*, now. We must record the great deeds of our time for those who come after us, as examples of heroism and Christian duty. We must take care to tell them fully and truly.

Ælflæd

Fully and *truly*? Does anyone believe that he or she does that in our time? Don't all our poems reinforce the status of the patriarchy and the oppression of women, minorities, and the working class? How can we talk about truth with meaning infinitely deferred?

Byrhtnoð

Look, dear, we've had this discussion a hundred times. Even the great Roman poet Horace said we should write to teach by delighting; the end of literature has always been to teach proper behavior to the next generation.

Ælflæd

Horace wrote that a poem should be *dulce et utile*, sweet and useful, but even he reinforced the phal-logo-centric party line. *Record* and *truth* retain their *différance*, both different and deferred, subject to the aporia between utterances and audience, my dear big bear of a husband. But don't worry: you come off well in the tapestry.

Byrhtnoð

Yes, my sweet little badger of a wife, you're right of course, and I thank you for the tapestry, but despite the infinite deferral of meaning, the structure of discourse, both in its literary and historical contexts, and the monomythic markers inherent in heroic meaning lend it unavoidable, archetypal patterns that we need if we're to affirm the *quidditas* of human nature and experience.

Ælflæd

Perhaps, sweet husband, but the act of interpretation, the *glyph* of thought translates the original experience, inevitably *deconstructs* . . .

Mæðhild and Godric (*together*)

Ahem! (Mæðhild continues *solo*.) Sorry to interrupt, but the Bishop expects my return as near as possible to the appointed time, and UPS riders won't wait indefinitely.

Ælflæd

Quite so. Sorry. Husband, shall we get to the story?

Byrhtnoð

Indeed. I'll need the help of some of the participants from either side, and together we can render an account of—"The Battle of Maldon" is it? Yes. Danes present?

Anlaf

Anlaf, leader of the Danes, present, with his messenger, Ivar.

Ivar

Ivar, present!

Byrhtnoð

Good. English soldiers present?

Byrhtwold

Aye, sir, Byrhtwold here, with Leofsunu to speak for the English!

Leofsunu

Leofsunu here. Yes, I was there for the battle.

Godric

Me, too.

Ælflæd

"I, too," Godric.

Godric

You weren't at the battle, Lady!

Ælflæd

No, I didn't mean I was there. It's your grammar again. You should say, "I, too, was there." Nominal case for the pronoun.

Godric

Grammar, right. All too formal for me.

Leofsunu

Hey, you're Godric? You weren't there! You ran off!

Godric

Like I've said before, I'm not that Godric! That was Odda's Godric. *I* fought there, to the bitter end.

Ælflæd

It's all right; I've got it now: not Godwine's brother Godric, but his other brother Godric. And use *as* for the conjunction, not *like*.

Godric

Frea help me. Not Godwine's brother at all. Godric, Æþelgar's son. Different entirely.

Byrhtnoð

Oh, *that* Godric. Yes, I remember you now. You fought bravely to the end. But don't blaspheme.

Godric

Finally, thank Oðin. I mean, thank God!

Mæðhild

So about the battle: what happened? I'm ready to record, and time is passing.

Byrhtnoð

I can tell you some of it. I began to put the young men in trim, counsel them where to stand, how to carry their shields. Most weren't soldiers, you know, just a few—the rest but farmers and townsmen. They pledged to fight with me even as the force of harrying Danes assembled across the water. Their messenger called out fiercely to us.

Ivar

"Stout seamen sent me, bade you yield gold and bright rings for safety. You'd do better to pay tribute than battle us head-on, cruel in conflict. No need to spill blood, if you speed the spoils." See? We can alliterate as well as you can! Then I said, "So peace for payment, and your leader, if he's listening, can ransom your residents. That's little to ask: all up the coast we've aired our demands. Pay up, and we'll sail in our ships, and peace be with you." That's all I said that day, other than "yah!" and "aaar!" and "ooh-ooh-ooh!"and other such yelling and taunting. I'm good at yelling and taunting. Would you like to hear some for the record?

Ælflæd

No, thank you.

Ivar

Too bad. I really do it quite well. Just a few blood-curdling battle calls? You'll be quite impressed, I assure you.

Mæðhild

Not necessary, in the interest of time, but thank you. I've written down what you said: it's clear and succinct.

Anlaf

I'm Anlaf, leader of the Danish expedition, and Ivar tells you truly. I'd told him what to say, and he said it just as he repeats it now. Ivar always had a great voice for shouting. I can tell you the next part. Then that tall fellow, Byrhtnoð, shouted back at us, spear and shield lifted over his head. Not a bad voice himself, for an Englishman . . .

Byrhtnoð

"Can you hear this, sea captain, what these folk say? Spear tips they offer, sharp heirloom swords. Come get them! You, messenger: give your men that welcome. Here waits an earl with his troop to defend Æþelred's earth. Heathen shall perish here. Too base it seems, I believe, to yield tribute unfought. Point and blade shall decide things between us, ere we go sniveling." Then I advanced the line to the shore. The tide was in, the path cut off. It seemed then too long until we should fight them. When the tide ebbed, they had only a thin causeway to cross, one at a time, each man easy to slaughter. Leofsunu saw it from the front line.

Leofsunu

Yes, I did. An admirable leader, Byrhtnoð stood there for us against the Vikings. We believed in him, ready to follow. We shot the first man who tried to cross. Young Wulfstan, son of Ceola, did it with his bow.

Ivar

He did—I saw it. They hadn't liked my message, but I told them the *truth*. (Aside to Anlaf) We're not going to get more of that "infinite deferral" stuff from the lady just because I said *truth*, are we?

Anlaf

Shh! Then I spoke to the English myself. I haven't the loud voice of Ivar, but I know these English and their sense of fair play. A thought struck me, so I called out to the tall one and asked a favor. You may call it cheating; I call it good sense. "You, big jarl," I yelled, "just let my soldiers cross the ford, and we'll have a nice fight over there on solid ground. What do you say?" Then I turned to Ivar.

(Anlaf and Ivar snigger together.)

Godric

We saw them sniggering, you know. We had them right where we wanted them, and they knew it, too. I looked at Leofsunu: "By Oðin's eye," I said, "like he's really going to let them cross! They must think we have bull's balls for brains. Then we all laughed aloud at the thought of Byrhtnoð just letting them march over as easily as you please.

(Godric, Leofsunu, and Byrhtwold laugh aloud together.)

Byrhtwold

"They must believe we're all either mad or scared to death of them," I said. "Why would we bother to listen to such foolishness, even after all their plundering?" Then Wulfstan picked off another of them with an arrow, and I armed my bow as well.

Byrhtnoð

I heard Byrhtwold say that, and I reached over and lowered his bow. I had already made my decision, and I spoke it out: "Right! Over you come, then!"

Leofsunu

I must admit I thought he was joking. But I saw his eyes, and I knew things were about to change for the worse. Byrhtnoð waved them on over. His spirit was too great to let them go without a fight, but he wasn't strong-willed enough to turn farmers instantly into soldiers against men like that. No one is. Their leader shrugged, surprised, and then those pirates began to cross, as though we had invited them to a picnic.

Anlaf

I couldn't believe it when I heard his words and saw he intended to yield us firm ground. I wondered if it was a trick. But something, maybe the gods, told me that he meant it, so we tightened our gear, and I ordered our lads over. I saw him arrange his folk in a defensive line, and I damn near laughed out loud: kids and old men, mostly, with a few soldiers here and there, most of them looking wary, a few frightened out of their shoes—I think they knew what they stood against. I expected the young one with the bow to shoot again—he aimed, but Byrhtnoð motioned him to wait for us to pass. The poor boy looked more disappointed than afraid.

Ivar

I was one of the first to cross—well, not the very first. Young Erik looked so eager and, frankly, not too smart. And I didn't trust that English lad with the bow to follow orders. Plus I needed a bit of time to think up some especially good taunting.

Anlaf

We crossed lickety-split, before Byrhtnoð could change his mind. I could already see ravens, circling about, perching in the trees, hungry for carrion. They sensed they had a feast ahead, and oh, we gave them one.

Byrhtwold

Then both sides let spears fly; shields caught sharp edges. Bitter was that battle, men falling on both sides. Young Wulfmær was wounded: he took war-death at his kinsman's side, sliced with weapons. Edward, I heard, slew one with his sword in retribution: Byrhtnoð thanked his chamberlain for the churl who fell at his feet. Steadfast stood the Englishmen, set to win glory.

Leofsunu

Then came a hardy one, raised spear against the earl, broke shaft against shield. The grand one, enraged, unleashed his weapon through the man's throat. Byrhtnoð blithely gave thanks to the Measurer above for that thrust, for his day's work. Then some soldier let fly from his fist a deadly dart; deeply it dug into Æþelred's thane. Wulfmær dropped him for that in defense of his kinsman, dead on the ground. Byrhtnoð drew blade, bright from its sheath, and struck his attackers: many accosted him, eager for spoils. Down fell the jeweled sword when they struck it from his hand, and quickly the pirates fell upon him. Without a weapon or means to wield it, the silver-haired soldier still drove on his troops. One last speech he directed to Heaven.

Byrhtnoð

"Thank you, Lord of hosts, for the joys I had in this world. Now I ask, mild Measurer, that you grant my ghost good journey, that my soul may come into your keeping, Lord of angels, and pass into peace. I pray that these hell-dwellers may not hinder it."

Leofsunu

Those heathen hacked at him, and the men beside him, Wulfmær and Ælfnoð, till all lay dead at the side of their lord.

Byrhtwold

Then flew the sons of Odda, no fight in them, Godwine and Godwig, and their brother Godric.

Godric

Not me!

Leofsunu

They fled their lord, hardly fitting, to save their lives, forgot the gifts their leader had given them, the many favors Lord Byrhtnoð had granted. Many speak boldly, but few stand the test in the moment of truth. So fell the ealdorman, Æþelred's earl; his hearth-men saw where their hero lay. The remainder pressed on, proud thanes, fearless men, for two reasons: give up the ghost or avenge their loved one. A man spoke from the turmoil, so I recall.

Byrhtwold

"Remember the oaths we made at the mead-hall, the boasts we broached in the hall of heroes. Now we can show who be brave. I'll call out my lineage, my great Mercian kin, descended from Ealhelm, the wise ealdorman. Nor they nor this folk shall scold that I fled this battle, now that my lord lies hewed on the field. That is greatest harm to me, for he was both my kin and my lord." That man spoke and attacked, and then spoke another. "Now that our lord lies dead, we build courage in one another, call each to carry an axe, a blade, a spear, a sword, till he can carry no more. The cowardly sons of Odda betrayed us, Godric among them!"

Godric

Not me!

Byrhtwold

"So fine a horse he took, when he rode off, that many a man thought it our lord, rending the folk and splitting our shield-wall. May it render him wretched!" I know not who said that, but then I heard Leofsunu answer, raising his shield.

Leofsunu

"I vow that I shall not retreat one foot's length from this spot, but I will go further, wreak vengeance for my friend-lord. No cause will the steadfast men of Stur-Mere have to twit me with words, that I slunk home lordless, but weapons must take me, edge and iron." And fight I did. Also at point stood Edward the Tall, ready and eager, and Dunnere, too, declared their desire to avenge their captain, kept heart in the fray, prayed God to allow their vengeance that day. So did Æþeric, noble comrade, brother of Sibyrht, split enemy shields, fierce in defense. Offa struck sea-soldiers, driving them down, fulfilling his pledge till he perished in war.

Godric

So did I!

Byrhtwold

Then fell Wistan, Thurstan's son: three he slew, till Wigelm's son laid him low. Oswold and Eadwold, the famous brothers, all the while urged soldiers and kinsmen to persist at need. Many the brave, unflagging in courage . . .

Godric

Then Byrhtwold spoke his famous words—I never heard better. I stood there beside him, swinging my sword.

Byrhtwold

"Spirit must be the surer, heart the keener, grit must be the greater, as our strength wanes."

Anlaf

I heard it myself, and that's a fact. Quoted it to Olaf when I met him later. May the ages remember it.

Byrhtwold

"Here lies our Elder, all forhewed, good man on the ground. Ever may he regret it who thinks to escape this battle-plain now. I have grown too old. For me, I choose to lie here at the last with my lord."

Anlaf

That was a bit too much. He might have left it where it was.

Ivar

Wasn't much battle left in them after that, though they fought on and died to a man.

Leofsunu

A few lived yet. Æþelgar's son Godric led a last charge, foremost among them, hacked and hewed. He was not that one who fled, but a better man.

Godric

Yes, yes! He remembers at last! Redemption! Thank Þor for it. To tell the rest, though, we didn't last long—just a few of us, tired to death, bloody and lost, but unyielding. When the battle finally ended, we had taken our share of the enemy with us, we few soldiers and farmers, enough to slow the raiding along the coast and save the towns to the south. It wasn't madness, that battle, or pride, as I see it now, though some say so: we did what we could against a superior foe. We lost bravely, and that's that.

Byrhtnoð

Maybe that's not quite all. Maybe we did something worth doing, set an example, gained some time, did deeds to remember.

Anlaf

If war is worth remembering. I had plenty of it. Enjoyed it at first, but it gets old as we do, and you begin to wonder, if you let yourself, why you did it.

Ælflæd

It's not that war is worthwhile, but that *something* we can do finally has value: facing the difficult, even the impossible, with a blithe heart. That's worth a tapestry.

Ivar

No one knows that better than we Norsemen do. You should hear the Icelandic sagas.

Byrhtnoð

We learned it, too, the hard way, and we tried to leave behind us more than that yet, not a count of corpses, but a sense of—though my wife may not believe as I do—*meaning*.

Ælflæd

No, my dear, in this case I do agree with you. If you can leave behind something of value and meaning, you've done as well as we humans can do. And you did, though I'd still call you mad for doing it. The poet, too, left something of value, and so do I with my tapestry. We all resist that terrible toll of mortality. Good luck to anyone who tries, and God . . .

Godric

Please tell me she's not going to say, "God bless us, every one."

Ælflæd

I was going to say, God help the lot of us.

(*All together.*)

Amen.

Mæðhild

If no one else has anything to add, that sounds like a wrap to me, folks, and I'll be on my way. I'll leave the vellum copy with you, and I'll offer your loving greetings to the Bishop. Well, as they say in London, "Cheers."

Godric

"Cheers"? People really say that? Sounds like the name of some silly pub.

Scene 3

Ellen

There you have it, folks, straight from Ely, under the auspices of *The Anglo-Saxon Chronicle*: "The Battle of Maldon" in all its historical glory. (Aside.) I wonder how much of that my editor will cut. (Full speech again.) Well. Be sure to listen for further reports in the coming years. 992 and 993 are sure to offer special excitement, particularly after the stirring account of 991. Remember: you can order copies of the *ASC* at your local diocesan office, though you may have to sacrifice the sheep yourself. If you have a favorite year, the diocese will normally have a spare folio, so you can place your order at only a nominal charge, for the benefit of the scribe's abbey. This is Ellen Ræd, and I hope to see you again for next year's report. Meanwhile, I'll be looking for another job to fill in the gaps: once a year doesn't pay much! And you, listeners: stay safe, pray hard, and keep that upper lip stiff. From *The Anglo-Saxon Chronicle* and Newcastle's Famous Ales, remember: Courage. And a bit of brains helps, too.

END

ST. NORBERT COLLEGE

A Look at Some New Lays of Beowulf:
The Misunderstood Monsters of Contemporary Popular Music

T.S. Miller

In spite of its rather modest influence on several intervening centuries of literary history, *Beowulf* appears just about everywhere in the cultural productions of the 20th and 21st centuries. The critical commentary has been extensive on the numerous literary works the poem has inspired, its various film adaptations, and even the surprisingly large number of comic book retellings, but the lively *Beowulf* tradition in popular music has received far less thorough consideration. There are several reasons, however, why we should find *Beowulf*'s influence on music of particular interest, not least of which being the complex and likely irresolvable debate about the relationship of the original poem to oral performance and oral tradition generally, a question that seems to fascinate the popular imagination as much as it does the average philologist.[1] Indeed, in recent years *Beowulf* in oral performance has become something of a minor craze: 2007 saw the release of Benjamin Bagby's dramatization of the poem on DVD, as well as a new translation by Dick Ringler designed specifically "for oral delivery" and also recorded as an audiobook. Of course, the abridged audio version of Seamus Heaney's epochal translation had made its own splash just a few years earlier, attracting a sizeable market share in the face of some criticism for its omissions.[2] The modern audience, in short, is no longer content merely to read *Beowulf*: we want to hear it.[3]

But what of those other oral translations of *Beowulf* that we may have heard of, but may also have never heard—rock operas, *bona fide* operas, heavy metal screamfests, meditative orchestral pieces, and crooning pop songs? After a survey of these "oral performances," I have concluded that popular music has been overlooked as a site of significant aesthetic engagement with the text, in that several of these compositions are more akin to sophisticated, self-conscious riffs on the poem like John Gardner's *Grendel* than many of our film adaptations, which so often seem like little more than excuses for "period" action sequences and maybe a few corrective sex scenes.[4] At the same time, even the best of these musical adaptations do betray a prevailing pop-culture desire to rehabilitate the marginal figure, and accordingly we hear sung of many a "misunderstood monster" in these new lays. Gardner himself is no doubt partly to blame—as is the wider trend that makes Frankenstein's monster our long-suffering bosom companion and vampires our dreamboat heroes—but what remains most striking is the extent to which these songs offer interpretations of the monsters suggested or at least permitted by the text of the original poem. I am interested, however, not so much in the relative "fidelity" of the songs in question, but in the novel ways in which they make use of *Beowulf* to examine the monstrous, and the ways in which these diverse usages might in turn illuminate our understanding of the range of the poem's popular reception. I will focus primarily on British rock group Marillion's power ballad "Grendel" (1982), itself a direct successor of Gardner's novel, and then a more pensive piece by American folk-rock band the Mountain Goats titled "Grendel's Mother" (1994), which seems fairly unique among *Beowulf* adaptations—though not quite all *Beowulf* scholarship—in giving Grendel's often exceptionally animalized mother the same "misunderstood monster" treatment. Amid the din of occasionally inarticulate anthems bearing the Beowulf and Grendel brands, we can find creative rereadings of the poem that reflect or parallel the ongoing attempts of medieval scholars to come to terms with the notoriously slippery monsters with which, alongside Beowulf himself, we must perpetually contend.

Before we proceed to the pair of songs I have singled out as especially worthy objects of critical scrutiny, we must briefly consider their respective contexts as both adaptations generally and musical adaptations specifically. To be sure, anyone diving into the heap of songs titled "Grendel" in search of complex engagements with the original poem will have to sift through a considerable amount of unintelligible, vague, and/or all-around lousy lyrics. And I will confess that I have consulted only a few of the recordings by the abundant musical groups—typically bands billing themselves as some hybrid of heavy metal's many subgenres—that have taken for their name either "Grendel" or "Beowulf": one of these latter has even unselfconsciously adopted the infamous heavy metal umlaut over the "u."[5] If I seem dismissive of this considerable segment of *Beowulf*'s afterlife in contemporary music, it is due less to a personal distaste for metal or industrial music, and more to the fact that, for the most part, these bands appear uninterested in the poem beyond the most generic pagan, heroic, or monstrous resonance that the onomastic allusion contributes to their identity of choice.[6] Representative of this tendency towards invoking the poem in only a superficial way is the perhaps most prominent of the Grendels, that is to say, the Dutch one, whose music belongs to a genre that Wikipedia describes as "Aggrotech."[7] Even their 2001 self-titled track "Grendel," for instance, consists chiefly of the hoarse repetition of a few generically "dark" and "monstrous" sentiments, with the exception of a passing reference to a swampy abode: "Back to the marshes / Back to the depths / Rejoice in madness / Till your dying breath / Only humanity will fall / Only humanity will fall." No doubt we could find such lyrics in any number of contemporary songs of the same and related genres, and they would hardly evoke *any* Anglo-Saxon heroic poem.

If we step back, however, and begin to understand works like Grendel's "Grendel" in relation to *Beowulf*'s larger adaptation history, we will see that this one song, at least, may have much more to tell us about the monster's, and indeed the poem's, evolution in music, representing a distinct branch of a salient trend across our monster's popular manifestations. Whether or not we can establish with any confidence that Marillion's "epic" ballad of roughly two decades earlier influenced the Dutch electro-industrial act, a quick comparison of the two songs will, if nothing else, reveal a common denominator of anti-establishment outrage tied, in music, to the figure of *Beowulf*'s most famous monster. We need not necessarily understand the Dutch duo as speaking in the voice of a particularly recognizable Gardneresque Grendel, but their use of the first person plural pronoun in one of the last lines in the song—"We'll make you see reality / And nothing more"—suggests that the band is assuming the voice of the monster as an instrument of demystification, as it were, albeit a demystification of an particularly violent sort; the only other use of the narratorial pronoun promises only, "We'll make you suffer / Till your dying breath." As much as Marillion's elaborate narrative differs in sound, structure, and content from this impressionistic monologue—perhaps a monologue addressed to a still-living thane dragged under the surface of the mere?—we will see that the slogan "We'll make you see reality / And nothing more" is precisely that of Marillion's own Grendel.

In Marillion's case, the anti-establishment, "pro-Grendel" theme of the song much more clearly participates in a history of "misreading" of Gardner's *Grendel*—misreadings, that is, from Gardner's perspective—as indeed many might wish to designate his own novel a (lamentable) misreading of *Beowulf.*[8] I will be using the term "misreading" not so much in the full Bloomian sense, though I do not view all misreadings in a negative light, nor do I think they should be ignored. Indeed, to a certain extent, it would seem difficult to judge what is or is not a misreading of a poem—whether the reading in question takes the form of a critical essay or a piece of music—when the most dedicated scholars cannot reach anything resembling a consensus on details as fundamental as its approximate date and immediate contexts of production and reading. I suppose I would prefer the terms "responsible reading" and "irresponsible reading," yet any attempt to pass such judgments definitively would drag us down into the murky mere of evaluating not only critical heft and substance but earnestness.

Nevertheless, responsible or not, in Marillion's "Grendel" and Grendel's "Grendel"—to say nothing of the more widespread appearance of the monster in metal—we see a reinscription of just what Gardner would call "monster values" (qtd. in Fawcett and Jones 635), a phenomenon not confined to his novel's popular reception, but rampant among his own reviewers and other critical interpreters. Although I have no wish to bog down my argument in the interminable debate about how to best interpret *Grendel*, it is important that we recognize that, since its first publication, critical reception of the novel has fallen into two sharply divided camps, the one that "misreads" the text as participating enthusiastically in the existentialist tradition, and then the one Gardner himself would and did sanction, which situates *Grendel* in violent opposition to that tradition in both philosophy and fiction.[9] Only recently have some scholars attempted to pave third ways through Gardner's existential labyrinth,[10] and Marillion very clearly set themselves in one of the two original camps, namely, that which understands Grendel as not only sympathetic but philosophically enlightened. I would only emphasize, again, that it is not only '80s rockers who "misread" *Grendel* in just this way, but an entire critical and popular tradition.

In short, while Gardner intended his novel as a critique of the various existentialist and nihilistic philosophies with which Grendel flirts, his work has quite naturally escaped him, as anyone so well-acquainted with Chaucer's *House of Fame* as Gardner should have anticipated. I am not overly concerned here with the ripple of effects this unsealable can of *niceras* has produced in Gardner criticism, but John William Sutton raises a relevant point in his apt summary of the novel's fate across popular media: "*Grendel* has become a springboard for those who seek to use this character as a subversive figure who can question traditional beliefs and values" ("Beowulfiana"). Of course, as Sutton puts it elsewhere with coauthor Michael Livingston, "we can have little doubt that each [reading of *Beowulf*] will say as much about the person doing the telling as it does about the poem itself" (11).[11] All Beowulfiana is a form of autobiography, to be sure, and the musical misreadings of the poem's monsters can show us much more than the fondness of heavy metal fans for monstrous iconography, if we trace the perhaps not so unlikely journey of the *mearcstapa* from Beowulf's nightmarish nemesis to Gardner's lovable if (possibly?) misguided antihero to progressive rock countercultural symbol.

Marillion's "Grendel," in brief, offers us but a single snapshot of the monster as depicted in Gardner's novel: we observe our familiar disillusioned Grendel only in his triumphant, self-righteous bloodlust, never in his moments of self-doubt and self-loathing. In freezing Grendel at precisely the moment when he boasts of his transformation into "Grendel, Ruiner of Meadhalls, Wrecker of Kings!" (80), Marillion's song conceals the fact that Grendel only rarely glimpses such a purpose, instead flirting with a number of different philosophies of being and meaning: solipsism, nihilism, Nietzscheism, and all the rest. Just over 17 minutes in length, the song is divided into four sections,[12] the first of which is somewhat disingenuously titled "Heorot's Plea and Grendel's Awakening," since it begins the narrative *in medias res*—much like Gardner's novel—with Grendel already awake and industriously terrorizing Heorot. The song portrays the Danes as murderous, benighted pagans who "stare blindly cross the sea" hoping for a hero that, tellingly, the narrator does not seem to think will ever arrive. In contrast to the generalized descriptions of part one, the following segment, "Grendel's Journey," seems to narrate a single approach to Heorot in the manner of celebrated passages like that describing Grendel's final expedition in *Beowulf*: "Ða com of more under misthleoþum / Grendel gongan, Godes yrre bær [Then from the moor under dark mists Grendel came walking; he bore God's wrath]" (710-1).[13] The third, titled "Lurker at the Threshold,"[14] brings Grendel up to a confrontation with Danish warriors, but, if Beowulf is present, we are not told. In the song's finale, the third-person narrator disappears and we instead hear Grendel condemn the Danes and justify his predations *in propria voce*, concluding with a repetition of the performative jussive phrase, "Let the blood flow." In other words, Grendel not only survives his ballad, but appears to live locked with the Danes in that curiously a-temporal twelve-year war, which here admits of no ending, not even Gardner's.

Any genealogy of the Marillion song in Gardner, then, must be a genealogy of omissions as well as borrowings, and omissions and borrowings from a text that has already read the original poem selectively: Gardner has certainly made the question of *Beowulf*'s reception much more complex across the board. After all, Livingston and Sutton seem quite right to contend that Gardner's *Grendel* represents "a marked turning point in Beowulfiana, after which these disparate materials tend to become far more sophisticated examples of social commentary" (2), a genuine "watershed moment" prior to which, in creative responses to the poem, "Beowulf is the hero *par excellence*, and...Grendel is a fiendish monster" (3). Indeed, Marillion vocalist Fish (Derek William Dick), also the author of the lyrics to "Grendel," has made no secret of his overarching debt to Gardner: "At the time of joining the band I was asked to provide lyrics for a long track the band had written with bits that had originally been in a song called *The Tower* etc. I was obsessed with a book called *Grendel* by John Gardner and the way that it points out that anything ugly is instantly scorned upon and seen as wrong" ("Market Square Heroes"). In fact, Gardner's influence is so pronounced and so profound that the song's engagement with the text of *Beowulf* may be almost entirely mediated through the novel, though I would note that the name "Heorot," at least, must have originated in a distinct *Beowulf* tradition, as Gardner refers to Hrothgar's hall only as "Hart." Even so, Grendel's introduction in the song as "earth-rim-walker" clearly echoes Gardner's favorite descriptions of the monster as "earth-rim-roamer" (7) and "world-rim-walker" (127). Moreover, Marillion's reference to one of Grendel's special charms—"Hounds freeze in silence bewitched by the reptile spell"—derives exclusively from Gardner's novel: "The dogs fall silent at the edge of my spell" (13). Finally, while one could list several more parallels, Marillion also takes care to mention Grendel's murder of children – "Heorot awaits him like lamb to the butcher's knife / Stellular heavens ignore even children's cries"—as does Gardner's Grendel, who flags the act as especially gratuitous in a potshot at Vonnegut: "A shadow looms over them (mine) and they're gone forever. So it goes" (142).

Other similarities between the two texts run far deeper, and in some ways—but only some ways—we can describe the song as a thematically "faithful" adaptation of (parts of) Gardner's novel. For instance, Marillion's Grendel's scorn for the Danes' "Wooden figures, pagan gods," reflects Gardner's monster's amusement at the "lifeless sticks" they worship (52), and both share a distinct distaste for empty boasts and speechmaking. In "Grendel," Grendel dismissively sings, "Well I've had enough of all your pretty pretty speeches"; while, in the novel, Gardner includes a pastiche of touchstone heroic sentiments derived from the text of *Maldon* and Wiglaf's speech outside the dragon's den, and his Grendel repeatedly rejects such "interminable orations" (81) as "long-winded, tediously poetic, all lies" (101). Both Grendels, however, are even more enraged by the Shaper's poetic falsehoods, as well as by the Wealhþeow figure, with the Marillion narrator judiciously pairing these two sources of irritation: "The shaper's lies his poisoned tongue malign with mocking harp

/ Beguiling queen her innocence offends his icy heart." Likewise, Gardner's
Grendel describes the queen as 'beautiful, as innocent as dawn on winter
hills," perforce "[tearing him] apart as once the Shaper's song had done" (100),
and he seems especially incensed by the particular species of fabrication that
entails "sly revisions of the bloody past" (102). Very like many adaptations of
Gardner's work, "Grendel" seizes on the monster's criticism of the original
poem's heroes, here and elsewhere, and thus the song's disparaging stance
on the petty, profiteering wars of the Danes resonates far more with *Grendel*
than with *Beowulf*:

> So you say you believe in all of Mother Nature's laws
> You lust for gold with your sharpened knives
> Oh when your hoards are gathered and your enemies left to rot
> You pray with your bloodstained hands at the feet of your pagan gods
> Then you try to place the killer's blade in my hand
> You call for justice and distort the truth.

In other words, the two Grendels resemble one another most nearly in their
common desire to deflate heroic culture in any way possible, to unmask, in
Marillion's terms, the "Heroes' delusion."

The only thing missing from Marillion's rendition of *Grendel* is the
parenthesis, that sort of self-pitying, self-critical hiccough—"(Her-kapf)"
(128)—that accompanies every major philosophical or moral statement
Gardner's monster might make. Indeed, the absolute self-righteousness of
Marillion's Grendel—"Why should I feel pity when you kill your own and feel
no shame / God's on my side, sure as hell, I'm gonna take no blame / I'm
gonna take no blame, I'm gonna take no blame"—we find belied in the very
first page of Gardner's novel, in which the eponymous monster describes his
vendetta against Hrothgar as "my idiotic war" (5). Nor does any semblance
of superiority tincture his criticism of the Danes: "Not, of course that I fool
myself with thoughts that I'm more noble" (6). While Marillion's Grendel lives
a purpose-driven if violent life, Gardner's spends his days in purposeless,
goalless anomie; in other words, whereas Gardner's Grendel recognizes his
irresistible impulse to kill as a pathology, "the sickness I can observe in myself"
(11), Marillion's Grendel finds a noble calling in making the Danes "pay in
blood for all [their] vicious slander." The passage from *Grendel* in which the
monster nearly kills the queen provides the best illustration of how Marillion
omits thematically crucial instances of parenthetical self-undermining: "I would
kill her and teach them reality. Grendel the truth-teacher, phantasm-tester! It
was what I would be from this day forward—my commitment, my character as
long as I lived—nothing alive or dead could change my mind!" (110). Then a
paragraph break, and the immediate deflation: "I changed my mind. It would
be meaningless, killing her. As meaningless as letting her live" (110). Note also
that in this passage Grendel toys with taking up the same purpose driving the
speaker of the Dutch Grendel's "Grendel"—"We'll make you see reality"—but

that both bands prefer to ignore how this solution to Grendel's existential crisis fails to satisfy him for even a moment.

Indeed, Marillion's Grendel is nothing if not convinced of his own righteous purpose, concluding the song with a reassertion of his self-defined role as instrument of divine justice: "Receive your punishment, expose your throats to my righteous claws / And let the blood flow, and [let the blood flow], flow, flow, flow." Marillion, in short, seem to accept the ontological explanation of the monster to which the Danes cling in *Grendel*, an explanation that Grendel himself scorns: "'This is some punishment sent us,' I hear them bawling from the hill" (13). The understanding of Grendel as a divinely-appointed avenger rather than a being cursed by God remains a minority view in *Beowulf* scholarship, but we can find it expressed in some quarters, as in an essay by Fidel Fajardo-Acosta that includes in its title the happy phrase "the Elusiveness of Grendel": "Grendel seems indeed a sort of manifestation of a divine decree against the way of life of the Danes" (206). And, looking past *Grendel* back to the original poem, Marillion's wonderful line "God's on my side, sure as hell" makes the always-tempting move of reconfiguring the sense of "Godes yrre bær" (711b) from he who carries the mark of God's wrath upon him to he who carries God's wrath in his claws and delivers it to the target of that wrath, as it were. In the last analysis dramatically different from Gardner's monster, *this* Grendel believes in both justice and truth.

But there is still the problem of Beowulf. Since "Grendel" never directs the audience to ponder the implications of Grendel's eventual defeat at a hero's hands when he had believed himself invincible, we must now ask whether we are to read any irony into Grendel's considerable self-possession in the song. After all, not only is this a Grendel without a good deal of Gardner, this is a Grendel without a Beowulf—a seeming impossibility in any retelling of the poem named for him, even a retelling once or twice removed. Although Marillion elegantly captures Heorot's despair—"Wooden figures, pagan gods, stare blindly cross the sea / Appeal for help from ocean fogs, for savior born of dreams"—the song again suppresses Gardner's monster's fear that the savior will indeed come: "Something is coming, strange as spring. I am afraid. Standing on an open hill, I imagine muffled footsteps overhead" (126). At the same time, we should keep in mind that in the novel our poor schizoid Grendel later dismisses the tales of a hero from across the sea as "lies" told to children (141): perhaps both monsters are simply suffering from denial, intermittent in one case and absolute in the other. In consequence, when Grendel insists in the last chapter of the novel that his own mortal wounding by Beowulf is the result of nothing but a chance accident, we can imagine that Marillion's Grendel would probably say much the same thing, for all of their philosophical differences. Marillion's consistently sympathetic stance towards their Grendel simply does not admit of the kind of ironic readings Gardner preferred for his own novel: if there is no Beowulf, as in the text of their song, it would seem that all things *are* lawful for a vigilante monster. Even were the savior to materialize from the fog as we readers of *Beowulf* know he must, all the evidence in the song would continue to uphold Grendel's righteousness; after all, the hypocritical warriors deserved their punishment, and their punisher will accept no blame.

Above all, Marillion uses Gardner's novel as justification to refashion Grendel as revolutionary *Übermonster*, but the song demands further examination in the context of the misunderstood monster tradition more generally, a tradition in which Gardner himself participates, and a tradition that includes the complex but parallel reception histories of monsters like Frankenstein's cast-off creature. The moment in *Grendel* that seems most obviously Shelleyan is, of course, Grendel's ill-fated attempt to join the revelers in the mead hall, which precisely reproduces the scene of Shelley's monster's entrance into the De Lacey cottage; Grendel's words even echo the James Whale versions of the story: "I sank to my knees, crying, 'Friend! Friend!'" (52).[15] In addition, this scene perhaps provides the only concrete connection to *Grendel* or *Beowulf* in American rock group Sunny Day Real Estate's own song "Grendel": "I wanted to be them / But instead I destroyed my chance." Marillion's "Grendel," however, avoids modeling the creature on Frankenstein in any such transparent way, in favor of a pastiche of misunderstood monstrosity that includes Caliban as well as more recently farrowed mooncalves like Tolkien's Gollum.[16] In fact, the band had originally chosen the name "Silmarillion" after Tolkien's unfinished saga, but quickly dropped the first three letters, according to Dave Wilson, in order "to avoid copyright issues" with the notoriously litigious Tolkien Estate (33). Because of the obvious influence of *Beowulf* on Tolkien and his works, Gollum and the original Grendel are often compared themselves,[17] and efforts to attenuate Gollum's own monstrosity have proceeded apace.[18] Particularly in light of Grendel's predominant characterization as misunderstood monster in popular music, it is no coincidence that Peter Jackson should have elected to feature a woeful ballad told from Gollum's perspective during the credits of his 2002 adaptation of *The Two Towers*: "And we will weep to be so alone / We are lost, we can never go home."

Of course, the impulse to "rehabilitate" these literary monsters is not limited to music,[19] and certainly not limited to popular culture at large, as we see especially prominently in Caliban's reception in both postcolonial literatures and postcolonial studies. In a review of Gardner's novel, Timothy Foote points out that, "[l]ike Shakespeare's Caliban, Grendel has learned to swear from listening to men" (1), yet Marillion—intentionally or otherwise—builds on the connection with the Shakespearean intertext in a way Gardner does not, in a kinder, gentler glimpse of Grendel's interior life: "Silken membranes span his path, fingerprints in dew / Denizens of twilight lands humbly beg him through / Mother nature's bastard child shunned by leaf and stream / An alien in an alien land seeks solace within dreams." This last image distinctly recalls Caliban's famous speech from the *Tempest*:

> Be not afeard. The isle is full of noises,
> Sounds, and sweet airs, that give delight and hurt not.
> Sometimes a thousand twangling instruments

Will hum about mine ears, and sometime voices
That if I then had waked after long sleep,
Will make me sleep again; and then in dreaming
The clouds methought would open and show riches
Ready to drop upon me, that when I waked
I cried to dream again. (3.2.130-8)

Moreover, the epithet "an alien in an alien land" aligns Grendel not with Cain but Moses (Exodus 2:22), almost the antitype of Cain, a repentant killer who goes on to become the great prophet and lawgiver. This reversal accords perfectly well with the conclusion of the song, which places the law squarely in Grendel's bloody but righteous claws, the hypocrites unfit to rule. Thus, in a more sophisticated way than the Dutch electronica duo, Marillion harnesses in Grendel the universal image of the misunderstood monster—no pun on Universal Horror intended—in order to drive home their anti-establishment critique.[20] Considering the reception of Grendel in rock and metal in this manner helps us understand why the Finnish metal band Grendel may have chosen to title their latest album *A Change Through Destruction*, rather than simply, say, *Destruction*. Although far from Gardner's intended meaning for his novel, Marillion's rereading sanctions neither existentialism or nihilism, instead simply finding Grendel not only well-suited to the "epic" impulse of (neo-)progressive rock, but also the perfect avatar of the anti-institutional.

While Marillion's version of Grendel's war has surely had the widest reach in the music world, lyrical compositions about Grendel continued and continue to be produced, albeit with a much lower profile. In the song "Grendel Reborn" (2007), for instance, somewhat smaller-time Second Life pop-star Barty Aum tells a surrealistic modern-day fable that seems to feature *Beowulf* as intertext only to invoke Grendel as an archetypal monster, in this new incarnation "a horrid beast from the genetical circus," a rapidly-growing devourer whose "father was darkness" and "mother was heat." Although Beowulf's name heralds the monster's arrival—"Out of the east came a Beowulf cry"—any resemblance between the two Grendels likely ends there. Likewise, the novelty song "Green'ich Grendel" (1965), covered as recently as 1994 by the Ranch Hounds but originally by Sam the Sham & the Pharaohs of "Wooly Bully" fame , stars a character named after the monster—"I know a chick Grendel is her name"—but who hardly seems monstrous in the least: "She wears shades on her baby blues / Digs folk rock and poetry too." And, although this interpretation still tempts me, I must concede that the song's refrain, "She's so far out / She's in," is probably not making any kind of statement about the marginalization of Grendel's mother and the later feminist reclamation of the marginal female, nor about the mainstreaming of the margins generally in academic literary criticism or otherwise. Yet, after having so obviously scraped the bottom of the barrel of pop-music Grendels, we should now turn our attention to this maternal monster, a monster so far out for so long that she does in fact, finally seem to have come into her own.

With a few significant exceptions—many of them recent—neither pop culture adaptations of *Beowulf* nor scholarship on the poem has been very kind to the being that, at some point in the story's reception history, became fully animalized as "Grendel's *dam*."[21] While the issue of her reception is surely more complex, Gardner has again helped establish this precedent with his depiction of a loathsome, inarticulate, and decidedly animalistic primal matron, a "[l]ife-bloated, baffled, long-suffering hag" who "never speaks" (11).[22] Accordingly, Karen Emanuelson seems correct to observe a general trend towards the intensification of the relative monstrosity of the maternal "brimwylf [sea-wolf]" (1599), even when the popular image of Grendel has become gradually more and more humanized: "Grendel's mother has been presented as a monster in most translations and re-tellings of the epic poem. Each depiction has strengthened the image of her as non-human, inherently evil and monstrous in appearance" (268).[23] In soaring defiance of this trend, however, is the 1994 Mountain Goats song "Grendel's Mother," which I will discuss in the context of a few related sympathetic takes on the "aglæcwif" (1259). The lyrics to "Grendel's Mother" were written by John Darnielle—the sole lyricist behind the band's prolific output and often its only performer— whom Sasha Frere-Jones of the *New Yorker* has described in superlative terms as "America's best non-hip-hop lyricist" (1), and whom Laura Barton of the *Guardian* has also lionized as "arguably the best lyricist of his generation." To be sure, the Mountain Goats have established a reputation as a hyper-"literary" outfit: not only is Darnielle surely one of the few recording artists to have both alluded to Dostoevsky ("Love, Love, Love," *The Sunset Tree*, 2005) and sampled T. S. Eliot ("I Wonder Where Our Love Has Gone," *Sweden*, 1995), but he also whimsically bestows EPs with titles like *Taking the Dative* (1994) and *Songs for Petronius* (1992)—not a bad choice, I suppose, for an arbiter of taste. In terms of its own immediate genesis, however, "Grendel's Mother" would appear to be nothing more than one of the many fine products of the standard Brit-Lit survey, according to an account of a live performance of the song: "Before treating the audience to 'Grendel's Mom,' Darnielle explains how he wrote the song during the last twenty minutes of British Lit, bitterly arranging lyrics while 'people ask[ed] questions just to prove they read the assignment'" (Sally). We can say with confidence, then, that Darnielle's take on Grendel's mother comes straight from the source, as it were, free, perhaps, of Gardner's mediation in a way few attempts to tease a misunderstood monster out of *Beowulf* can be.

If we have seen how the Grendel of heavy metal and '80s rock in part emerged from a prior construction of monstrosity already existing in or readily appropriable by those genres, so too does Darnielle's vision of the disaffected monstrous in "Grendel's Mother" represent but one facet of a broader fascination with the concept, though, in his case, it is perhaps a somewhat more personal one. The extensive lyrical corpus of the Mountain Goats includes several album-spanning song cycles, members of which are typically flagged by a recurring collocation in song titles or lyrics, but I would suggest that we can also see the outline of a more nebulous sort of "monster cycle" beginning to take shape alongside those already identified. Indeed, Darnielle makes no secret of the fact that he has *always* been interested in monsters: "My English thesis was gonna be about monstrosity as a concept. But I wound up writing it on Joan Didion instead" (Barton). Moreover, an especially large number of monstrous *narrators* appear in Darnielle's music, even if we restrict ourselves to the "genuine" monsters, that is, passing over those who are simply human beings behaving monstrously. Of course, we don't need the *Beowulf*-poet with his slippery designation "aglæca" to remind us that the two are connected, and Darnielle will often narrate from the perspective of, say, a rapist, a murderer, or an all-around violent and destructive person: "Everyone's a monster," declares the narrator of "Letter from Belgium" (*We Shall All Be Healed*, 2004), "That's cool with all of us."[24] And Darnielle seems keen to give every monster its hearing-out.

For the example most manifestly relevant to our marginalized Others in the Grendelkin, I would point to the narrator of Darnielle's "Creature Song," a (misunderstood? repentant?) Caliban who concludes his rather un-Browningesque monologue, "No harm intended / No harm / Oh brave new world / that has such people in it / Oh brave new world / Brave." In the music of the Mountain Goats, then, we see a particular approach to the Hollywood trope of the misunderstood monster grounded as firmly in literary sources as in celluloid, and the entire tradition acts as another key intertext alongside *Beowulf* and (perhaps) *Grendel*. The original release of "Creature Song" was roughly contemporaneous with "Grendel's Mother," but monstrosity has not drifted far from Darnielle's mind since, despite his abandonment of such staples of his music as his signature lo-fi recording style, which his 2002 album *Tallahassee* marks. In a 2006 release, Darnielle spins a story about a breakup that births a kind of Frankenstein's monster, and distinctly of the misunderstood, James Whale variety. His song "If You See Light" opens with a framing metaphor that quotes the final scenes of the 1931 film—"When the villagers come to my door / I will hide underneath the table in the dining room / Knees drawn to my chest"—but the narrator leaves us himself left "Waiting for the front door to splinter / Waiting all winter." The album on which the song appears, *Get Lonely*, develops the conceit of post-breakup monstrosity over several songs; according to Darnielle, *Get Lonely* in fact originated, among other things, as "a projected group of songs about monsters" (Heater).[25] The Frankenstein motif continues in both "Song for Lonely Giants" and "New Monster Avenue," which concludes with the line, "All the neighbors come on out to their front porches, waving torches." Nor have later albums shied from depicting *literal* monsters: 2008's *Heretic Pride* features the track "How to Embrace a Swamp Creature," a song about another down-and-out (though presumably still allegorical) fen-denizen feeling "out of [his] element" and unable to breathe. This album has a broader pulp/horror theme: it opens with a track titled "Sax Rohmer, Pt. 1" and concludes with "Michael Myers Resplendent," rounded out in the middle with "Lovecraft in Brooklyn." The song "Tianchi Lake" also paints us a picturesque scene complete with a friendly enough lake monster: "Backstroking on the surface, moonlight on its face / Floats the Tianchi Monster, staring into space." In an explicatory comic included in the album's promotional press kit and available online, Darnielle writes—quite earnestly, it would seem—that "[t] he Mountain Goats consider themselves friends to all lake and river monsters everywhere whether they exist or not"; Darnielle proves himself equally kind to our often friendless "merewif [water-woman]" (1519).

But perhaps the most interesting of the Mountain Goats's marginalized monsters may be found in their most marginalized tracks, which Darnielle has only made available through various methods of limited or unofficial release. For example, a demo that failed to make *Heretic Pride*, "The Mummy's Hand," returns us to the world of Universal Horror, and summons from across the aeons the voice of yet another lonesome, mournful monster: "I spent several thousand years down here all alone / No way to stand the lonely old ache in my bones." Finally, Darnielle returns to the *locus classicus* of misunderstood monstrosity in "Bride," a track excluded from the 2009 album *The Life of the World to Come*, which itself retains hints of the monstrous in the form of witches and zombies: "Bodies reassembling down where the worms crawl / Make your own friends when the world's gone cold" ("Hebrews 11:40"). "Bride" is a meditation on Whale's famous sequel *Bride of Frankenstein*—"Designed for one another / We lay tied to our slabs / While the same electricity that gave us life / Crackles through the lab"—which relies heavily on the repetition of the male creature's final words in the film, "We belong dead." Darnielle has hinted on the band's online forums that he plans to "cannibalize" the song into a future work ("New song" 6), but for now these two complementary hymns to Universal Horror remain buried, monsters in Darnielle's closet, his very own brood of *mearcstapan*.

It seems more than clear that a fascination with recovering the voice of the monster has been an overriding preoccupation of the lyricist of "Grendel's Mother," but we must now ask why Darnielle has chosen this particular monster. The Mountain Goats song, rather than using the misunderstood monster for any kind of institutional critique, instead explores the character as an emblem of, well, motherhood: *this* lonesome monster is lonesome because she is a bereaved mother, and as such the song stands as an attempt to transform the sea-wolf of the poem into a she-wolf, perhaps of the Capitoline variety.[26] On the most basic level, "Grendel's Mother" takes the form of a familiar monologue ostensibly directed at Beowulf—or perhaps even her victim Æschere, incriminated with Beowulf—but that monologue is distinguished by a decidedly "maternal" mode of address that ironically implicates Beowulf with Grendel as both "wayward sons." The ambiguity in the addressee centers around the suppressed violence of the repeated and admittedly animalistic maternal image, "I will carry you home in my teeth," which, here in the song's conclusion, could apply equally well to the young pup Grendel, or to the decapitated corpse of a thane—the only one in the poem whom Grendel's mother does carry home in her teeth—or to a hero against whom she is making a solemn threat:

You can stand up or you can run
You and I both know what you've done
And I will carry you home
I will carry you home
I will carry you home in my teeth.

Speaking firmly to the hero as if he were a child caught in the act—"You and I both know what you've done"—Grendel's mother makes a vow to treat the slayer of her son in the same manner we might imagine she would retrieve her Grendel, who has regrettably caught his death for poaching on mankind. (Many of Grendel's mothers warn him against just such bad behavior, including Angelina Jolie.) In fact, the description of her addressee's behavior in the mead hall – "In the great hall you drink red wine / You chew meat off the bone"—would work fairly well as a free translation of "þæt banlocan, blod edrum dranc, / synsnædum swealh [bit into the bone-lockers, drank blood in streams, swallowed great morsels]" (742-3a), with "red wine" acting as a wonderfully monstrous kenning for Grendel's own beverage of choice. In short, while the song belongs to a long tradition of adaptations associating Beowulf and the monster with which he grapples, to my knowledge we have not seen one that effects the association in just this way: through patient, subdued reprimanding by a knowing mother-figure.

That Grendel's mother cannot be reproving her "real" biological son on the strictly literal level we see confirmed in lines that reference his death: "I laid my son on bier, I burned the wreath / Fire overhead, water underneath." Of all the translations and adaptations of the poem I have consulted, in my opinion Darnielle—*pace* Heaney—has here given us one of the more poetic renderings of that memorable collocation "fyr on flode [fire on the water]" (1366), the terrible wonder that dances nightly on the surface of the monsters' mere. In its opening lines, "Grendel's Mother" also provides yet another idiosyncratic explanation for the phenomenon of the mere's illumination, but I suppose it is no more outlandish than any of the others: "The cave mouth shines / By pure force of will / I look down on the world / From the top of this lonesome hill." Commentators have long tried to rationalize the supernatural image of "fyr on flode" as foxfire or a will-o'-the-wisp—that is, a stack of rotting wood or a puff of marsh gas—but Darnielle insists that, no, no, it's Grendel's mother who's responsible: "By pure force of will."[27] In fact, this explanation seems a fitting creative counterpart to Edward B. Irving's suggestion that "Grendel's mother is the mere, in fact" (114). But most striking about Darnielle's take on the mere is his association of its description with a funeral—and not simply any funeral, but Grendel's. The rhyme "burned the wreath"/"water underneath" makes the (I think) unique move of tying the image to a funeral bier or ship cremation, or even the full-fledged *fyr-on-flode* "Viking burial" with which pop culture is so enamored. And here, also, the mere remains the ultimate *locus ab-amoenus*, the same place of death it is in *Beowulf*, but, rather than the place that confronts the hart or the hero with death, the mere has become the place of death and *grieving*, grieving for a lost son.

The unusual image of Grendel's mother participating in the very same type of funeral rites that the Danes and the Geats perform for their own fallen heroes is remarkable for many reasons, not least of which being the way in which Darnielle thereby aligns Grendel's mother even more closely with other lamenting parents in *Beowulf* like Hildeburh, or even the figurative father of "The Father's Lament" (ll. 2444-2462a). Mary Lou Reside, who argues in an unpublished thesis that as a powerful woman Grendel's mother becomes a "casualty" of the perpetuation of male heroic culture, has also made such a comparison: "Grendel's mother stands with Hildeburh lamenting at the funeral pyre, the pyre on which lie both Hildeburh's son and her brother, giving her songs their power to heal the pain of death" (8).[28] Even Kevin S. Kiernan has lent his support to this association, in an essay that further tracks the ways in which the *Beowulf*-poet—long before Darnielle—presents Grendel's mother in human terms: "Hildeburh and Hengest, bereaved mother and avenger, together foreshadow the behavior of the *ides, aglaec-wif*" (27). In other words, as an independent aesthetic response to the *Beowulf*, "Grendel's Mother" nevertheless serves as a lyrical translation of a range of critical readings of the poem, even those advanced by heavyweight scholars like Kiernan: "Her grief seems as real as Hrothgar's, and her response, swift life-for-life vengeance, is (mutatis mutandis) as heroic as Beowulf's. Our client has, in fact, both legal and textual precedent for her attack on Heorot" (27).[29]

With plenty of precedent in the scholarship, then, Darnielle has conjured up an irresistible new image of Grendel's mother as a patient but stern parent, bereaved and grieving yet determined to pursue justice with a cool head, rather than blinded by bloodlust and vengeful rage. "Grendel's Mother" is not a simplistic rewriting of the narrative such that Grendel or his mother becomes the aggrieved party and the hero turns out to be the real monster: instead, the killer Beowulf, the killer Grendel, and the killer in his avenger find themselves on equal terms. Thus, when Grendel's mother describes her approach to Heorot—"I come naked and alone"—Darnielle communicates her feelings of both bereavement and powerlessness, but also sets her on identical footing with Beowulf, "naked and alone" being precisely how Beowulf always insists on fighting. Moreover, the outrageous anachronism in the song's first half—"And you can run, and run some more / From here all the way to Singapore / But I will carry you home in my teeth"—obscures the more subtle, and I should think no less deliberate, anachronism that dots our generic medieval Europe with excessively advanced fortifications: "I beat down the new path to the castle."[30] These deliberate anachronisms mirror the tissue of past and present in *Beowulf*, a poem produced by a Christian chronicler of a departed heroic age; in Darnielle we have a postmodern chronicler of that same age, and most everything else since.

Up to this point I have perhaps overemphasized the uniqueness of "Grendel's Mother" as a creative response to the poem, because we may in fact find a strikingly (if superficially) similar song hidden in the filk tradition, a typically more or less amateur strain of folk music associated with science fiction fandom. "Grendel," a song by Pegasus Award-winning filk artist Kathy Mar, also gives voice to a grieving Grendel's mother, and, although it has kept a much lower profile, likely limited to close-knit filk circles, it predates the Mountain Goats song by at least a few years, having been first recorded in 1988. Just as we might expect a known monster-lover like Darnielle to approach Grendel's mother with atypical sympathy, we might expect an empowered female filker like Mar to likewise eschew both the animalistic and the highly sexed representation of Grendel's mother so popular in Hollywood. As Kathleen Forni suggests in her articles on both Graham Baker and Robert Zemeckis's *Beowulf* films, the interests of a lucrative young male demographic might encourage this latter representation of Grendel's mother, while discouraging in the mainstream treatments like Mar's, which encourage identification with the monster in her role as—of all things—a mother.[31]

In spite of their similarities, the filk song is far jauntier than "Grendel's Mother," and, while not entirely parodic, Mar's song suffers, I feel, from a tongue-in-cheek folk style that detracts from the real gravity of the parental grief on which it reflects.[32] Further unlike Darnielle in approach, Mar recuperates the mother's character at the expense of the son, and that from the very beginning of the song: "Dumb as dirt and twice as mean, such a son makes mother crazy / Foul as sewers I have seen, ugly, loutish, large, and lazy / That's the child I've had to raise, what's a mom to do / Drag him in an ocean cave and stay to watch him too." The chorus allows for an even more instructive comparison with "Grendel's Mother," since in subject matter it comes very near to Darnielle's striking account of a funeral scene: "Son of mine you've been a disappointment since your birth / Now I've had to bury you in this cold Northern earth / I know you would be sorry if you weren't so very dead / But you never listened to a word I said." While the phrase "bury you in this cold Northern earth" can strike a real note of pathos, and the hint of wistful reproof from "Grendel's Mother" surfaces here in the final line, the previous line obviously undercuts the high seriousness of the burial with the flippant phrase "so very dead," which I can only imagine generating titters and chuckles in performance. The stoic resolve of the song's final stanza, if again diluted by some unaccountable levity, nevertheless confirms that Mar's heart seems to be in approximately the same place as Darnielle's: "When I found my wine was spiked it was far too late to aid him / Though there wasn't much I liked I was often glad I made him / So I must avenge him now, what's a mom to do / If he was yours anyhow I'll bet that you would too." To my ear, Mar's persistently playful stance towards her subject matter—I hesitate to describe it as "folksy"—causes the song to compare unfavorably with Darnielle's as a serious approach to imagining the perspective of a marginalized, aggrieved figure of monstrosity, but it remains quite noteworthy for its not so uncanny anticipation of later revenge ballads like Darnielle's that dignify Grendel's mother.

I use the phrase "revenge ballads" in the plural, because one final significant deposition of Grendel's mother remains to be discussed, namely, Marijane Osborn's magnificently titled poem "Grendel's Mother Broods Over

Her Feral Son," which appeared in a recent issue of the *Old English Newsletter*. Throughout this essay, I have attempted to demonstrate how often certain creative rereadings of *Beowulf* can independently parallel certain other critical interpretations, and in Osborn's poem we may observe the reverse (obverse?) of this process, in effect allowing us to see in the confluence of both trends that they are probably one and the same. Osborn's poem positions Grendel's mother—still nameless, but no longer voiceless—as a castoff fling of "High Halfdane": "He raped me, then he spoke of love, then cut / my tongue out so that I could not betray / him and his men, whose plans I knew, in words" (20). We see that, like Darnielle and Mar, Osborn is eager to supply Grendel's mother with a voice, but she chooses to address the issue of the character's silence in the original poem—and perhaps in its reception history—in a more sophisticated manner, explaining why she should be "a mother inarticulate as a wolf" through recourse to this clever analogue to the tales of Philomela and Shakespeare's Lavinia (21). In contrast to the two songs, Grendel's mother addresses her still-living son in order to incite him to vengeance, sending him to his death as duty requires, rather than lamenting his deviant violence. Of course, as Roy M. Liuzza puts it in his concise introduction, Osborn's poem "takes a fine point of philology" as inspiration (20), and, in contrast to Darnielle's fast-and-loose way with history, her poem functions in large part as an extrapolative exploration of a historical conception of revenge as reconstructed from modern scholarship. Nevertheless, her basic creative motivation seems not too distantly removed from, say, Roger Avary's own claim that his inspiration for the retelling of *Beowulf* that eventually became the Zemeckis adaptation originated in a careful reading of the poem and its narrative omissions: "Perhaps scenes had been added to spice up the tale. And perhaps, as I increasingly suspected, critical elements had been left out, edited by the passage of time" (5). Moreover, Osborn's reorganization of *Beowulf*'s family trees naturally turns Hrothgar into Grendel's brother, reflecting the same desire to fill the vacuum of Grendel's paternity that we see in so many adaptations of the poem, Avary and Neil Gaiman's script of course prominently included. Osborn's poem is certainly the more rigorous and the more "plausible" of these two exercises in counterfactual literary history, but they represent analogous engagements with the text, which alter it (fruitfully or otherwise) according to different artistic goals and the expectations of different audiences.

I am not necessarily arguing here that "Grendel's Mother" and Osborn's poem are of comparable aesthetic quality—and I am certainly not arguing that her work, both creative and critical, approaches any kind of equivalency with something like the Zemeckis film—but these three lyric compositions in the voice of Grendel's mother would seem, at the least, most productively studied together. In spite of similar motivations and several other shared characteristics, each work reaches a different audience: a distinct subset of the speculative fiction community, the body of indie-minded college students—and slightly aged former college students—that constitute the bulk of the Mountain Goats's fan base,[33] and then the rather modest by comparison circulation of an academic publication like the *Old English Newsletter* (I do not wish to imply any kind of hierarchy here). Considered together, these compositions demonstrate how Umberto Eco's distinction between the sins of mass media "fantastic neomedievalism" and "responsible philological examination" has become increasingly difficult to parse across various hybrid reading and viewing communities (63), depending on the extent to which scholarship may inform necessarily speculative creative works, and, I suppose, on how "fantastic" we may wish to judge some of the more baroque critical fads of the past few decades. Arguably, Eco himself had already begun to participate in this blurring of the two with novels like *The Name of the Rose*, and I do think a blurring or blending is a more appropriate description of the state of affairs in modern medievalisms than the "oscillation" between two poles that Eco identified (63).

By way of illustration, and to return to Grendel himself for a moment with our trio of maternal lullabies still in mind, we can also find thoroughly dispersed across modern literary culture—in the mass marketplace, the "highbrow" literary world, and the academy—that impulse to reclaim Grendel the fearsome "mearcstapa" as an outcast closer to the pitiable "eardstapa" of a text like *The Wanderer* (6). While Heaney's translation does very little in the way of rehabilitating Grendel's "troll-dam" (xiv), he reserves much more sympathy for Grendel himself, whom he describes "a mixture of Caliban and hoplite" (xviii).[34] And, while the Zemeckis film bludgeons us rather artlessly with the theme of the commonality of hero and monster—with Beowulf in fact declaring himself a monster on numerous occasions[35]--Livingston and Sutton rightly emphasize that works "that muddle the moral clarity of good hero against evil monster are largely indebted to Gardner, but they also highlight a theme that may be lurking in the original poem" (10). Stanley B. Greenfield, for one, suggests "a touch of the monstrous in the hero" (294-5), and, while he is content to prove only that the poet speaks of *Beowulf* in superhuman terms, leaving him one of the "good monsters" (297), many other scholars have not stopped there.[36] More than anything, the growing confluence (and conflicts) of popular media, scholarship, and primary texts themselves have irrevocably altered the ways in which this poem is read, and indeed Liuzza speaks to these sorts of issues when he explains the editorial decision to publish Osborn's poem as in part "a reminder that old works of literature like *Beowulf* will continue to matter to contemporary readers only if we have the courage to apply not just philological skill and critical discernment, but also emotional intelligence and creative imagination, to our interpretation of them" (20). Although her approach rests on a much firmer foundation in a lifetime of study and scholarship, Osborn's poem, especially in the context of the direct predecessors discussed here, illustrates the same impulse we see across the field of popular music: the impulse to hear *Beowulf* anew, and in new ways.

Will the proliferation of musical Beowulfiana begin to slow as the Zemeckis film and its concomitant media campaign fade from the collective pop consciousness? I should expect not, if only because the explosion of *Beowulf* productions for stage and song largely preceded its release. More significantly, the continued presence of *Beowulf* and/or *Grendel* in AP English classes across the U. S., combined with the increasing use of media technologies like YouTube and the increasing ubiquity of inexpensive video cameras, will also undoubtedly continue to inspire, facilitate, and widely circulate new aesthetic responses to a poem that once narrowly survived complete destruction in a single manuscript copy. Today on YouTube, for example, one can already find a cover of the Mountain Goats's "Grendel's Mother" by unsigned alternative band Stillicide, who themselves update the old mid-'90s track by sampling Heaney reading Heaney. And then there are those videos perhaps favored with fewer views but no less interesting for it in the context of the poem's reception history, videos that feature musical compositions like "Avenging Grendel," a performance by three high school students with lyrics by a Tamlyn Miller. This a cappella trio consists of Grendel's Mother, Sea Serpent 1, and the indispensable Sea Serpent 2, and the lyrics contain a series of (tragically) heroic boasts against Beowulf's life: "Beowulf is gonna go down / Beowulf is gonna drown." It should be apparent that the oral *afterlife* of the poem has rapidly become far more complex than any early proponents of the oral-formulaic theory could have imagined, and these new lays of Beowulf do deserve a listen in all their variety, if only for the astonishing scope of that variety—and lest they suffer the same lonesome fate as the spurned and mistreated monsters they imagine.[37] If some of our 20th and 21st-century *scops* have decided to switch out the harp for the acoustic guitar, we must still recognize what they are and what they mean: new Shapers of *Beowulf*, and new shapes for *Beowulf*.

UNIVERSITY OF NOTRE DAME

NOTES

1   After the endlessly divisive question of the poem's dating, the problem of its relative orality and "literacy" has likely been the second most fiercely argued point of contention in *Beowulf* scholarship, if not in all of Anglo-Saxon studies. While something resembling an uneasy consensus has been reached, any affirmative statements on the oral character of the poem remain couched in fairly circumspect language, as John Niles's representative summation illustrates: "While the question of the mode of composition of the original poem will probably never be resolved, the text as we have it bears the traces of an oral verse-making technique as well as features typically associated with an oral-traditional mentality" (144). For a more complete history of the debate, see the references in Sorrell, "Oral Poetry and the World of *Beowulf*," or see the discussion in the introduction to *Klaeber's Beowulf*, clxxx-clxxxiii.

2   Not only was the original CD marketed somewhat duplicitously as containing "unabridged selections," but Douglas Ryan VanBenthuysen, while he speaks highly of Heaney's translation, has also lamented the negative, generally flattening effects of the omissions: "Taken as a whole, the omissions in Heaney's audio *Beowulf* eliminate much of the social, historical, cultural, geographical, and other contexts in which the main action of the poem takes place. They obliterate major themes such as the role

of women, the relationship between the Christian and Germanic worlds, and the role of nobility, and they tend to oversimplify and even resolve key ambiguities that often appear when these themes surface in the poem" (162).

3   Again, we see this impulse within the academic community and without. Ward Parks has even called for the scholar-driven production of "authoritative" audio versions of medieval texts, both for pedagogical purposes and, more contentiously, as "primary sources on which literary critics can ground research and interpretation" (103).

4   Scholarly opinions on the film adaptations of *Beowulf* seem to range from bemusement to fascinated acceptance to contempt -- I know, for example, that at least one of the editors of the latest Klaeber edition has expressed absolutely no desire to see the Robert Zemeckis film -- but one must conclude that Zemeckis and Neil Gaiman probably meant well enough in some respects; for a fairly sympathetic view of the filmic redefinition of the hero, see Noone, "The Monsters and the Heroes." In this particular case, I am most persuaded by Kathleen Forni's more balanced analysis of the production and its process of adaptation, which she sees as "influenced by the popular reception history of *Beowulf* and by the pressure to make a commercially viable product," and in the result of which she ultimately finds "a disquieting fusion of graphic violence and moral conservatism" ("Popularizing High Culture" 46).

5   There also seems to have been a short-lived Maryland act named "Grendels Arm" [sic] ("Petition to Reunite Grendels Arm"), and I was pleased to discover an album by Pete Castle that pays a different kind of homage to Grendel with the title *Mearcstapa*, a collection of "traditional songs" described on the label's website as "English music with a European accent." For a far more meticulous sorting-out of, for instance, all the Grendels and Beowulfs on the global music scene, see the online bibliography of "Beowulfiana" collected by John William Sutton, which also offers brief annotations of several other musical adaptations I will not be examining here. For example, omitted from this discussion is Howard Hanson's 1925 choral piece "The Lament for Beowulf," as well as the extensive if not critically well received tradition in opera and musical theater, for which see Lisi Oliver, "A Banner Year." Oliver focuses primarily on the Irish Repertory Theatre's *Beowulf* (2005) and the Triad Theatre Company's *Brother Wolf* (2006), but also covers several earlier productions as well as the Los Angeles Opera's *Grendel: Transcendence of the Great Big Bad* (2006). For a more comprehensive treatment of this latter, see Frantzen, "Grendel's Ride in LA," which takes a rather dim view of, among other things, "[t]he creative team's antipathy to heroism" (31). Finally, postdating Oliver's piece is the Banana Bag & Bodice's Off-Off-Broadway *Beowulf: A Thousand Years of Baggage* (2008-9). I ask pardon for my failure to engage with this recent spate of musical adaptations of *Beowulf* only because I understand that Oliver is at work on a book-length study concerning just such representations of the Anglo-Saxon world on the musical stage.

6   The exception here would be the underground Italian black metal band Grendel, which has recently released a pair of concept albums, titled *Beowulf* and *Dragon's Awakening*, that retell the poem in tracks like "The Golden Palace of Heorot," "The Mother of the Orc," and "Beowulf's Funeral Pyre." Unfortunately, after repeated listening I cannot make out enough of the lyrics to determine how selectively or carefully the source material has been adapted, or to judge the depth of engagement with the narrative generally.

7   I will have to take the anonymous author's word for this piece of information, as well as for the definition given for Aggrotech, "an evolution of electro-industrial and dark electro with a strong influence of techno that first surfaced in the mid-1990s."

8   Although the novel was generally well-received among academics and the public alike—and to such an extent that it is still frequently inflicted on high school students alongside their obligatory helping of *Beowulf*—not all Anglo-Saxonists embraced Gardner's idiosyncratic rereading of the poem. For example, I imagine Raymond Tripp's judgment of the novel is only somewhat tongue-in-cheek: "When the late John Gardner presented us with a maladjusted teenage Grendel, I was unconvinced, even offended" (43).

9   For two examples of what I will call the "intentionally accordant" camp, see Stromme, "The Twelve Chapters," and, more recently, Fawcett and Jones, "The Twelve Traps." Both of these articles are attempts to identify the philosophical position and/ or "heroic ideal" examined in each chapter, based on that chapter's corresponding astrological sign.

10   Although Robert Merrill concedes that "there is a real question as to whether Gardner's several aims can be reconciled," he ultimately sides with Gardner, obliquely suggesting a comparison with Milton's notorious reception history—f rom Blake to Philip Pullman—to explain where things went wrong for Gardner, as it were: "His rhetorical strategy is first to seduce us into identification with Grendel, then to reveal the terrible consequences of believing what Grendel believes. He wants to surprise us into virtue, or at least self-examination, by challenging our most basic assumptions" (171). Merrill makes his comparison between Grendel and Milton's Satan only in passing, but here he even echoes the title of Stanley Fish's *Surprised by Sin*, and, whether intentionally so or not, his proposed solution to the dilemma strongly resembles Fish's own solution to a similar critical divide in Milton studies. Coming from a rather different (deconstructionist) angle, Anna Kowalcze critiques the "sympathetic" critical camp's slavish adherence to Gardner's intentionality (see especially 36-9), and her point is well taken that Gardner scholars who defend his authorial intent have insisted upon a curiously restrictive reading of the novel in light of modern attitudes towards the original poem: "The history of *Beowulf* criticism shows that even though the network of the epic has been framed to fit theoretical demands/presuppositions of its readers/critics, the long strife for an ur-meaning inherent to the poem has been abandoned in favour of more 'open' interpretations. In the Gardnerian reading of *Grendel*, however, there has been no acceptance of the polysemous meaning of the text" (43). Robert Morace, in a talk titled "W(h)ither Gardner Studies," anticipates Kowalcze's criticism of Gardner scholars by a few years and from within their own community, but himself prefers a Bakhtinian approach to the author's works (he is also concerned more generally with Gardner's artistic aims as explicated in *On Moral Fiction*). Finally, Mark Pedretti, also acknowledging that Gardner was always "dismayed that his text should be so 'misread' into an endorsement of what he considered to be nihilism," attempts a Nietzschean synthesis that would reconcile both the anti-existentialist and pro-postmodernist currents in the text. If none of these "third ways" is entirely satisfying, it is probably due to the complexity of, as George Gaudette puts it in a superb paper title, "The Problem of the Abyss in John Gardner's Fiction."

11   The essay from which this quotation is taken remains the most comprehensive survey of Beowulfiana in print, and, happily, Livingston and Sutton even devote a few descriptive sentences to Marillion's tale of "a defiantly subversive Grendel, straight out of Gardner's novel" (8). Although they barely scratch the surface of the interpretive problems of this song and its larger context among other oral performances, they rightly emphasize that "[m]usic constitutes another major category" of Beowulfiana (9).

12   The authenticity of these division titles may be in some doubt: the liner notes for the remaster of the album *Script for a Jester's Tear* do not include them, but the lyrics

posted on the band's official website do. Regardless, distinct musical styles internally delineate the divisions.

13   Unless otherwise noted, all quotations from the poem are taken from *Klaeber's Beowulf*, 4th ed., and all translations are my own.

14   The description of Grendel as "Lurker at the threshold" also appears in the lyrics, but I will assume that Fish did not intend too complex a reference to the unfinished H. P. Lovecraft novel of that title, which could change the nature of the monster considerably, that is, as a being requiring an invitation to enter. I think, then, that we need not make too much of the phrase, although a general figurative portrayal of Grendel outside the hall as a creature lurking in a kind of Lovecraftian outer darkness would be apt enough.

15   Susan Strehle also singles out this scene as a "literary echo of Frankenstein's monster" (95), and makes a further connection between the Shaper's music and the guitar with which the old man De Lacey inadvertently charms the monster. W. P. Fitzpatrick also suggests Grendel's kinship with Mary Shelley's Promethean monster, though he understands Gardner's novel even more specifically as a "grisly parody of the Romantic *Prometheus Unbound*" (5). We should also keep in mind that Gardner himself also wrote a 1969 poem titled "Frankenstein"—which begins, "The myth is unchained: it staggers north, / insane" (505)—as well as, of all things, a libretto for an operatic version of *Frankenstein* (1975).

16   Verlyn Flieger in fact argues that Gardner himself "took Gollum and made him (by way of his medieval/postmodern equivalent) the hero of his own story in *Grendel*" (26).

17   For the most recent discussion of this monstrous conjunction, see Nelson, "Cain-Leviathan Typology in Gollum and Grendel." For an early example—indeed, a study among the very earliest Tolkien criticism indexed by the *MLA International Bibliography*—see Winter, "Grendel, Gollum, and the Un-Man." Eugenio M. Olivares-Merino also attempts to illustrate the various relationships between the two monsters in an imposing diagram that further maps Sméagol onto Cain and Frodo onto Beowulf (204).

18   See, for instance, Callaway, "Gollum: A Misunderstood Hero," or Arthur, "Gollum as Hero."

19   As Forni suggests, Graham Baker's location of Grendel's paternity in Hrothgar, replicated in the Zemeckis version, in part brings Grendel in line with more familiar monsters: "While Baker's Grendel is just as destructive as the original, his violence and bad behavior are motivated, like other famous neglected offspring such as Shakespeare's Edmund or Caliban, or Frankenstein's monster, by a quest for paternal recognition or attention." ("Graham Baker's *Beowulf*" 248).

20   In 1981, roughly a year before the original release of Marillion's B-side, Ken Pickering and Keith Cole's *Beowulf: A Rock Musical* first saw performance. Sutton's analysis of the piece is quite intriguing in the context of my argument about Marillion's song: "*Beowulf, A Rock Musical* is meant for school-aged children, and is notable for its depiction of Grendel as a black-hearted, cockney punk rocker—a clear reaction against the punk's place as a '70s and '80s anti-establishment icon" ("Beowulfiana"). In other words, within months of one another, two very different groups of British musicians cast Grendel as an anti-establishment icon in their music—but the one celebratory of this role and the other condemning him for it, as a "revolting" creature "rotten right to the core" and "covered in slime" (5). Naturally, although Grendel's mother is equally revolting, at first she responds to the trappings of punk in an appropriately maternal fashion:"Oh, for cryin' out loud, what's he on about—you're a pansy, mate—you're no

son of mine—first you want your hair dyed green and red, and now you want pierced ears" (11).

21   Paul Acker stresses that "[t]he use in the critical literature of the term 'Grendel's dam,' to suggest her animal aspect and a connection with 'the devil and his dam' of folklore, is not strictly speaking supported by the poem's usage, which calls her Grendel's 'modor' 'mother' (e.g., 1258) and 'mage' 'kinswoman' (1391)" (709-10 n.6). Nevertheless, the conception that Grendel's mother is somehow more inhuman than her offspring remains deeply ingrained in translations of the poem as well as in the criticism, as we see in Norma L. Hutman's analysis of the three monsters: "Gardner chooses the monster who stands, obviously, closest to men, rejecting both Grendel's mother *who is principally beast* and hence less than man and the dragon which is in Gardner's terms extra-temporal and in traditional lore superior in power to man" (25; emphasis mine). More recently, there have been some feminist attempts to recuperate the vilified female in the figure of Grendel's mother; for a survey of these efforts and the tradition they oppose, see Hennequin, "We've Created a Monster," 503-4, but an article by Christine Alfano exemplifies the strong form of this argument: "I believe that this woman-as-monster motif is a relatively recent construct that translators, lexicographers, and literary critics have superimposed upon *Beowulf,* thereby rewriting both character and text" (1); "She finds herself implicated in her child's monstrosity, as unchallenged assumptions subsume her maternal role within a son's identity" (12). Furthermore, it is interesting to note that, even in Michael Crichton's *Eaters of the Dead,* a novel so determinedly rationalistic that it translates the fire-dragon into a line of torches, the matriarch of the wendol remains a "mother-*creature*" (166; emphasis mine).

22   *Grendel, Grendel, Grendel* (1981), that good-humored but ill-conceived adaptation of Gardner's novel into what appears to be an animated family film, both preserves this characterization of Grendel's mother and unfortunately contains enough musical numbers to lie within the purview of this article. Strangely, even though Grendel's mother remains an inarticulate beast sequestered off-screen in a pit for most of the film, the incongruous song over the opening credits uses her perspective and a rich, throaty voice that sings of "mother-love," further anatomizing her affection for her son's "every hair, every scale, every tooth," etc. "Your mother needs you, Grendel," the disembodied voice coos, describing herself as "listening nightly at the door for you," but the song consists largely of the repetition of Grendel's name, and I think contributes little to any real effort to reconfigure his mother's place in the story: after the credits finish, the ethereal voice disappears back into the animal silence of Gardner's "fat, foul bulk" (9). But don't miss Peter Ustinov as Grendel, especially his existentialist duet with a chorus of tap-dancing clams.

23   For example, Emanuelson goes on to note, with appropriately Anglo-Saxon understatement, that Crichton's cannibal witch doctor in *Eaters of the Dead/The Thirteenth Warrior* "is not what most people would think of as a good person" (270). Similarly, in Sturla Gunnarsson's *Beowulf & Grendel,* while her son appears more or less like a large human possessing the rudiments of speech, Grendel's mother is pallid, foul, mute, and downright unearthly. Also mutely monstrous are the winged creature in Syfy's made-for-TV movie *Grendel* and the "hell-dame" of the literally no-budget *Beowulf: Prince of the Geats,* the film also known as "Black *Beowulf.*" I even picked up a copy of the 2009 self-published novel *Grendel's Mother* hoping for a more inspiring treatment of the titular monster, but discovered that she is introduced in the prologue as a tentacle monster that sexually violates a ship full of men. Indeed, most disturbing to some critics is the specific trend in which female sexuality itself becomes implicated with the monstrous, as Forni notes of both the Graham Baker and Zemeckis films, where

Grendel's mother becomes "a predatory, shape-shifting seductress (with the concomitant notion that female sexuality is monstrously destructive)" ("Popularizing High Culture" 49). In Baker's production, the actress is literally a Playboy Playmate, and Zemeckis, of course, not to be outdone by some sci-fi exercise in high bizarrerie, chose Angelina Jolie as his own arch-temptress. (If nothing else, as a colleague of mine has quipped, the image of universal sex symbol Jolie sauntering across her mere-hall provides yet another new interpretation of that protean image of *fire* on the water.)

24   Incidentally, before Heaney published his translation of *Beowulf*, Darnielle composed a song titled "Tollund Man" that complements the complaints of his more literally monstrous narrators. In contrast to Heaney's poem of the same name, which is arguably as much about Heaney's own life as the experience of the titular preserved primeval, the Mountain Goats song gives voice to the bog-man as a condemned man of few words bidding farewell to the world: "I was sitting at the edge of the marsh / When the council came to bring me the news / They handed me a bowl of cooked wild grasses and they / Gave me the ceremonial shoes / Goodbye young Danish women / Goodbye Danish sky / Goodbye cold air, I am going away / Goodbye, goodbye, goodbye" (*Sweden*, 1995). Compare the composition on the same subject by English hard rock band the Darkness, titled "Curse of the Tollund Man" and analogous to Marillion's "Grendel" in tone and moral stance, just as "Tollund Man" resembles Darnielle's more contemplative monstrous reflections: "Rise did the Tollud Man / To unleash the terror / Upon everyone that he saw / The curse of the Tollund Man / Nothing worse than that."

25   In late 2005, presumably while working on an early version of *Get Lonely*, Darnielle also hinted at his monstrous designs: "I think I'd like to tell a few stories about sad monsters now" (MacIntosh).

26   Perhaps not so incidentally, Rome-o-phile Darnielle also seems to have a fondness for the story of Romulus and Remus, and his crowd-pleaser "Up the Wolves" (*The Sunset Tree*, 2005) contains the following lines: "Our mother has been absent / Ever since we founded Rome / But there's gonna be a party when the wolf comes home."

27   Zemeckis et al. prefer to place the blame on bioluminescent dinoflagellates; Alexander M. Bruce suggests that the phrase is "a description of the Northern Lights, the *aurora borealis*" (106); and, most recently, Christopher Abram has argued that we should understand "fyr on flode" as a skaldic "periphrasis for 'gold'" (201).

28   Jane Chance has taken a somewhat different approach to the relationship between Hildeburh and Grendel's mother: "Later that night, Grendel's mother, intent on avenging the loss of her son in the *present*, attacks Heorot, her masculine aggression contrasting with the feminine passivity of both Hildeburh and Wealhtheow" (100). Rather than argue that either Hildeburh or Grendel's mother serve as model women, Chance goes on to explain that "three females characters appear [...] to convey dialectically the idea that women cannot ensure peace in the world" (106).

29   Compare Keith P. Taylor's more radical argument that, "by referring to Grendel's mother as *ides aglæcwif*, the *Beowulf*-poet emphasizes not the physical monstrosity, but the inherent nobility of Grendel's mother" (14).

30   Darnielle has also written a kind of companion piece to "Grendel's Mother" titled "The Anglo-Saxons," itself a comprehensive enough (if not completely disingenuous) disquisition on early British social history, which revels in conveying bits of information like the following: "They used to paint their bodies blue / A couple of them might be distantly related to you / According to Caesar, they shaved their entire bodies / Except for the upper lip, and the head." In his defense, Darnielle does apologize for some sins of historical inaccuracy in the *Ghana* liner notes: "I blush with shame every time I hear

it: the liberties this lyric takes with matters of historical record are inexcusable. The Picts painted their bodies blue, not the Anglo-Saxons. The Romans, visiting England with a view to expanding the empire, took note of this unusual practice. Centuries later, a singer in California would note that 'Yeah, the Picts!' didn't have the same ring to it as 'Yeah, the Anglo-Saxons!' One hopes, perhaps vainly, that the 'all you'd get/alphabet' rhyme offsets the glaring inaccuracies at play here."

31   I would note that, despite the derisive jokes we've all heard -- whether at the expense of the gilded Jolie tottering on stiletto hooves, or her son, some sort of dragon/ Oscar-statuette Transformer -- even this sexualized reading of Grendel's mother is not without precedent in the numberless volumes of *Beowulf* criticism, which is surely approaching Library of Babel proportions. Gwendolyn A. Morgan, for example, has suggested (prior to the release of any of the Hollywood adaptations) that "the poet equates the aggression of Grendel's Mother to sexual invitation which, unless he resist the temptation, will consume the male" (58-9).

32   Compare Oliver's more favorable analysis of the Irish Repertory Theatre's presentation of Grendel's long-suffering mother in their version of *Beowulf*: "Then we have the more successful of two interpolated scenes: Grendel's (baritone) mother in the mere complains to her dying son that he was never much good at anything, and now she has to finish the work he began. This grumbling mere-witch provides a welcome and comic change from the frequent modern portrayal of Grendel's mother as victim" (23). I will confess that I am not entirely certain which portrayals of Grendel's mother Oliver may be referring to here, and the balance -- at least in popular culture -- still seems to weigh heavily against sympathy for the character.

33   Apparently Darnielle's appeal extends to at least Stephen Colbert's generation; see the October 6, 2009 episode of *The Colbert Report*, in which the host makes no secret of his serious fan status.

34   Conor McCarthy, emphasizing that "Heaney's advocacy of the outcast is long standing," fairly describes the poet's tempered sympathy for Grendel: "Sometimes these outcast or marginal figures are projections of the poet; always they are treated with sympathy, even when, as with Grendel and Philoctetes, that sympathy is not unqualified" (163).

35   For a lengthier discussion of the slippage between monstrosity and heroism in the film, as well as Gaiman's other work, again see Noone, "The Monsters and the Heroes." In brief, an identification of the hero with the monstrous also appears in Gaiman's poem "Bay Wolf," a retelling of the poem "as a futuristic episode of 'Baywatch' for an anthology of detective stories" with a werewolf in the title role (*Smoke and Mirrors* 26), as well as in his novella "The Monarch of the Glen," notable for some softer images of "Grendel's mum" (338): "She sat on the bank, with her son's head in her lap. She took a packet of tissues from her handbag, and spat on a tissue, and began fiercely to scrub at her son's face with it, scrubbing away the blood" (333). Jennifer Kelso Farrell has also noted how recent adaptations of *Beowulf* consistently "[blur] the boundaries between good and evil" (935).

36   We could point to Fajardo-Acosta's own monograph, *The Condemnation of Heroism in the Tragedy of Beowulf*, which stresses "the duality of the hero's character" as man and monster (14). S. L. Dragland also stresses Beowulf's "symbolic identity with monsters" (609), and Grendel's with mankind, insisting that the poet "closely associated the monstrous with the human" (617). Likewise, the poet's use of the word "aglæca" to refer to Grendel and the dragon as well as Beowulf and Sigemund has often fueled such interpretations (to the chagrin of some etymologists); Marion Lois Huffines, for example, understands the word as indicating "a moral decline on the part of monsters

and heroes" (80). The appropriate definition of the word remains a matter of some controversy, for which see *Klaeber's Beowulf,* 169, 893n., as well as the glossary.

37   Lest my occasionally polemical tone suggest that medievalists have entirely ignored these musical adaptations of Beowulf, I should note that the 2010 Kalamazoo conference witnessed—although sadly I did not—"a beautiful cover of 'Grendel's Mother'" by none other than Jeffrey Jerome Cohen, Dan Remein, and Brantley Bryant (Cohen).

WORKS CITED

Abram, Christopher. "New Light on the Illumination of Grendel's Mere." *Journal of English and*
Germanic Philology 109.2 (2010): 198-216. Print.

Acker, Paul. "Horror and the Maternal in *Beowulf.*" *PMLA* 121.3 (2006): 702-16. Print.

Alfano, Christine. The Issue of Feminine Monstrosity: A Reevaluation of Grendel's Mother."
Comitatus 23 (1992): 1-16. Print.

Arthur, Elizabeth. "Above All Shadows Rides the Sun: Gollum as Hero." *Mythlore* 18.1 (1991):
19-27. Print.

Aum, Barty. "Grendel Reborn." *When the Meteor Hits.* Midnight Owl Records, 2007. Digital
download.

Avary, Roger. Foreword. *Beowulf: the Script Book.* With Neil Gaiman. New York: Harper
Entertainment, 2007. 3-13. Print.

Bagby, Benjamin, perf., and Stellan Olsson, dir. *Beowulf.* Koch Vision, 2007. DVD.

Baker, Graham, dir. *Beowulf.* 1999. Dimension, 2000. DVD.

Barton, Laura. "'I was a very pretentious young writer.'" *Guardian.co.uk.* Guardian News and
Media Limited, 15 Feb. 2008. Web. 16 May 2010.

Bourne, Ralph. *Grendel's Mother.* Tucson: Wheatmark, 2009. Print.

Bruce, Alexander M. "Beowulf 1366a: Fyr on flode as the aurora borealis?" *Archiv für das*
Studium der Neueren Sprachen und Literaturen 159.1 (2007): 105-9. Print.

Callaway, David. "Gollum: A Misunderstood Hero." *Mythlore* 10.3 (1984): 14-7, 22. Print.

Chance, Jane. *Woman as Hero in Old English Literature.* Syracuse: Syracuse University Press,
1986. Print.

Cohen, J. J. "Memories of Kalamazoo (2010 Edition)." *InTheMedievalMiddle.com.* J. J. Cohen,
17 May 2010. Web. 19 May 2010.

Colbert, Stephen. "*The Colbert Report* 6 Oct. 2009." *Colbertnation.com.* Comedy Partners,   2010. Web. 14 June 2010.

Crichton, Michael. *Eaters of the Dead: The Manuscript of Ibn Fadlan, Relating His Experiences*
with the Northmen in A. D. 922. New York: Alfred A. Knopf, 1976. Print.

The Darkness. "Curse of the Tollund Man." *Curse of the Tollund Man.* Atlantic Records UK, 2004. Digital download.

Darnielle, John. "The Mountain Goats—'Heretic Pride' Press Kit." *Thejeffreylewissite. com*. Jeffrey Lewis, 2008.

_____. "New song" *Mountain-goats.com/forums*. The Mountain Goats, 2 June 2009. Web. 14   June 2010.

Dragland, S. L. "Monster-Man in *Beowulf*." *Neophilologus* 61 (1977): 606-18. Print.

Eco, Umberto. *Travels in Hyperreality: Essays*. San Diego: Harcourt Brace Jovanovich, 1986.
Print.

"Electro-industrial." *Wikipedia: The Free Encyclopedia*. Wikimedia Foundation, Inc., 12 May
2010. Web. 12 May 2010.

Emanuelson, Karen. "Head-Hunting Witch Doctor, Blood-Sucking Porn Star (and Other
Portrayals of Grendel's Mother)." *The Image of Violence in Literature, Media, and
Society II*. Ed. Will Wright and Steven Kaplan. Pueblo: Society for the Interdisciplinary
Study of Social Imagery, CSU-Pueblo, 2007. 267-72. Print.

Fajardo-Acosta, Fidel. *The Condemnation of Heroism in the Tragedy of Beowulf: A Study in the
Characterization of the Epic*. Lewiston: E. Mellen Press, 1989. Print.

_____. "Intemperance, Fratricide, and the Elusiveness of Grendel." *English Studies* 73.3 (1992):
205-10. Print.

Farrell, Jennifer Kelso. "The Evil behind the Mask: Grendel's Pop Culture Evolution." *Journal of
Popular Culture* 41.6 (2008): 934-49. Print.

Fawcett, Barry, and Elizabeth Jones. "The Twelve Traps in John Gardner's *Grendel*." *American
Literature* 62.4 (1990): 634-47. Print.

Fish. "Market Square Heroes EP—Grendel." *Marillion.baldyslaphead.co.uk*. Fraser Marshall,
2010. Web. 12 May 2010.

Fitzpatrick, W. P. "Down and Down I Go: A Note on Shelley's *Prometheus Unbound* and
Gardner's *Grendel*." *Notes on Contemporary Literature* 7.1 (1977): 2-5. Print.

Flieger, Verlyn. "A Postmodern Medievalist?" *Tolkien's Modern Middle Ages*. Ed. Jane Chance
and Alfred K. Siewers. New York: Palgrave Macmillan, 2005. 17-28. Print.

Foote, Timothy. "Books: The Geat Generation." Rev. of *Grendel* by John Gardner. *Time.com*.
Time Inc., 20 Sept. 1971. Web. 14 June 2010.

Forni, Kathleen. "Graham Baker's *Beowulf*: Intersections between High and Low Culture."
Literature/Film Quarterly 35.3 (2007): 244-9. Print.

_____. "Popularizing High Culture: Zemeckis's *Beowulf*." *Studies in Popular Culture* 31.2 (2009): 45-59. Print.

Frantzen, Allen J. "'Hrothgar Built Roads': Grendel's Ride in LA." *Old English Newsletter* 39.3
(2006): 27-35. Print.

Frere-Jones, Sasha. "The Declaimers: Two Rock Bands That Want to be Heard." *The New*
  Yorker 16 May 2005. *Newyorker.com*. Condé Nast Digital, 2010. Web. 12 May
  2010.
Fulk, R. D., Robert E. Bjork, and John D. Niles, eds. *Klaeber's Beowulf and the Fight at*
  Finnsburg. 4th ed. Toronto: University of Toronto Press, 2008. Print.
Gaiman, Neil. "The Monarch of the Glen: An *American Gods* Novella." *Fragile Things:*
  Short Fictions and Wonders. 2006. New York: Harper, 2010. 284-339. Print.
_____. *Smoke & Mirrors: Short Fiction and Illusions*. New York: Avon Books, 1998.
Gardner, John. "Frankenstein." *The Kenyon Review* 31.4 (1969): 505-6. Print.
_____. *Grendel*. 1971. New York: Vintage Books, 1989. Print.
Gaudette, George. "'To Nothing, or Everything': The Problem of the Abyss in John
  Gardner's
  Fiction." *Proceedings of the First Annual John Gardner Conference*. Ed. Jim
  Fessenden.
  West Chester, PA: Jim Fessenden, for John Gardner Society, 1999. 73-9.
  Genesee.suny.edu. George Gaudette, 23 June 1998. Web. 11 May 2010.
Greenfield, Stanley B. "A Touch of the Monstrous in the Hero, or Beowulf Re-
  Marvellized."
  English Studies 63.4 (1982): 294-307. Print.
Grendel [Dutch]. "Grendel." *Inhumane Amusement*. NoiTekk, 2001. Digital
  download.
Grendel [Finnish]. *A Change Through Destruction*. Firebox Finland, 2008. CD.
Grendel [Italian]. *Beowulf*. Narok Records, 2005. CD.
_____. *Dragon's Awakening*. Northern Horde Records, 2010. CD.
Gunnarsson, Sturla, dir. *Beowulf & Grendel*. 2005. Starz/Anchor Bay, 2006. DVD.
Hanson, Howard. "The Lament for Beowulf, Op. 25." 1925. *Symphony No. 3/Elegy/The*
  Lament
  For Beowulf. Philips, 1991. CD.
Heaney, Seamus, trans. *Beowulf: A New Verse Translation*. 1999. New York: W.W.
  Norton &
  Co., 2001. Print.
_____. *Beowulf*. Highbridge Audio, 2000. CD.
Heater, Brian. "Searching for John Darnielle." *PopMatters.com*. PopMatters Media, Inc.,
  11 Jan.
  2007. Web. 12 May 2010.
Hennequin, M. Wendy. "We've Created a Monster: The Strange Case of Grendel's
  Mother."
  English Studies 89.5 (2008): 503-23. Print.
Huffines, Marion Lois. "OE *aglaeca*: Magic and Moral Decline of Monsters and Men."
  Semasia
  1 (1974): 71-81. Print.
Hutman, Norma L. "Even Monsters Have Mothers: A Study of *Beowulf* and John
  Gardner's
  Grendel." *Mosaic* 9.1 (1975): 19-31. Print.
Irving, Edward B., Jr. *A Reading of Beowulf*. New Haven: Yale University Press, 1968.
  Print.
Kiernan, Kevin S. "Grendel's Heroic Mother." *In Geardagum* 6 (1984): 13-33. Print.
Kowalcze, Anna. "Disregarding the Text: Postmodern Medievalisms and the Readings
  of John Gardner's *Grendel*." *Year's Work in Medievalism* 17 (2002): 33-55. Print.

Livingston, Michael and John William Sutton. " Reinventing the Hero: Gardner's *Grendel* and the Shifting Face of Beowulf in Popular Culture." *Studies in Popular Culture* 29.1 (2006): 1-16. Print.

Lyon, Nick, dir. *Grendel*. 2007. Sci Fi Pictures. Syfy. 22 May 2010. Television.

MacIntosh, Dan. "The Medicinal Headphones." *PopMatters.com*. PopMatters Media, Inc., 17
Aug. 2005. Web. 25 May 2010.

Mar, Kathy. "Grendel." 1988. *Plus Ça Change/Plus C'est la Même Chose*. DragonsGate Music,
2000. CD.

_____. Lyrics to "Grendel." *Xocolatl.com*. Kathy Mar, 2009. Web. 14 June 2010.

Marillion. "Grendel." 1982. *Script for a Jester's Tear*. EMI Records Limited, 1997. CD.

_____. "Script for a Jester's Tear -- Grendel." *Marillion.com*. Marillion, 2010. 14 June 2010.

"*Mearcstapa*." *Steel Carpet Music*. Steel Carpet Music, 1999. Web. 21 May 2010.

McCarthy, Conor. *Seamus Heaney and Medieval Poetry*. Rochester: Boydell & Brewer, 2008.
Print.

Merrill, Robert. "John Gardner's *Grendel* and the Interpretation of Modern Fables." *American*
Literature 56.2 (1984): 162-80. Print.

Miller, Tamlyn. "Avenging Grendel." *YouTube*. 9 Feb. 2006. Web. 12 May 2010.

Morace, Robert. "W(h)ither Gardner Studies?" *Proceedings of the First Annual John Gardner*
Conference. Ed. Jim Fessenden. West Chester, PA: Jim Fessenden, for John Gardner
Society, 1999. 49-62. *Genesee.suny.edu*. Robert Morace, 23 April 1998. Web. 11 May
2010.

Morgan, Gwendolyn A. "Mothers, Monsters, Maturation: Female Evil in *Beowulf*." *Journal of*
the Fantastic in the Arts 4.1 (1991): 54-68. Print.

The Mountain Goats. "Bride." Unreleased. Mountain-goats.com, 2009. Digital download.

_____. *Get Lonely*. 4AD, 2006. CD.

_____. *Ghana*. 3 Beads of Sweat, 1999. CD.

_____. "Grendel's Mother." *Zopilote Machine*. 1994. 3 Beads of Sweat, 2005. CD.

_____. "Hebrews 11:40." *The Life of the World to Come*. 4AD, 2009. CD.

_____. *Heretic Pride*. 4AD, 2008. CD.

_____. "Letter from Belgium." *We Shall All Be Healed*. 4AD, 2004. CD.

_____. "The Mummy's Hand." 2005. Unreleased. *KEXP.org*. KEXP, 2010. Streaming download.

_____. *The Sunset Tree*. 4AD, 2005. CD.

_____. *Sweden*. 1995. Shrimper Records, 2000. CD.

Nelson, Brent. "Cain-Leviathan Typology in Gollum and Grendel." *Extrapolation* 49.3 (2009):
466-85. Print.

Niles, John D. "Reconceiving *Beowulf*: Poetry as Social Praxis." *College English* 61.2 (1998):
143-66. Print.

Noone, Kristin. "The Monsters and the Heroes: Neil Gaiman's *Beowulf*." Forthcoming in *Weird Fiction Review* 1 (2010). Print.

Olivares-Merino, Eugenio M. "A Monster That Matters: Tolkien's Grendel Revisited." *Myth and Magic: Art According to the Inklings*. Ed. Eduardo Segura and Thomas Honegger. Zollikofen, Switzerland: Walking Tree, 2007. 187-240. Print.

Oliver, Lisi. "A Banner Year for Beowulf on the Boards." *Old English Newsletter* 39.3 (2006): 22-6. Print.

Osborn, Marijane. "Grendel's Mother Broods Over Her Feral Son." *Old English Newsletter* 39.3 (2006): 20-1. Print.

Parks, Ward. "Song, Text, and Cassette: Why We Need Authoritative Audio Editions of Medieval Literary Works." *Oral Tradition* 7.1 (1992): 102-15. Print.

Pedretti, Mark "Gardner and Nietzsche: Towards a Post-Ethical Aesthetic Morality of Fiction: A Paper Loosely Based upon 'The Tragic Monster: Towards a Nietzschean Grendel,' from the Berkeley Undergraduate Journal, Fall 1996." *Proceedings of the First Annual John Gardner Conference*. Ed. Jim Fessenden. West Chester, PA: Jim Fessenden, for John Gardner Society, 1999. 109-17. *Genesee.suny.edu*. Mark Pedretti, 21 May 1998. Web. 11 May 2010.

"Petition to Reunite Grendel's Arm." *MySpace*. MySpace.com, 2010. Web. 12 May 2010.

Pickering, Ken, and Keith Cole. *Beowulf: A Rock Musical*. London: Samuel French, 1982. Print.

The Ranch Hands. "Green'ich Grendel." *Turban Renewal: A Tribute To Sam The Sham & The Pharaohs*. Norton, 1994. Digital download.

Reside, Mary Lou. "Witches and Women of Power: The Price of Making a Hero in *Beowulf*." MA thesis. Simon Fraser University, 1991. Print.

Ringler, Dick, trans. *Beowulf: The Complete Story: A Drama*. University of Wisconsin Press, 2007. CD.

———. trans. *Beowulf: A New Translation for Oral Delivery*. Indianapolis: Hackett Pub., 2007. Print.

Sally. "The Mountain Goats and Bower Birds." *UndressMeRobot.com*. Undress Me Robot, 29 April 2007. Web. 18 May 2010.

Sam the Sham & the Pharaohs. "Green'ich Grendel." 1965. *Wooly Bully/Li'l Red Riding Hood*. Collectables, 2004. CD.

Shakespeare, William. *The Tempest*. *The Norton Shakespeare*. Ed. Stephen Greenblatt. New York: W. W. Norton & Company, 1997. 3055-107. Print.

Sorrell, Paul. "Oral Poetry and the World of *Beowulf*." *Oral Tradition* 7.1 (1992): 28-65. Print.

Stillicide. "Stillicide: Grendel's Mother." *YouTube*. 27 Nov. 2006. Web. 12 May 2010.

Stitt, Alexander, dir. *Grendel, Grendel, Grendel.* Victorian Film, 1981. VHS.

Strehle, Susan. "John Gardner's Novels: Affirmation and the Alien." *Critique* 18.2 (1976):
    86-96.
    Print.

Stromme, Craig J. "The Twelve Chapters of *Grendel.*" *Critique* 20.1 (1978): 83-92.
    Print.

Sunny Day Real Estate. "Grendel." *Diary.* Sub Pop, 1994. CD.

Sutton, John William. "Beowulfiana: Modern Adaptations of *Beowulf.*" *Rochester.edu.*
    John
    William Sutton, 2009. Web. 12 May 2010.

Taylor, Keith P. "*Beowulf* 1259a: The Inherent Nobility of Grendel's Mother." *English
    Language
    Notes* 31.3 (1994): 13-25. Print.

Torrini, Emiliana. "Gollum's Song." *The Lord of the Rings: The Two Towers.* Reprise /
    Wea,
    2002. CD.

Tripp, Raymond. "Grendel Polytropos." *In Geardagum* 6 (1984): 43-69. Print.

VanBenthuysen, Douglas Ryan. "Seamus Heaney's Audio *Beowulf*: An Analysis of the
    Omissions." *Defining Medievalism(s).* Ed. Karl Fugelso. Cambridge, England:
    Brewer,
    2009. 161-84. Print.

The Wanderer. The Cambridge Old English Reader. Ed. Richard Marsden. Cambridge:
    Cambridge UP, 2004. 327-34.

Wegener, Scott, dir. *Beowulf: Prince of the Geats.* David Garrison Productions, 2008.
    DVD.

Wilson, Dave. *Rock Formations: Categorical Answers to How Band Names Were Formed.*
    San
    Jose: Cidermill Books, 2004. Print.

Winter, Karen C. "Grendel, Gollum, and the Un-Man: The Death of the Monster as an
    Archetype." *Orcrist* 2 (1967): 28-37. Print.

Zemeckis, Robert, dir. *Beowulf: Director's Cut.* 2007. Paramount, 2008. DVD.

Debilitating Dracula:
Vampires as Illness Metaphor from the Middle Ages to the Present Day

Aspen Hougen

In many ways, the vampire in folklore and literature is a cipher, acting as a metaphor for a host of different concepts. Among other things, the vampire can and has been read as a representative of social otherness, of queer and/ or illicit sexuality, and of the racial and class outsider in colonial discourse. Of all the metaphorical parallels which can be drawn in vampire literature, perhaps the most readily apparent is that between the vampire and the disease sufferer. Vampirism, after all, produces a host of unhealthy symptoms: allergy to sunlight and common substances, altered complexion, lack of pulse and respiration. It interferes with the appetite, causing a compulsive craving for unnatural food. And, of course, vampirism can be spread through contact with the bodily fluids of an infected person, producing these same symptoms in the next victim. Vampirism, frequently referred to as a "curse," can just as accurately be called a contagion.

This metaphorical link is no accident. From the earliest folklore through to the present day, our representations of vampires have reflected our attitudes towards the sufferers of infectious disease—and as our attitudes have changed, our representations have also shifted. Early vampire stories drew on medieval notions of contagion as divine punishments for wrongdoing, positioning the vampire as an evildoer whose curse was the result of moral failings. For centuries, this attitude persisted in vampire lore, but in recent decades vampire stories have shifted away from this model of sufferer-as-sinner and towards representations of vampires as victims of contagion, often innocent of any personal wrongdoing. The changing face of the vampire through the centuries—from resurrected evildoer to monstrous force of nature to, ultimately, a sympathetic victim—is not merely the product of evolving genre expectations; it results from a change in the metaphor informing the stories themselves, a change which results in turn from a developing scientific understanding of how and why sickness spreads from one person to another.

Sufferers as Sinners: Illness and Medieval Morality

It is, of course, an oversimplification to speak of "the medieval attitude towards infectious disease" as if there were any one such attitude. Theories about contagion and beliefs about the sufferers of infectious disease were numerous and varied throughout the Middle Ages, with physicians, clergy, and laypeople alike ascribing to a variety of beliefs depending on time, place, and context, and no single framework for understanding illness and contagion can be referred to as *the* medieval understanding of these ideas. We can, however, take notice of the persistence and prevalence of one such viewpoint as it appears in medieval thought: that which views illness, and particularly infectious disease, as a punishment from God.

According to this viewpoint, illness can occur either as a byproduct of man's fallen and sinful nature or as the result of an explicit violation of the Judeo-Christian moral law. Individuals may be chosen to suffer from infection because they have done wrong, or because they live in a community that has done wrong. Even if lip service is paid to the innocence of individual victims by placing the blame on original sin, the strength of the correlation between sin and suffering still results in an implicit understanding that victims cannot be entirely innocent—after all, they are still human and thus still bear the guilt of original sin. The result is an atmosphere of blame which negates the possibility of an innocent sufferer—anyone who suffers illness must, by the logic of this viewpoint, have done something to deserve it. While this viewpoint is evident at various points throughout the medieval period, it can most easily be seen by focusing on the treatment of two specific infectious diseases which had special prominence at that time: the bubonic plague and leprosy. In both cases, the sufferers were framed by some observers as sinners deserving of their fates—in the case of Plague, victims were understood as being punished for communal or original sin, while victims of leprosy were believed to be suffering as a result of personal sin.

Of all epidemic and infectious diseases prevalent in the Middle Ages, Plague was by far the most daunting to those who might become its victims. Perhaps unsurprisingly, the Plague came to be seen as something more than an illness—it took on a reputation as an act of God. Although medieval secular medicine had its own theories regarding the cause and spread of the Plague, these explanations "were, of course, consonant with the idea that the primary cause was God's will. Nor would medical explanations necessarily have been perceived as at variance with explanations, much favored by preachers and moralists, that attributed the plague to God's displeasure with general human sinfulness" (Siraisi 129). In the case of Plague, victims could be seen as falling ill as the result of wickedness—usually that of mankind or of specific communities, but occasionally that of the individuals themselves. The calls to repentance made by those who held this viewpoint made it clear that mankind (including the victims) was at fault for the illness; it was, in some sense, justly deserved as a punishment for wrongdoing, and the sufferers were not entirely innocent of blame, inasmuch as they had a share in the assumed sins of their community and in the original sin of humankind.

If the paradigm of sufferer-as-sinner is present in the treatment of Plague victims, it is even more clearly evident in the attitudes towards the sufferers of another infectious illness which dramatically figured in the cultural landscape of the Middle Ages: leprosy. The assumed correlation between leprosy and wickedness is an ancient one; leprosy is sent as a divine punishment in several Biblical accounts, such as that of Uzziah, who is struck with leprosy as a punishment for pride.[1] Medieval Christianity thus inherited a tradition of viewing leprosy as a tool of divine retribution, and it is unsurprising that the disease represents one of the most prominent examples of the assumed link between bodily illness and spiritual iniquity. As one scholar put it, "[l]eprosy in the Middle Ages was a disease of the soul as well as the body, and although the leper carried many burdens, few were so heavy as his reputation for immorality. He contracted his reputation along with his disease, for the stigma inevitable followed the illness. The association of leprosy and sinfulness was as persistent as the disease itself" (Brody 107). Lepers were seen as a threat to society not only because of their physical contagion, but because of the moral decay associated with their condition; thus, they were shunned not only because the healthy might catch their illness, but because the morally upright might catch their assumed depravity. Furthermore, this assumption of moral decay accompanying the physical decay of the disease led to the disease being seen as a punishment for immorality, even if the assumption of immorality followed the diagnosis, rather than vice-versa. In this way the leper (more so even than the victim of Plague) was positioned as a figure suffering for his sins-not an innocent victim, but one who was deserving of this punishment from God.

This attitude towards infection and illness persisted into the early modern era and beyond. It was still evident, for example, in the writings of the seventeenth-century plague years, when pamphleteers sought to call their readers to repentance for the sins that had called the Plague down on their towns and cities. In these writings, as with writings from earlier Plague outbreaks, the pamphleteers draw an undisputed correlation between infectious disease and wickedness, both personal and social. The Plague is referred to as "[God's] sword" (Allen 70) and "a broom in the hands of the Almighty" (62), and it is made clear in that God is using these tools to dispose of those who have angered him. Only repentance on a mass scale can eliminate the infection and restore health to society. The inference is clearly the same as that seen in earlier time periods: bad people get sick—and when innocents get sick, it is clearly still due to someone's sins.

Heretics and Monsters: Vampires as Sinners in Traditional Folklore

The notion of illness as a punishment for wickedness is mimicked in early vampire folklore, where the vampire is most often an individual who behaved wickedly in life, died unshriven, or committed suicide, or, in some cases, one for whom proper burial rites were not performed. Throughout the body of legends that form the basis of modern vampire tales, a common theme arises: the vampire is a figure of wickedness, being punished for earthly sins. Much as the victim of infectious disease deserves his suffering, so, too, does the vampire deserve his; overwhelmingly, the vampire of medieval folklore is a monster, without innocence and beyond redemption—and he is frequently rendered thus through his own misdeeds.

The suicide victim is especially favored in medieval stories as a candidate for resurrection as a vampire—unsurprisingly, given the overwhelming stigma attached to the act of suicide by medieval Christianity. Killing oneself represented an ultimate act of both despair and pride, a rejection of God's mercy as well as a flaunting of his power to decide the human lifespan; it furthermore deprived the victim of any chance to confess and be absolved of the sin of self-murder. In light of this view of suicide, it is easy to understand why the victim would be seen as deserving of punishment for this unabsolved sin—punishment which could only be rendered by post-death transformation into a monster. Of course, suicides were not the only candidates for a vampiric fate; according to the folklore of various times and regions, a number of offenses committed before death might cause a person to return as a vampire. One scholar's list of those likely to rise again includes the following: "'the godless...evildoers, suicides, in addition sorcerers, witches...robbers, highwaymen, arsonists, prostitutes, deceitful and treacherous barmaids and other dishonorable people'" (qtd. in Barber 30). The list is ponderous, but it can be reduced to a simple formula: those who committed grievous sins deserved a monstrous punishment after death.

However, just as Plague victims were sometimes understood to be suffering for communal or universal sins rather than their own, in some cases vampires were seen as suffering for the sins of others. This is most evident in the cases of those who become vampires through the bite of another vampire, but there are also other transgressions which might cause the deceased to rise again, most notably incorrect or incomplete burial practices. Suicides, of course, often fall into this category, since they were traditionally barred from Christian burial; but murder victims, those who died in epidemics or on battlefields, and others whose bodies were not properly interred are all traditional folkloric candidates for vampirism, as are those who, while buried, did not have their funerary rites properly conducted. As Paul Barber notes, "even babies may be doomed to a condition of vampirism through the action, or inaction, of others. Commonly this is reported of children who die without being baptized" (37). In these cases, it is not necessarily the deceased's own sins for which they are being punished—it is the violation of social customs by others in dealing with their bodies. This fact, however, does not cause the vampire to be seen with pity or as an innocent victim: in all cases, the vampire is a monster and a figure of wickedness, suffering as the direct result of the breaking of social codes.

In fact, the correlation between wickedness and vampirism is the most constant element of medieval vampire lore; while the causes and symptoms of vampirism vary depending on the tale, the vampire is virtually always framed as a person being punished for some misdeed. The influence of this link between vampirism and sin was powerful and far-reaching; in some parts of Russia, for example, the notions of 'heretic' and 'vampire' became so closely linked that the same word, *eretnik*, was used to denote both (Oinas 433). In the medieval stories where they had their beginnings, vampires *are* evildoers; those who violated the codes of society (or who had those codes violated on their behalf) are doomed to continue doing evil after their deaths. An unquiet afterlife is the punishment for a wicked life, and the vampire deserves no sympathy for this justly earned fate. Even in tales where vampirism is spread through the bite, the victim deserves no pity; he is still a threat to others because of his contamination and becomes just as evil and dangerous as the one who infected him. Vampire and victim alike remain monstrous. There are no innocents.

It is clear, then, that the cultural attitude towards traditional depictions of vampires bore strong similarities to societal view of the victims of leprosy, Plague, and other infectious diseases. In both cases, the affliction was seen to be the result of and punishment for wrongdoing, and the individual thus afflicted posed a danger to society because of it. More than the similarities between physical symptoms or modes of transmission, it is this central parallel which makes the vampire such a strong metaphor for the victim of disease—and it is this metaphor which persisted from the medieval roots of vampire folklore through the early modern era and into the nineteenth century, strongly shaping the ways in which vampire stories were told.

Germ Theory and *Dracula:* a Shift in Perspective

With the passage of time, scientific and medical advancements began to cast serious doubt on the concept of illness as a punishment for moral failings. Germ theory and other breakthroughs offered proof of concrete, natural causes for disease, entirely separate from questions of good or evil. By the end of the nineteenth century, research had made it clear—to the medical community if not to society at large—that the victims of infectious disease had been targeted not by supernaturally inflicted punishment, but by the morally neutral forces of the germ and the virus. An innocent was just as likely to fall sick as a sinner. Culturally, the medieval notion of illness as a punishment remained active, but scientific evidence presented a considerable challenge to what had previously been considered an incontrovertible fact.

While theories of disease were being refined by scientific research, vampire tales were also undergoing a process of refinement. The nineteenth century saw vampires move from their folkloric beginnings into the realm of the novel, culminating with the publication in 1897 of Bram Stoker's *Dracula*, the novel from which almost all modern vampiric representations take their cues. It was Stoker who cemented in the public imagination the figure of the master vampire: evil, relentless, and deadly, a threat so potent he is himself a force of nature, like an earthquake—or an epidemic, for Dracula's curse is contagious, and those he feeds upon become in many respects no less monstrous than he. In this respect, *Dracula* carries on the tradition of the vampire as a cursed sinner, one whose infection with the vampiric plague both results from and leads to moral and spiritual decay—made evident by the aversion Dracula and his victims have to holy symbols such as crucifixes and communion hosts.

Despite all the ways in which *Dracula* reinforces the image of the vampire/infected person as a monster to be feared and destroyed, it still shows traces of the ambiguity introduced to the vampire/illness metaphor by medical advancement. While those Dracula targets become vampiric monsters themselves, there is a window of time after their initial exposure when the infected can still be saved. Witness, for example, the ultimately unsuccessful attempt to save Lucy Westenra.[2] While Lucy is ultimately beyond saving, the effort expended on trying to rescue her from the curse is telling. No longer is infection seen as an incontrovertible punishment for wrongdoings; there remains the possibility of undoing the damage before it becomes permanent.

Of course, these attempts at salvation become useless once the vampire's victim has succumbed to full-blown infection. While Lucy is not yet fully a vampire, she might still be saved, but once she has succumbed, she becomes just as evil as Dracula himself, a threat to the non-infected who must be destroyed as soon as possible. Even Mina Harker, the novel's most innocent character, is compromised by vampiric infection; if she is not 'cured' by the destruction of Dracula, she too will become monstrous and beyond redemption. At this stage in the development of vampire lore, the possibility of a vampire who is *not* monstrous—a victim rather than a villain—does not yet exist, but the ambiguity towards those who are not yet fully turned points back to the newfound medical understanding of infection as a morally neutral event. Vampires—and disease sufferers—may still represent a feared threat to the uninfected; but the vampire/illness metaphor now allows for the possibility that some of those who are infected do not deserve their fate.

Innocent Monsters: the Rise of the Suffering Vampire

With the coming of the twentieth century, disease theory continued to progress as improvements in medical technology made it more and more possible to observe, trace, and combat the spread of contagious disease. Societal attitudes towards infection followed suit, albeit at a much less rapid rate; while the idea of contagion as punishment for moral failing never entirely lost its cachet with the general public, it did find itself joined by other, more scientifically-supported paradigms. However, the vampire-as-illness-metaphor was much slower to evolve. The firm hold which *Dracula* had on the public imagination persisted, and the numerous adaptations, homages, and knockoffs it inspired contributed to a static vision of the vampire as an evil to be combated, with victims who were only sympathetic *before* their transformation from human to vampire was complete. This was the vampire as it existed in the first three quarters of the twentieth century.

In the last thirty years, however, shifts in the societal attitude towards disease and in popular representations of vampires have become much more pronounced. The specter of AIDS and other pandemic diseases has grown more widespread, and while societal viewpoints linking infection to immorality persist (especially in the case of AIDS infection)[3] the impact these diseases have had on innocents has become increasingly impossible to ignore. With the rise of phenomena such as African AIDS orphans and schoolchildren falling victim to SARS and H1N1 influenza, it has become impossible to ignore the fact that contagious disease is not a punishment for wrongdoing. Over this same time period, and in the face of these changing perceptions, pop-cultural representations of vampirism have undergone a dramatic shift: where vampires were once thoroughly evil disease vectors, they are now just as frequently represented as sufferers— even as innocent victims—of the plague they might potentially spread to others.

The 2006 Kurt Wimmer film *Ultraviolet* is one of many texts which present this new vision of the vampire/sufferer. In the film, vampirism is caused by a highly contagious virus, which temporarily gives the infected person increased stamina, greater strength, and more acute senses, but also leaves him sensitive to sunlight, in need of regular blood transfusions, and with lifespans which are "much shorter" than the human average—"twelve years maximum from infection to death." In fact, the deadly progression of the virus itself is the most clearly destructive aspect of vampirism in *Ultraviolet*. The "vampires" of the *Ultraviolet* universe acquire blood through transfusion rather than injection – an apparently victimless process, posing no threat to normal humans.

The film's main character, Violet (played by Milla Jovovich), is shown in flashback at the moment of her infection: as a nurse who is pregnant with her first child. This picture of double innocence—the pregnant mother and the noble healthcare worker—is abruptly shattered when Violet is infected with the "hemophage virus." Taken into government custody, Violet's transformation from human to vampire is accompanied by medical experimentation and the forced termination of her pregnancy. When Violet escapes from government custody, she reinvents herself as a ruthless avenger—one who by her own admission "hate[s] humans with every fiber of [her] being." But despite this hardened Action Girl persona, Violet is, more than anything, a victim—of human prejudice, of medical torture, and, of course, of the blood-borne pathogen which is slowly killing her.

Other vampires in the film show a more villainous attitude (including a willingness to wipe out normal humankind through biological warfare) but Violet, the main character (and thus the vampire with whom the audience has the most contact) rejects this course of action, ultimately choosing to battle the virus itself (and its creator) rather than the uninfected segment of the population. For all her violent tendencies, this rejection frames Violet as, ultimately, an innocent—one who retains her moral compass and inherent goodness despite numerous persecutions and the suffering caused by her disease.

This sympathetic view of vampire-as-sufferer is present in other modern vampire media as well. Charlaine Harris' Southern Vampire series (and the HBO series *True Blood*, based on Harris' novels) take place in a universe where vampires present themselves to the world at large as innocents who wish to live peacefully alongside mainstream society. Harris' vampires suffer from the traditional symptoms of vampirism—allergies to silver and sunlight—but their blood also has aphrodisiac and hallucinogenic properties which make it highly marketable on the illegal drug market. Because of this, the vampires in Harris' universe often fall victim to human criminals, who attack them with the intention of draining and selling their valuable (infected) blood.[4] This purposeful inversion of the classic relationship between vampire and human, predator and prey, leaves the reader/audience with little choice but to see the vampires as the innocents. The vampire is, again, not only sufferer but victim.

Edward Cullen of the *Twilight* books is yet another example of the trope of vampire-as-innocent. In fact, Cullen is doubly innocent in his infection: he is initially infected with influenza during the 1918 epidemic, only to be "saved" by his infection with vampirism.[5] Furthermore, Cullen and his vampire "family" abstain totally from human blood (a position remarkably common among the innocent vampires of popular media), and, while he continues to view himself as a "monster," the audience is clearly meant to doubt that classification. Indeed, the rise of Edward Cullen as the most well-known vampire protagonist of current literature perfectly demonstrates the shift in vampiric representations over the course of the last thirty years—from bloodthirsty villains to innocent and even noble victims.

Debilitated Dracula: The Master Vampire as the Ultimate Victim

As the medieval association of illness with sin and transgression has been challenged by modern medical paradigms which insist that moral character and disease are not mutually exclusive, surely it only makes sense that *some* vampires might come to be portrayed as sufferers rather than sinners. But what of the master vampire? Surely if any figure in vampire fiction is likely to retain the medieval connection between infection and monstrosity, it must be Dracula, the master vampire himself.

But no—even Dracula is not immune to this shift in attitude. In modern vampire tales, even the master vampire himself can suffer because of his infection. More remarkably, Dracula can be positioned as a victimized character. This scenario, in which the ultimate vampiric threat is reframed as a debilitated sufferer, heralds the final breakdown of the medieval paradigm of infected person as monster. Here, even the most monstrous of the infected suffers for his curse, rather than gaining power from it; and this suffering proves to be a humanizing element, casting a sympathetic light on all the victims of the disease, even on Dracula himself.

This scenario plays out in the 2008 film *The Librarian: Curse of the Judas Chalice*. The plot of this comedic action-adventure centers on the search for the titular chalice, a relic which the film's villains intend to use to resurrect the desiccated corpse of Vlad Dracul. To help them in their search, the villains abduct a college professor, Emil Laszlo (played by Bruce Davison). Laszlo, an old man who depends on unwieldy braces and crutches in order to walk, is framed for most of the film's narrative as an unwilling and largely powerless pawn of the villains, sympathetic to the hero's quest to prevent Dracula's resurrection. It is only towards the end of the film that Laszlo reveals his true identity and nature—he, and not the corpse uncovered by the villains, is the true Count Dracula. His paralyzed legs and aged appearance are the result of his drinking the blood of a cholera victim. Feeding on the blood of others, traditionally the source of all Dracula's power, is the source of *this* Dracula's weakness—he is "trapped in [his] withered body," a victim of his vampirism.

True, the Dracula of *Judas Chalice* is far from an *innocent*: he continues to feed on the blood of the living, and ultimately proves to be the true villain of the film who must be defeated in the climactic battle. Nevertheless, for the majority of the film this Dracula appears more as victim than as villain – and this representation prevents the audience from seeing Laszlo/Dracula as an entirely soulless monster. The shift here is subtle, but it mirrors the shift from monsters to sufferers which has already been demonstrated in the depiction of vampires in general.

Furthermore, there is at least one incident in modern vampire stories which takes this portrayal of Dracula one step further, presenting him not only as a sufferer, but as a harmless and sympathetic victim rather than as an antagonist. This is the standalone issue story "House of Dracula," written by Mark Millar and drawn by John Paul Leon for *Liberty Comics* #1.[6] The story opens with the tagline, "For five centuries, Count Dracula was a scourge of all mankind. Now retired, he lives alone in a council flat in South London."

The Dracula of Millar's "House of Dracula" is an old man—reclusive, introspective, and struggling with the effects of age and loneliness. He watches daytime television, shops for single-serving frozen pizzas, and frets to his doctor that he isn't getting enough vitamin D. Mocked by a gang of neighborhood boys throwing stones at his windows, Dracula does not descend to take bloody vengeance: he watches from behind half-drawn curtains and wonders where their parents are. Finally, he dines alone and retires by seven-thirty, musing on immortality. In light of this banal existence, the final line of Dracula's running internal monologue has an air of tragedy: "Forever can feel like a very long time some days."

In "House of Dracula," we see a Dracula who is no longer a monster or villain of any kind, merely a sad old man wrestling with his crushing loneliness. Despite the throwaway reference to his days as "scourge of all mankind," Dracula here evokes no feelings of terror or loathing, but rather those of pity and sadness. Indeed, Millar's portrayal humanizes Dracula to the point that he effectively *becomes* human—his life and his loneliness are no different than those an elderly human being would face in his situation, except that Dracula's immortality contributes the added specter of a lonely life without any possible end. The villain, the monster, has entirely disappeared. All that remains is Dracula, alone in his council flat with the suffering his infection causes him.

Conclusion: The Future of the Vampiric Victim

Of course, incidences of Dracula as sufferer, victim, and/or pathetic figure are at this point the exception rather than the rule (as evidenced by the fact that two of the phenomenon's most notable examples occur in a made-for-television movie and a single-issue comic book). For the most part, Dracula continues to be represented as a force of nature, powerful and almost entirely unsympathetic—but the same could have been said about vampires in general for much of their history. Only in recent years has a shift in the popular imagination allowed for vampires to take on sympathetic traits and roles beyond that of the villain; it is therefore unsurprising that sympathetic representations of the master vampire should only recently follow suit. In support of this, works such as *Judas Chalice* and "House of Dracula" show clear indications that the changing attitude towards the vampire in pop culture is now being extended to the master vampire himself. Just as the changes in feeling over the course of the twentieth century made the innocent vampire possible, shifts in cultural attitudes over the course of the twenty-first century will no doubt make room for more sympathetic portrayals of Dracula.

This is not to suggest that our shifting cultural attitudes towards vampires herald the eradication of the sufferer-as-sinner paradigm, either in vampire fiction or in the culture at large. Medieval notions linking illness and sin, infection and monstrosity, have not completely vanished from society, just as the vampire-as-monster has not vanished from our vampire lore. These ideas remain with us, often in incredibly subtle ways, and they continue to influence social discourse on topics such as epidemic disease and the right to healthcare. In many ways, modern American society still views the sick as deserving of their sickness. However, our cultural attitudes towards illness and infection continue to shift away from this black-and-white paradigm, and the ways in which the metaphor of vampirism expresses those cultural attitudes also continue to shift and change. Where it once showed us only monsters, the metaphor now has room for sympathetic vampires, and even a sympathetic Dracula. We have no way of knowing how our cultural understandings of disease might develop in the future: but vampires, after all, are immortal. They will stay with us, changing (often in surprising ways) to mirror our shifting ideas of illness and infection.

MONTANA STATE UNIVERSITY

NOTES

1   2 Chronicles 26: 19-21
2   An attempt which, incidentally, employs both medieval and modern medical practices—the former in the use of flowers to try and ward off infection, the latter in the use of numerous blood transfusions, still a cutting-edge medical therapy at the time of the novel's publication.
3   For an excellent discussion of the American moral attitude towards AIDS and its relation to medieval moral traditions, see Peter Lewis Allen's *The Wages of Sin*, particularly Chapter 6.
4   This is, in fact, how the protagonist first meets Bill, her vampire love interest; she saves him from a pair of blood-thieves in the opening chapter of *Dead until Dark* , the first novel in the series.
5   *Twilight*, Chapter 14.

6   A benefit anthology published by Image Comics on behalf of the Comic Books Legal Defense Fund.

WORKS CITED

Allen, Peter Lewis. *The Wages of Sin: Sex and Disease, Past and Present*. Chicago: U of Chicago P, 2000. Print.
Barber, Paul. *Vampires, Burial, and Death: Folklore and Reality*. New Haven, CT: Yale UP, 1988. Print.
Brody, Saul Nathaniel. *The Disease of the Soul: Leprosy in Medieval Literature*. Ithaca, NY: Cornell UP, 1974. Print
Harris, Charlaine. *Dead until Dark*. New York: Ace Books, 2001.
Librarian: Curse of the Judas Chalice, The. Dir. Jonathan Frakes. TNT, 2008. DVD.
Meyer, Stephanie. *Twilight*. New York: Little, Brown, 2005.
Millar, Mark. "House of Dracula." *Liberty Comics #1*. Art by John Paul Leon. Berkeley, CA: Image, 2008. Print.
Oinas, Felix J. "Heretics as Vampires and Demons in Russia." *The Slavic and East European Journal*, 22.4 (1978):433-441. *JSTOR*. Web. 7 May 2010.
Siraisi, Nancy G. *Medieval and Early Renaissance Medicine*. Chicago: University of Chicago, 1990. Print.
Ultraviolet. Dir. Kurt Wimmer. Sony Pictures, 2006. DVD.

Purged by Fire:
The Influence of Medieval Visionary Literature on
Post-Apocalyptic Science Fiction

Peter Johnsson

> Woe unto us if we let these days [in this world] go by without completing
> our purgation and must later be purged by that most cruel of fires, quicker
> and more violent than any that one can imagine in this life! – Guerric of
> Igny, 5th sermon on purification.[1] The atom bomb is the most Christian
> thing we've ever invented. – Ray Bradbury.[2]

For the past century, a recurrent concern has been that, sooner or later, a
catastrophe will destroy humanity, probably one of its own making. This is
the central theme of a very popular variety of science fiction, aptly called
"Apocalyptic." This genre is both deeply introspective and philosophical, and
imbedded within it exists a perhaps even more complex subgenre known as
post-Apocalyptic science fiction. As this oxymoronic name implies, the latter
deals with the world *after* an Apocalyptic event—usually an atomic one. As
such, it centers around a small population of survivors who, though faced with
a horrible wasteland, are seemingly bent on turning their lives into a living
hell. Yet, what makes post-Apocalyptic science fiction so complicated is that
it is inherently illogical. Whereas simple Apocalyptic science fiction generally
exists as a warning against self-destruction, the post-Apocalyptic subgenre
elicits a strange fascination, bordering on desire, with the idea of an impending
holocaust. The sci-fi writer John Varley laid this bare in his 1984 short story,
"The Manhattan Phone Book," stating that:

> We all love the After-the-bomb stories. If we didn't why would there be
> so many of them? There is something attractive about all those people
> being gone, about wandering in a depopulated world, scrounging cans of
> Campbell's pork and beans, defending one's family from marauders. Sure it
> is horrible, sure we weep for all those dead people, but some secret part of
> us thinks it would be good to survive, to start over. Secretly we know we'll
> survive. All those *other* folks will die.[3]

That this subgenre is both romanticized and inherently fantastical perhaps
should not come as a surprise, considering that no one, after all, knows what
will happen after the world ends. Nevertheless, Post-Apocalypticism manages
to engage more fans than perhaps any other single genre of science fiction.[4]
Currently, the subgenre is experiencing a surge in popularity with increasing
numbers of movies, books, and games produced every year. The larger aim of
this paper is to elaborate on the popularity of this complex genre.

    Curiously, post-Apocalyptic science fiction bears some striking similarities
to medieval visions of Purgatory. Both deal with themes of life-after-death and
"adventure and adversity, suffering and excitement, and most importantly, a

profound theological warning wrapped in the joyful solace of communion with the departed and hope for our own sinful selves."[5] I intend to illuminate these similarities by elaborating upon the origins of the concept of Purgatory as a product of popular imagination rather than theological debate, thereby making it possible to reiterate it in narrative conventions within the modern culture of science fiction.[6] Since the concept of Purgatory lacked a solid basis in scripture, a purely theological basis proved too difficult to be convincing. Therefore, Purgatory evolved primarily as a literary depiction. The imagery of Purgatory was based, in large part, on pre-Christian depictions of the underworld and the cleansing qualities of fire. Even though the doctrine experienced little concrete expansion during the period between the sixth and the twelfth centuries, the landscape of Purgatory reached maturity during this time in the explosion of visionary depictions called *visio*. This genre of visionary writing can be traced back to the *Dialogues* of Pope St. Gregory the Great and reached its culmination with Dante's *Purgatorio*. It relied on specific imagery which both enthralled and horrified readers, and, as the genre became recognized as an effective didactic tool for teaching morals, it gained popularity. By the 13th century Purgatory became official church doctrine, albeit meeting with some reluctance. Following its official Church sanction, Purgatory diminished and was transformed in the turmoil of the Reformation, and its imagery consequently stagnated. Nevertheless, it was able to survive because of its connection to the popular belief of radical eschatology and the place of both as part of a common European culture of sin and fear.[7] After the subgenre of post-Apocalyptic science fiction was born in the nineteenth-century work *The Last Man*, by Mary Shelly, it came to incorporate much of the same imagery of medieval Purgatory, which offered a release from the fears and anxieties of the modern world. Today, the anxieties of a post-9/11 world have resulted in a steady rise of post-Apocalyptic science fiction. Some of the most popular additions to the genre include the publication and subsequent dramatization of Cormac McCarthy's critically acclaimed *The Road*, and the explosively popular *Fallout* computer game franchise. Today's post-Apocalyptic science fiction relies heavily on imagery from medieval visions of Purgatory because they represent the means for redemption and freedom from the anxieties of a modern world which permits a degree of hope for a more innocent future—one purged by fire.

Although no scholars have firmly established the connection between medieval Purgatorial visions and post-Apocalyptic science fiction, that between post-Apocalyptic fiction and medieval concepts in general has been argued among literary scholars. Dominic Manganiello, in his article "History as Judgment and Promise in 'A Canticle for Leibowitz,'" illustrates how Walter M. Miller's work uses clearly medieval elements of cyclical History to project his vision of a reborn world.[8] Furthermore, Miller himself has on occasion noted the similarities between pre-Christian underworld myths and post-Apocalyptic fiction.[9] In addition, Brian Stableford has argued for a theoretical connection between Apocalyptic science fiction and an obsession with sin and redemption.[10]

Among historians, the connection between the popular imagination of the Middle Ages and science fiction has often been made in recent works on Medievalism. Notably, Angela Weisl, in her book *The Persistence of Medievalism*, points out that much of modern popular subculture is heavily influenced by the remnants of its corresponding medieval culture.[11] A possible connection between these two worlds was even hinted at by the preeminent scholar on Purgatory, Jacques le Goff, who concluded his *The Birth of Purgatory* with a cryptic note that "Paradises are projections of this worldly dreams and hells are projections of fears for which a new kind of imagery has been invented. Our Apocalypse is nuclear destruction; and a part of mankind has already endured the terrifying experience."[12] This quote might at first seem a reference to Hiroshima and Nagasakhi, but it could equally be a reference to the subject of his book, the medieval visionaries of Purgatory.

Part of the appeal of Purgatory was that it incorporated much from older, pre-Christian religious notions of an Afterlife which survived in folk traditions of the Middle Ages. In specific, the notion of ritual purgation incorporating fire—especially in connection with entering a sacred space—was wide spread in the ancient and Classical world, with examples in Zoroastrianism and the Roman cult of the goddess Vesta.[13] The common purgatorial image of a narrow path or bridge is prominent among ancient Persians, who believed in a "bridge from earth to heaven and on this bridge the dead are subject to tests of strength and skill which have a moral connotation."[14] But, without a doubt, the greatest pre-Christian literary influence on concepts of Purgatory was the first-century Roman epic poet, Virgil. The sixth book of Virgil's *Aeneid* depicts the mythical hero Aeneas' journey into the underworld, a compartmentalized place complete with a vestibule, a field of the tombless dead, the river Styx, fields of tears, and a final meadow, which features a fork in the road to either the hellish Tartarus or the Elysian fields.[15] Furthermore, Virgil hints at a Roman notion of Purgatory, stating that "when we on the last day are lost to the light we do not shed away all evil or ills that the body has bequeathed to us poor wretches....Therefore we souls are trained with punishment and pay with suffering for old felonies...the stain of sin is cleansed for others of us in the trough of a huge whirlpool or with fire burned out of us."[16] Soon after the writing of the *Aeneid*, the notion of an afterlife filled with a cleansing fire was also featured in early Christian belief.

The notions of sacred fire and Purgation nonetheless were slow to take hold in Christianity and achieved only a very unsteady shape before the advent of Christian other-worldly visions. The earliest notion of Purgatory was suggested in the Gospels. Both Matthew and Luke mention John the Baptist's prophetic statement that, "one who cometh after me ... who will baptize you with the Holy Spirit and with fire."[17] This baptism with fire would absolve the sins of mankind. A similar explanation was provided by St. Paul, who stated "the fire shall try every man's work of what sort it is." Furthermore, "he himself shall be saved; yet some as by fire."[18] This was later expanded upon by St. Augustine, who initially envisioned Purgatory as a "middle place," where minor, venial, sins might be punished. St. Augustine also speculated that this middle place—distinct from Heaven and Hell—was where those, whom he described as "not wholly good" and "not wholly bad," might go when they die.[19] Nevertheless, the doctrine of Purgatory remained very much speculative and ill-defined until the 13th century. Despite the Biblical and theological foundation for Purgatory, the notion of Purgatory proved extremely difficult to support, much harder than both Heaven and Hell, which could easily be explained as absolute good and absolute evil. Distinct from these, the "middle place" of Purgatory could only be envisioned through the use of fantastical imagery—through otherworldly visions.

The maturation of Purgatory could take place, separately from theological debate, because of the literary tradition of Purgatorial *visio*, started by the sixth-century Pope, Gregory the Great, who used *exempla* to reach the imagination of the lay masses. When considering the descriptions of the otherworld, we must remember that these were not considered literary inventions at the time but, rather, were conceived of as real events by the people of the Middle Ages. These visions were seen as real out-of-body experiences, in which the visionary traveled—spiritually or bodily—to another level of existence and then returned with his or her description and scars.[20] Furthermore, since the visionary was usually drawn into Purgatory because of his own sinful nature, he, and his journey, could serve as a model for others who might share in the same sins, a so-called *exemplum*. Gregory the Great recognized the usefulness of these stories, stating that, "those who had heard of the torments of Hell but still refused to believe were to see these realms with their own eyes."[21] This soon became the official impetus behind *exempla* writing, and according to one twelfth-century writer, the impetus of Gregory's purgatorial homilies was to "improve the simple folk."[22] Consequently, these *visio* came to incorporate imagery—some gruesome—from folk beliefs and span literary genres, all of which made them even more appealing to the masses. The end result was a belief in Purgatory that rested more on imagination than on doctrine. This created a self-perpetuating cycle, in which the *visio* spurred the imagination, and imagination prompted still more visions and texts. Eventually, visionary literature became a staple in hagiographic and religious literature because it allowed for eyewitness accounts of the convoluted and ill-defined afterlife. The popular nature of the *visio* was perhaps best evidenced in the fact that they spread to virtually every genre, from poetry to chronicles.[23]

In this early period, it was in lay literature that the image of Purgatory developed, relying heavily on pre-Christian themes, especially those of a burning river and a narrow path or bridge to salvation. In addition to Gregory the Great, the earliest example of *visio* came from Gregory of Tours. In his *Decem libri historiae*, Gregory of Tours describes the very brief vision of Sunniulf, the abbot of a monastery in Puy-de Dome. Sunniulf's revelation includes "a certain river of fire, into which men...were plunged like so many bees entering a hive...[and] all were shouting out that they were being burned very severely. A bridge led over the river, so narrow that only one man could cross at a time."[24] A similar vision was later recounted by St. Boniface, who claimed that the protagonist of the *exempla* in question, Wenlock, had seen Jerusalem on the other side of the bridge, and that those who fell off bridge to be tormented in the river of fire below came out "clean and shining."[25] Many other *visio* of this time involve similar themes of a bridge, cleansing fires, and the eventual transition to paradise. Yet, curiously few writers were able to explain this place or even name it. The first writer to offer a theological explanation to go along with his *visio* was Bede. His *exempla* entailed a place very similar to that of Sunniulf and Wenlock, but Bede also inserted a cryptic explanation of the place by having his daemons exclaim, "this is not Hell as you imagine." Continuing St. Augustine's hypothesis, Bede claimed that there could exist some place for those who "because of their good works are predestined to share the fate of the elect but who, because of certain evil works, have left the body in a unclean state, [and] are taken after death by the flames of purgatorial fire and severely punished."[26] As the *visio* literature became more and more popular, and the stories replicated throughout various genres, the *exempla's* usefulness as a clerical tool began to be recognized.

In the high Middle Ages, monks and later mendicant friars expanded Purgatorial visions to be even more appealing to the masses. Indeed, by this time it seemed to have become more or less accepted that all, including those "made perfect by their goodness, go into the torment of Purgatory, and that after this suffering they enter into glory."[27] Purgatory had become open, and indeed required, for everyone who sought salvation, and the result was a renewed creativity in the writing of *visio*. Representative of the wide range in this period were *The Vision of Tundale*, the story of *The Gast of Gy*, and the enormously popular *Saint Patrick's Purgatory*.

Saint Patrick's Purgatory became the model for later *visio* and established Purgatory as a departmentalized landscape. It built on an early legend of St. Patrick finding an opening to Purgatory where penitents could enter and be purged of their sins. That this story survives in over one hundred and fifty manuscripts in Latin alone, as well as in over three hundred translations and adaptations in almost every European vernacular, attests to its remarkable popularity.[28] The original story of the Irish knight Owein's journey into Purgatory was written down in 1153, as *Tractatus de Purgatorio Sancti Patricii*, by the Monk H, who claimed to have been relaying the vision from the Cistercian monk Gilbert, who hired Owein as a guide while in Ireland. The vision elaborated on previous themes by including a detailed description of the topography of Purgatory itself. The first feature of its landscape is of a gate that required any passing through it to undergo the trial of purgation before a return was possible. The landscape itself was divided into four large fields filled with suffering. In the first field, Owein encountered a dark desert where he was whipped by a cutting wind. The subsequent fields were equally massive and desolate, each filled with new means of torture—dragons, serpents, and daemons. In the last area, Owein entered a large structure where men and women were suspended from iron hooks and dipped into vats of boiling metal. *Saint Patrick's Purgatory* also adds an element of romance to the *visio*: Owein enters Purgatory as much as an "aggressive" and "intrepid" questing knight as a penitent—his sins were never even described.[29] All these themes that became staples of Purgatorial writing.

Much of the appeal of Purgatorial *visio* lay in the use of gruesome vivid imagery, but its real strength was its flexibility, which enabled it to be merged with many different genres. A gradual shift to more hellish depictions of Purgatory accompanied its rise in popularity and new use as preaching tool. The types of torments facing sinners, as well as the horrible appearance of the daemons inhabiting the realm, became increasingly highlighted. *The Vision of Tundale*, the second most popular *visio* of the high Middle Ages, was what might be called the 'gore-fest extraordinaire' of purgatorial visions—so much so that it remains one of the few *visio* to actually be illuminated as *Les Visions du chevalier Tonda*.[30] In it, the knight Tundale must not only witness the torments of Purgatory but actually experience them himself, which makes him a surprisingly sympathetic character. Tundale also is one of the first 'witnesses' to list specific sins for each punishment; for example, sexual sins were punished by dismemberment and roasting of the offending parts, and covetous sinners were bitten repeatedly by lions, snakes, and adders. The earlier bridge motif also appears repeatedly in Tundale's *visio*. Yet, while the visions of Owein and Tundale relied heavily on the "popular taste for [the] grotesque and horrific," other genres were also incorporated in order to reach a popular audience.[31]

The story of *The Gast of Gy* is different from most other accounts of Purgatory since it is a mix between a traditional *visio* and a medieval ghost story. Curiously, *The Gast of Gy* presents a "rational and compassionate context in which Purgatory emerges as a doctrine of hope rather than horror."[32] This might be because it represents Dominican views of Purgatory, and also possibly because it was designed to present a convincing theological defense of Purgatory, still a highly suspect pseudo-doctrine. The *exempla* of the story is the Gast—ghost—of Gy, a man who is suffering in Purgatory and comes back to haunt his wife. In his description, Gy described a "Common Purgatory" where everyone suffers together[33] and which was of a contradictory nature, "occupies na stede bodily" yet, it has "rayne, and slete, haile and snaw.[34] The punishment Gy suffered was to be "taken as companion" by fiends "disfigured in horrible ways" who torment him by giving him false hope.[35] Again, the concept of a cleansing fire was asserted when Gy stated that he suffered a pain as "in flame of fire" but unlike "hellfire [which] is bodily and eternal, ... Purgatory fire has no power to destroy me ... but to pain me for my sins."[36] As the versatility of such *visio* developed, it was now in the 12th century that the doctrine of Purgatory was again taken up and developed independently and outside of literature.

The next step in the evolution of Purgatory resulted from the recognition of twelfth-century of the need to include the dead in the community of believers. Coming out of the monastic world where the *visio* literature was so prominent, St. Bernard was the first theologian to incorporate Purgatory in his sermons, stating that, "[i]t is justly said that the souls that suffer in these Purgatory places, run hither and yon in dark and dirty places, since in this life they were not afraid to inhabit these places in thought."[37] Furthermore, Bernard infused a new element into Purgatorial doctrine when he observed, "we confess not only that we sympathize with the dead and pray for them, but also that we wish them the joy of hope. "[38] This reflects the wide acceptance of the idea that the living could act as intercessors for the suffering dead through prayer. This became the Cistercian view of Purgatory, taken up again by Bernard's successor, Guerric of Igny, who asserted that only very few were "perfect enough to have accomplished the purgation."[39] In contrast, the Dominican view of purgatory was expanded by Thomas Aquinas who underlined the necessity of purgation as part of the debt owed to divine justice. Furthermore, Thomist doctrine established the correspondence between each soul's stay in purgatory and their level of moral status.[40] Yet, despite the growth of theological support, the doctrine of Purgatory remained suspect. So much was it debated, that, when the papacy did finally officially sanction it at the 1274 council of Lyon, it was only amidst much suspicion that "the belief was being swamped by vulgar and superstitious piety, to fear of an other world so close to popular folklore and to popular sensibility an other world defined more by the imagination than by theory."[41] Perhaps this fear was not unfounded, considering that Purgatorial imagery tended to go its own way rather than remain within the confines of official dogma. Indeed the doctrine of Purgatory not only led to increasing conflicts with heretical groups such as Waldensians—who refused to acknowledge the doctrine—but also became a vehicle for social criticism.[42] Into this atmosphere of half-hearted acceptance came perhaps the most popular account of Purgatory ever written, Dante's *Purgatorio*.

Dante's *Purgatorio* was the first move away from traditional *visio* literature towards a more ordered view of Purgatory, one more in keeping with the Church's views. In his depiction, Dante relied heavily on older imagery from the *visio*, but he was also influenced by both Classical sources—especially the *Aeneid*—and Church teaching. Dante's Purgatory was, logically enough, a mountain which one needed to ascend in order to pass from Hell to Heaven and expanded to include the area before the actual entrance gate, thereby creating a sort of waiting-room for those waiting to enter. In his 'ante-Purgatory,' Dante placed the excommunicated, the indolent, and the negligent rulers. Purgatory itself was divided into seven terraces—one for each of the seven deadly sins. The most interesting feature Dante added to its landscape were constant reminders of the sins for which the penitents were being punished, usually carvings in the rock wall or disembodied voices and visions. Dante was very concerned to suit the punishment to the sin; hence the proud had to grovel in the dirt, the slothful had to be in perpetual motion, the gluttonous starve, and the lustful burn in flames. The notion of a special purgatorial fire reached its apex in Dante's writing, where the poet's final ordeal before passing into heaven was to burn in a pillar of flame that does not "singe a single hair."[43] Although the landscape was slowly changing into something perhaps closer to what the

Church wanted, it was not until the great purge of popular culture and religion during the Reformation that the image of Purgatory was irreparably altered.

The Reformation greatly affected the popular conception of Purgatory, either by suppression or abstraction. The Protestant denial of Purgatory, closely following that of the earlier groups such as the Waldensians, asserted that only Heaven and Hell existed, and that they could not be visited. This resulted in a sort of censure of popular imagination in regard to the afterlife, as evidenced in *Hamlet*, when the ghost of Hamlet's father states, "But that I am forbid to tell the secrets of my prison house, I could a tale unfold whose lightest word would harrow up thy soul, freeze thy young blood, make thy two eyes like stars from their spheres ... But this eternal blazon must not be to the ears of flesh and blood."[44] In Catholicism, Purgatory did not fare much better: the imagery stagnated in this period as the clergy moved to a less material conception of it. Because the Church tightened its control over outlets of religious speculation, most visionaries either became heretics or mystics, as in the case of St. Catherine of Genoa. Catherine's *Treatise on Purgatory* explained that punishment was not a place, but a state devoid of God's love, using this analogy: "The hungry souls in Purgatory...though they do not see as much of the bread as they wish, hope to see it and fully enjoy it one day."[45] The end result was that in the newly reformed Catholic Church, Purgatory became not a place but a state where, "Church dogma specifies neither the location nor the penalties to which souls are subjected, these being matters left up to the individual opinion."[46] Following the Reformation, the fantastical imagery of Purgatory was increasingly reined in, forcing it to retreat into the recesses of popular imagination whence it had originated.

The survival, and eventual transformation, of Purgatory were possible because of the societal anxieties with which it dealt. The punishment that was enforced in Purgatory had to fit the crime, which became increasingly important in the high medieval period. Therefore, Purgatory increasingly mimicked the legal system of the time,[47] encompassing the same criteria as punishment: remorse, repetition, and personal or public penance befitting the crime. Similarly, the reward for this penance took the form of rebirth and forgiveness. The notion of rebirth was perhaps most strong in Dante's *Purgatorio*, where new souls are told, "Run to the mountain, shed that slough [referring to snake's skin] which still does not let God be manifest to you!"[48] The washing away of sins, therefore, allowed for a new beginning in a better state of existence. This became part of the Purgatory of the oppressed masses, since it was a place which did not recognize the social order of this world, but rather existed as a place where everyone underwent appropriate punishment, regardless of rank or status.[49] This was because "[t]he other world was to eliminate the injustices and inequalities of this one."[50] In this way, Purgatory crossed paths with popular Revolutionary Eschatology. As described by Norman Cohn, Revolutionary Eschatology rested on a central belief that this world was dominated by evil and that only the true "Saints of God" could overthrow this evil; "then the saints themselves, the chosen, shall in turn inherit dominion over the whole earth."[51]

In the popular imagination, this was only possible through the same kind of cleansing Purgatorial fire that burns away only sins. This preoccupation with sin was also a fundamental part of the Western culture of guilt.[52] In this way, the same impulses that gave birth to the imagery of Purgatory, a longing for redemption from sins and a second chance for salvation, created a sense of *communitas*, "the idea that souls are equal with regard to salvation ... which shows the citizens their place in the redemptive scheme."[53] Thus, Purgatory, and by extension the Apocalypse, became a vehicle of social criticism by those powerless in society. In addition, this belief maintained an inherent "potential for community and unification, often lost within a modern technological society, [which] transcends categories that separate people and instead provide[s] a shared community experience."[54] In this way, the only means by which to transform the world into a better place was through a punishing cataclysm, modeled on the belief in purgatorial fire.

The subgenre of post-Apocalyptic science fiction emerged out of the anxieties of modern society and a resultant longing for a different world. The post-Apocalyptic subgenre was born in the midst of the Romantic movement, with Mary Shelly's 1826 novel, *The Last Man*. The Romantics sought to escape post-enlightenment positivism and to create a "new dialectival spatio-temporal scheme through the sublime and imaginative transcendence.[55] As such, they idealized a blending of the past with quasi-utopian and pastoral imagery. The post-Apocalyptic world, then, represented the Romantics' dream of escaping an uncaring modern world and a return to an idealized past.[56] Soon afterwards, the discovery of X-ray and radiation by Roentgen and Becquerel enabled an "age of miraculous rays and no longer unsplittable atoms," as well as weapons of "miraculous potency."[57] These new inventions remained mythologized and misunderstood by an unenlightened public, but nevertheless the Apocalypse no longer resided in God's hands but in humankind's. In the shadow of the horrors of the 20th century, the belief in a world after the Apocalypse became increasingly popular and even normalized: the Holocaust, the atom bomb, and that "Apocalyptic fulcrum of the century," the Cold War.[58] During this time, the post-Apocalyptic scenario "came to seem less fantastic"[59] in new novels such as *Star Man's Son* (1952) and *A Canticle for Leibowitz* (1959). The advent of cinema further spurred the genre, especially in the late sixties and early seventies with movies such as *Planet of the Apes* (1968), and *Omega Man* (1971). Indeed, in the secular postmodern era, it became no longer necessary for the New Jerusalem to be a new world, but rather "a new way of understanding the old world."[60] Yet, at the same time, what made the post-Apocalyptic vision of this time different from the purely apocalyptic one was that it maintained a degree of hope, and most stories in the subgenre actually have optimistic endings.

The recurring imagery of Purgatory in post-Apocalyptic science fiction comes from its core message of hope, in the knowledge that mankind will survive and emerge, stronger, into a new paradise. The landscape of the post-Apocalypse is "the Wasteland," a landscape filled with "the decaying detritus of a mechanical civilization that had lost the means to service and maintain its machines. The machines themselves turned into raw materials ... before they are reclaimed by the natural world."[61] Just as Dante's carvings reminded the sinners of their misdoings in his Purgatory, this reflects the sins of the world purged. Hence, the landscape plays an extremely important role in post-Apocalyptic stories, combined with the constant theme of the journey through the wasteland. Just as the protagonists of the *visio* traveled through the landscape of Purgatory, so does the hero of these stories: both to provide an overview of the disaster, and also to serve as an ordeal of purgation. The motivation for this journey is usually the hope of family and community, and the goal re-establishing a new community, representative of redemption.[62] Therefore, despite being a deadly and hostile place, the wasteland is not meant to be Hell, where despair is the defining quality, but rather an adapted Purgatory, a "construction of a new mythology of moral responsibility."[63] In this Purgatory, the anxieties of the 21st century—loss of family values and a sense of community—can be redeemed.[64]

Cormac McCarthy's *The Road* relies heavily on themes from Purgatorial *visio* in order to show that man's sins can be redeemed through caring for others. The landscape of *The Road* is one of total devastation: "the country as far as they could see was burned away, the blackened shapes of rock standing out of the shoals of ash and billows of ash rising up and blowing down country through the waste."[65] Through this landscape runs the road, the one last path to salvation, which is represented by the ocean in the south. All along this road, the main characters—a man and his son—encounter "mumified dead," with their "flesh cloven along the bones, ligaments dried to tug and taut as wires. Shriveled and drawn like latter day bogfolk.[66] Sometimes, the dead are even melted into the road: "figures half mired in the black top clutching themselves, mouths howling ... where they struggled forever in the road's cold coagulate."[67] The landscape, the corpses, and the ash all serve as reminders of the sins that created this wasteland, hinted at in the father's recollection of how, when disaster struck: "the frailty of everything [was] revealed at last. Old and troubling issues resolved into nothingness and night....Within a year there were fires on the ridges and deranged chanting, the screams of the murdered. By day the impaled on spikes along the road."[68] In the face of the unspecified disaster, mankind turned on itself rather than come together. Even the father shares in this sin when he refuses to help the other survivors the pair encounter, so he too must atone for his sins in this world—only the boy remains innocent. The sins of mankind lie in the failure to care for one another and, instead, to prey on one another.

As in many post-Apocalyptic stories, the theme of cannibalism in *The Road* is a grotesque symbol of the sin of modern society in its willingness to exploit others. Food often plays an important role. In *The Road*, the protagonists are constantly starving, living off what little provisions they can salvage. This is part of their penance, since the other option—in which those unworthy of salvation engage—is cannibalism. Such distinguishes the elect and the damned, the "good guys" and the "bad guys":

Boy: 'We wouldn't ever eat anybody, would we?'
Man: 'No of course not.'
Boy: 'even if we were starving?'
Man: 'We're starving now.'
Boy: 'But we wouldn't'....Because we're the good guys. And we're carrying the fire.'[69]

The fire which the father and son "carry" is Purgatorial fire, representing their purity in never having eaten human flesh, which is what makes them worthy of salvation. The penance of the main characters is therefore to starve nearly to death in order to atone for the sin of an uncaring modern society—an ironic punishment in which the consumer becomes, literally, consumed. [70] In Purgatory, cannibalism is a common punishment performed by daemons against the sinner who is often being eaten or bitten by monsters; even Owein ran into a group of "misshapen" daemons who laughed and mocked him, before roasting him in the blaze on a spit.[71] The "bad guys" in *The Road* are thus purgatorial daemons, constantly hunting for people to consume. Their appearance betrays their nature:

> An army in tennis shoes, tramping. Carrying three-foot lengths of pipe with leather wrappings....the phalanx following carried spears or lances tassled with ribbons, the long blades hammered out of truck springs in some crude forge up country....Behind them came wagons drawn by slaves in harness and piled with goods of war and after that came the women...and lastly a supplementary consort of catamites.[72]

This depiction bears striking similarities to the vision of Walcelin, who saw "a great army...a great crowd on foot appeared carrying across their necks and shoulders animals and clothes of every kind of furnishing and household goods that raiders usually seize as plunder. But all lamented bitterly and urged each other to hurry." This crowd is also accompanied by groups of women and monks.[73] The turning point of the novel comes when the father learns compassion from his son and, for the first time, regrets mistreating a fellow penitent who stole from the pair. This is followed by the ultimate sacrifice of the father, in order to save his son, and the son's eventual salvation in joining a community of "good guys."[74]

The promise of familial love and the rebirth of community is also equated to salvation in the computer Game *Fallout 3*, the latest in a four-part franchise. Here, the player takes on the role of the main character who must venture out into the devastated wasteland of Washington D.C in search of his or her father, James. Again, the landscape of the wasteland plays an enormously important role, as much of the game is spent wandering and surviving the harsh terrain and monsters. The adventure begins in "the Vault," an underground complex inhabited by survivors and the post-apocalyptic version of Dante's ante-Purgatory: the sinners here are separated from the trials of Purgatory proper and must only wait for salvation—when the outside is safe enough for them to emerge. The gate of the Vault, too, imitates Dante's gate in the loud sound it makes when opening, echoing how "the pivots of that sacred gate fashioned of heavy metal resonant turned slow inside their sockets. The rolling roar was louder and more stubborn than Tarpeias."[75] Once out in the devastated wasteland, the player is faced with a series of quests, often involving moral dilemmas. In this way, the wasteland becomes an "identity-challenging space" where the players can discover how their ethical choices measure on a "Karma" scale.[76] These quests almost always involve either rescuing individuals or helping communities to survive, while revealing clues to James' whereabouts. After James is found, a surprise twist in the plot leads him to sacrifice himself for the ultimate goal, known as "Project Purity"—the salvation of the wasteland by removing radiation from its water.[77]

In *Fallout 3*, radiation becomes a symbol of the cleansing purgatorial fire, permeating its wasteland and rendering it similar to Owein's dark desert, a "wasteland [where t]he soil was black and the land dark [with…]a burning wind….blowing which seemed nonetheless to pierce his body with its harshness."[78] Just as food was a source of moral pollution in *The Road*, in *Fallout 3*, the food is radioactive. The Purgatorial fire of radiation is, furthermore, a corrupting and painful substance that reveals the true character of the sinners it touches. Just as the cannibalistic "bad guys" in *The Road*, the mutated monsters and raiders (most of them once ordinary people or creatures) of *Fallout 3* take on the role of daemons, while at the same time reflecting the sins of the modern world. The ever-present villains in the game, the Super-mutants, were created through the "big dip" into vats of "FEV," or Forced Evolution Virus, a process which echoes both the vats of molten metal of Sir Owein and the monster of Tungdale's vision who "devours souls in its fiery gullet, digests them, and then vomits them up."[79] However, in the end the true role of radiation is as a means of purgation. The main character must enter it one last time—and consequently die—in order to wash away the last of the player's sins and allow him to sacrifice himself in order to complete "Project Purity."

The ultimate success of the post-Apocalyptic genre lies in its ability to place its audience in the role of an intercessor and force them to recognize their own sinful nature. The medieval concept and imagery of Purgatory are thus reborn, resting on the belief of the world's rebirth through the purgation of the old one. The point of post-Apocalypticism is not to warn against what might happen, but rather to illustrate "what we are doing to ourselves," because *we* caused the Apocalypse.[80] The medium through which this is conveyed might have changed—from out-of-body visions to popular fiction— but the anxiety over the same anti-communal sins has not. This is because the essential western culture of fear persists into the 20th century, where we have "reentered this 'country of fear,' and following a classic process of 'projection,' we never weary of evoking it in both words and images."[81] Through seeing the modern characters struggle and suffer our own worst nightmares in such stories as *the Road*, we are ourselves reminded of our own sins and partake of their sacrifice—in the case of *Fallout 3*, the player actually becomes the character and thereby shares even more in the Purgatorial trials and tribulations. In this way, this modern subgenre places its audience in the same role of intercessor as in the medieval *visio*, by making us hope and pray for the salvation of the seemingly damned. In so doing, the modern doctrine of Purgatory, found in post-Apocalyptic science fiction, represents a means by which the population of a modern society can envision an release from the constraints and anxieties of this world, as they are given the possibility of a new beginning, just as their medieval forbears had envisioned before them.

SAN FRANCISCO STATE UNIVERSITY

NOTES

1   Quoted in, Jaques le Goff, *The Birth of Purgatory*, trans. Arthur Goldhammer,(Chicago: University of Chicago Press, 1984) 139.
2   Ottawa Citizen, aug 27, 1985, b10, Quoted in Dominic Manganiello, History as Judgement and Promise in 'A Canticle for Leibowitz'" in *Science Fiction Studies*, (Vol 13, No.2, Jul., 1986) 165.
3   John Varley, "The Manhattan Phone Book," in *Bangs and Whimpers: Stories about the end of the world*. Ed. James Frenkel, (Lincolnwood, Ill. : Lowell House, c1999) 181-2.
4   Peter Nicholls ed, "Holocaust and after," in *Science Fiction Encyclopedia*, (N.Y. : Doubleday, 1979) 581.
5   Edward Foster Ed., "Introduction" in *Three Purgatory Poems*,(Kalamazoo : Medieval Institute Publications, 2004) 10.
6   This follows the argument about medievalisms proposed by Angela Weisl. Angela Jane Weisl, *The Persistence of Medievalism: narrative adventures in contemporary fiction*, (New York : Palgrave Macmillan, 2003) 12
7   Cf. Jean Delumeau "Sin and Fear: the Emergence of a Western Guilt Culture in the 13th-18th Centuries," Trans. Eric Nicholson, NY: St. Martin's, 1990.
8   Dominic Manganiello, History as Judgement and Promise in 'A Canticle for Leibowitz'" in *Science Fiction Studies*, (Vol 13, No.2, Jul., 1986)
9   Cf, Walter. M, Miller, "Introduction," in *Bangs and Whimpers: Stories about the end of the world*. Ed. James Frenkel, (Lincolnwood, Ill. : Lowell House, c1999)
10   Brian Stableford "Man-made catastrophes" in *The End of the World*, Eric S. Rabkin, Martin H. Greenberg, Joseph D. Olander ed. (Carbondale : Southern Illinois University Press, c1983)
11   Angela Weisl, *The persistence of Medievalism: narrative adventures in contemporary culture*. (New York : Palgrave Macmillan, 2003)
12   Jaques le Goff, *The Birth of Purgatory*, transl. Arthur Goldhammer,(Chicago: University of Chicago Press, 1984) 360.
13   Jacques le Goff notes that this kind of fire was known to "wipe out the part period of existence and makes a new period possible." Le Goff, *The Birth of Purgatory*, 8.
14   Le Goff, *The Birth of Purgatory*, 19.
15   Vergil. *The Aeneid*, transl. Robert Fagles, (New York : Viking, 2006) VI
16   Vergil, *The Aeneid*, VI.
17   Matt. 3:11, also Luke 3:16 (NRSV).
18   1 Corinthians 3:13-15 (NRSV).

19   The "non valde bon" and "non valde mali." St. Augustine, *Enchiridion*, PL 40.265.

20   Cf. Robert Easting, "Introduction" in *Annotated bibliographies of old and middle English literature III: Visions of the other world in middle English*, (Cambridge, U.K. ; Rochester, N.Y. : D.S. Brewer, 1997)

21   St. Gregory the Great, *Dialouges*, transl. Odo John Zimmerman, (New York: Fathers of the Church inc., 1959) 4.36.

22   Marie De France, "Preface" in *Saint Patrick's Purgatory: a Poem*, transl. Michel J Curley, (Binghamton, N.Y. : Medieval & Renaissance Texts & Studies, 1993) 49. Marie later in her epilogue also states that she herself translated sir. Oweins travels so that "it might be intelligible and suited to lay folk." 171.

23   Cf Eileen Gardiner, *Medieval Visions of Heaven and Hell: a source book.* (New York : Garland Pub., 1993)

24   Gregory of Tours, *Decem libri Historiae*, transl. Lewis Thrope, (Harmondsworth: Penguin, 1974) IV.33

25   St. Boniface, *The letters of Saint Boniface*, transl. Ephraim Emerton, (New York : Columbia University Press, 2000) 25-31.

26   Quoted in Le Goff, *The birth of Purgatory*, 101.

27   Marie de France, "Preface," 55.

28   Foster "Introduction to Sir Owain" in *Three Purgatory Poems.* 112.

29   The text explicitly states this by describing Owein as "novam igitur, Miliciam aggressus miles noster, licet solus, intrepidus tamen." Quoted by Le Goff, *The Birth of Purgatory*, 195.

30   Currently at the Getty museum, and Available at http://www.getty.edu/art/gettyguide/artObjectDetails?artobj=1771

31   Foster, "Introduction to Tundale's vision," in *Three Purgatory Poems*, 188.

32   Foster, "Introduction to the Gast of Gy," in *Three Purgatory Poems*, 15.

33   *Gast of Gy*, in *Three Purgatory Poems*, 552-4

34   *Gast of Gy*, 558-9.

35   *Gast of Gy*, 600-608.

36   *Gast of Gy*, 1703, 1756-8

37   St. Bernard, *Sermon for St. Andrew's day* quoted in Le Goff, *The Birth of Purgatory*, 145.

38   Ibid, 145.

39   Guerric of Igny, *5th sermon on purgation*, quoted in Le Goff, *The Birth of Purgatory*, 139

40   Le Goff, *The Birth of Purgatory*, 269.

41   Le Goff, *The Birth of Purgatory*, 240.

42   Curiously, The Waldensians, and other similar heretical groups, claimed instead that purgation of sins must take place in this world, before death and judgment. Le Goff, *The Birth of Purgatory*, 331

43   Dante, *Purgatorio*, transl. Jean and Robert Hollander, (New York : Anchor Books, 2004) Canto XXVII, 27.

44   William Shakespeare, *Hamlet*, Burton Raffel, ed. (New Haven : Yale University Press, 2003) I.5.13-22.

45   St. Catherine of Genoa,"Treatise of Purgatory," in Purgation *and Purgatory: the spiritual dialogue*, transl. Sege Hughes, (New York ; Ramsey, N.J. : Paulist Press, 1979) 76.

46   Le Goff, *The Birth of Purgatory*, 13. Also Delumeau points out that the sufferings of purgatory became increasingly described as "unimaginable." Delumeau, *Sin and Fear*, 392.
47   Le Goff, in fact, argues that Purgatory *could not* exist before the creation of a structured, feudalistic, society and the subsequent projection of that society onto Purgatory. *The Birth of Purgatory*, 215.
48   Dante, *Purgatorio*, Canto II 122-3.
49   Purgatorial visio were known for including famous names, again especially Dante was a master at this.
50   Le Goff, *The Birth of Purgatory*, 21.
51   Norman Cohn, *The Pursuit of the Millenium: Revolutionary Millenarians and Mystical Anarchits of the Middle Ages*. Fairlawn: Essential Books, 1957) 21.
52   Cf Delumeau, *Sin and Fear*.
53   Weisl, *The Persistence of Medievalism*, 119-20.
54   Weisl, *The Persistence of Medievalism*, 18.
55   Elizabeth Fay, *Romantic Medievalism: History and Romantic literary ideal*, New York: Palgrave, 2002, 11.
56   Fay, *Romantic medievalism*. 168.
57   Brian Stableford, "Man-made catastrophes," 107.
58   Kirsten Moana Thompson, *Apocalyptic Dread: American film at the turn of the millennium*, (Albany : State University of New York Press, c2007) 7.
59   Nicholls,"The Holocaust and after," 582.
60   Elizabeth Rosen, *Apocalyptic Transformation: Apocalypse and the Postmodern imagination*. Lanham : Lexington Books, 2008. Xii
61   Gary Wolf, "The Remaking of Zero," in *The End of the World*. 2-3.
62   Wolf, "The Remaking of Zero," 10.
63   Stableford, "Man-made catastrophes," 103.
64   Cf. Thompson, *Apocalyptic Dread*.
65   Cormac McCarthy, *The Road*, (New York : Vintage Books, 2006) 14.
66   McCarthy, *The Road*, 24.
67   McCarthy, *The Road*, 190-1.
68   McCarthy, *The Road*, 33.
69   McCarthy, *The Road*, 128-9.
70   A similar theme is also present in George A. Romero's zombie horror movies, Cf. Linnie Blake ed., "Consumed Out of the Good Land" in *The Wounds of Nations: Horror cinema, historical trauma, and national identity*, (New York : Palgrave, 2008)
71   "Sir Owein," in *Medieval Popular Religion: 1000-1500, a Reader*, John Shinners ed.,(Peterborough: Broadview Press, 1997) 521
72   McCarthy, *The Road*, The Road, 92.
73   "Walcelin's vision of Purgatory," in *Medieval Popular Religion: 1000-1500, a Reader*, 247-48.
74   Macarthur, The Road, 286.
75   Dante, Purgatorio, Canto IX, 133-36.
76   Massimo Maeietti, "Player in Fabula: ethics of interaction as semiotic negotiation," in *Computer games as a sociocultural phenomenon: games without frontier, wars without tears*, Andreas John-Sudmann and Ralf Stockman, ed. (Basingstoke [England] ; New York : Palgrave Macmillan, 2008) 100.
77   *Fallout 3*. (Bethesda Game Studio, 2008)
78   "Sir Owein" in *Medieval Popular Religion: 1000-1500, a Reader*, 521.
79   Quoted in Le Goff, *The Birth of Purgatory*, 190.

80   Stableford, "Man-made catastrophes," 133.
81   Delumeau, *Sin and fear*, 96.

WORKS CITED

Primary sources:

Dante. *Purgatorio*. Trans. Jean and Robert Hollander. New York: Anchor Books, 2004.

Fallout 3. Bethesda Game Studio, 2008.

Delumeau, Jean. *Sin and Fear: The Emergence of a Western Guilt Culture*. Trans. Eric Nicholson. New York: St. Martin's Press, 1990.

Gardiner Eileen. *Medieval Visions of Heaven and Hell: a source book*. New York: Garland, 1993.

Gregory of Tours. *Decem libri Historiae*. Trans. Lewis Thorpe. Harmondsworth: Penguin, 1974

Gregory the Great. *Dialogues.*. Trans. Odo John Zimmerman. New York: Fathers of the Church,inc., 1959.

Marie De France. *Saint Patrick's Purgatory: a Poem*. Trans. Michel J Curley. Binghamton, NY: Medieval & Renaissance Texts & Studies, 1993.

McCarthy, Cormac. *The Road*. New York: Vintage Books, 2006

St. Boniface. *The Letters of Saint Boniface*. Trans. Ephraim Emerton. New York: Columbia UP, 2000.

Shakespeare, William. *Hamlet*. Ed. Burton Raffel. New Haven: Yale UP, 2003.

Shinners, John ed. *Medieval Popular Religion: 1000-1500, a Reader*. Peterborough: Broadview, 1997. St. Catherine of Genoa. *Purgation and Purgatory: the spiritual dialogue*. Trans. Sege Hughes.   New York, Ramsey, NJ: Paulist Press, 1979.

Vergil. *The Aeneid*. Trans. Robert Fagles. New York: Viking, 2006.

Secondary sources:

Blake, Linnie. *The Wounds of Nations: Horror cinema, historical trauma, and national identity*. New York: Palgrave, 2008.

Cohn Norman. *The Pursuit of the Millennium: Revolutionary Millenarians and Mystical Anarchist of the Middle Ages*. Fairlawn, NJ: Essential Books, 1957.

Easting, Robert. *Annotated Bibliographies of Old and Middle English Literature III: Visions of   the Other World in Middle English*. Cambridge, UK; Rochester, NY: D.S. Brewer, 1997.

Foster, Edward, ed. *Three Purgatory Poems*. Kalamazoo: Medieval Institute Publications, 2004.

Frenkel, James, ed. *Bangs and Whimpers: Stories about the end of the world*. Lincolnwood, IL: Lowell House, 1999.

Goff, le Jaques. *The Birth of Purgatory*. Trans. Arthur Goldhammer. Chicago: U of Chicago P,   1984.

John-Sudmann, Andreas and Ralf Stockman, eds. *Computer Games as a Sociocultural Phenomenon: games without frontier, wars without tears*. New York: Palgrave Macmillan, 2008.

Manganiello, Dominic. "History as Judgment and Promise in 'A Canticle for Leibowitz'" in *Science Fiction Studies* 13:2 (Jul. 1986) , 159-69.

Nicholls, Peter, ed. *Science Fiction Encyclopedia*. NewYork: Doubleday, 1979.

Rabkin, Eric S., Martin H. Greenberg, Joseph D. Olander, eds. *The End of the World*. Carbondale: Southern Illinois UP, 1983.

Rosen, Elizabeth. *Apocalyptic Transformation: Apocalypse and the Postmodern Imagination.* Lanham : Lexington Books, 2008.

Thompson, Kirsten Moana. *Apocalyptic Dread: American film at the turn of the millennium.* Albany: State University of New York P, 2007.

Weisl, Angela Jane. *The Persistence of Medievalism: narrative adventures in contemporary fiction.* New York: Palgrave Macmillan, 2003.

Unburied Corpses:
The Violence of the Past in William Morris's Froissartian Poems

Gerald Nachtwey

It is difficult to say just what William Morris (1834 - 1896) is best known for. All of his biographers draw a picture of a man so energetic that he could not find sufficient outlets on which to lavish his creativity.[1] As an undergraduate at Oxford, Morris became friends with the Pre-Raphaelite artist Edward Burne-Jones, with whom he formed an informal group known as the Brotherhood that was devoted to reviving the medieval— and specifically "Gothic"—traditions of English art and architecture. The artistic and literary works produced by the Brotherhood sought to combine medievalist revivalism with social activism; many of these works were published in the group's short-lived periodical, *The Oxford and Cambridge Magazine*. All the members of the Brotherhood were influenced by the "Christian Socialist" writings of John Ruskin, but it was Morris especially who saw in Ruskin's *The Stones of Venice* a mechanism through which a distant medieval past could influence England's industrial present. Morris's medievalism informed his relationship with the elder Pre-Raphaelite artist Dante Gabriel Rossetti, but it would also lead, thirty years later, to his involvement with the English Socialist movement.[2] That connection might seem odd, given that Pre-Raphaelitism was essentially a reactionary movement in art, while socialism was politically radical, especially in the late Victorian Era. However, the connection makes sense when one considers the fact that both Ruskin and Morris blamed England's industrial economy for turning craftsmen and artisans into "workers" and the products of human ingenuity into "commodities." Beyond this attitude towards the economy, though, Morris also inherited from Ruskin—but greatly elaborated—a sense that the past would become inescapable if it remained inaccessible: as the ultimate site of the origin of society's ills, the past would haunt society's present only as long as it remained untapped for potential remedies. It was Morris's understanding of how the past could interact with the social present—his understanding that it *could* interact with that present in concrete ways—that informed many of his literary works, from the fantastic and lengthy *The Earthly Paradise*, to the politically charged *A Dream of John Ball*.

Long before debates about the historicity of literature began in universities, Morris had a clear notion that there was something inherent in the genre of medieval romance that could allow historical truths to be known directly. In speaking of her father's works, Morris's daughter May once asked, "What does romance mean? I have heard people miscalled for being romantic, but what romance means is the capacity for a true conception of history, a power of making the past part of the present."[3] To say that the past is "part of the present" can only be figurative unless it participates in a Romantic mysticism, but May Morris's comment neither makes an appeal to mysticism, nor seems troubled by the need to resort to figuration: indeed, her father's continued fascination with romance was fueled by his attempts to forge relationships between history and literature, between a material present and an imagined past.

Morris was not alone in seeking such relationships. The historian J.A. Froude, writing in the nineteenth century, described the activity of medieval scholarship as a way of giving the dead a voice: "They cannot come to us, and our imagination can but feebly penetrate them. Only among the aisles of the Cathedral, only as we gaze upon their silent figures sleeping on their tombs, some faint conceptions float before us of what these men were when alive; and perhaps in the sound of bells, that peculiar creation of the medieval age, which falls upon the ear like the echo of a vanished world."[4] Froude's comment constructs human mortality as the primary barrier to historical understanding, and he suggests that "imagination"—like May Morris's "romance"—can overcome that barrier. As recently as 1936, C.S. Lewis expressed a modified version of Froude's comment when he said of allegorical literature that, "The study of this whole tradition may seem, at first sight, to be but one more example of that itch for 'revival', that refusal to leave any corpse ungalvanized, which is among the more distressing accidents of scholarship."[5] Lewis's "distress" demonstrates how, by the early twentieth century, scholars were uncomfortable with the desire to bring the dead back to life; while this revivification remained a figurative *raison d'être* for historical research, its mystical implications were too distracting for an increasingly positivist enterprise.

However, even after scholars became regularly conscious of how their ideological predispositions shaped their methodologies, the metaphor remained. Paul de Man might as well have been answering Froude as he parsed another nineteenth-century poem that confronted the problem of reading the past, Shelley's *Triumph of Life:* "to read is to understand, to question, to know, to forget, to erase, to deface, to repeat—that is to say, the endless prosopopoeia by which the dead are made to have a face and a voice which tells the allegory of their demise and allows us to apostrophize them in our turn."[6] By the time de Man wrote those words, literary theorists were under the powerful influence of what Gabrielle Spiegel has called "the linguistic turn," the assertion that social structures, even modes of thought, cannot pre-exist our linguistic articulation of them. Spiegel has used this assertion to try to remove the metaphor of "giving the dead a voice" from medieval research, to acknowledge that because of "the mediating force of language in the representation of the past . . . there is no direct access to historical events or persons, so that all historical writing, whether medieval or modern, approaches the past via discourses of one sort or another."[7] Yet, even those "discourses" are only a more theoretically sophisticated way of talking about the sorts of diachronic relationships that are suggested by May Morris's "true conception of history."

The Romantic metaphor of making the dead speak has tenaciously persisted because it is theoretically useful. Stephen Greenblatt once compared the process of historical mediation with the discovery of the ghost in Act One of *Hamlet*. He asserted that when cast into the realm of human history, reading is less of a profound conversation between the living and the dead and more of a haunting.[8] The "haunting" of both readers and works by the legacy of violence is one way of approaching the violence found in so much of the chivalric literature of the late Middle Ages. Victorian medievalists found many exemplars of self-discipline and "refined" love in medieval romance, but they also struggled with its violence—a violence which frequently complicated nineteenth-century conceptions of a "code" of chivalry. Speaking of the role Arthurian romance played in this process, Jonathan Freedman has already observed that, "Arthurianism entered Victorian culture as many things at one and the same time: for Rossetti and the Pre-Raphaelites, it embodied an exoticism at once native and strange; for Tennyson, it provided a parable of ideal imperial order and an image of that order's decadence; for Morris, it represented a haven of intense, vital experience, and a reflection of the cruelty and violence intrinsic to the exercise of social authority."[9] It was not just the "cruelty and violence" of the Arthurian legends that informed William Morris's poetic exploration of past and present, however.

In his first full volume of poetry, *The Defense of Guenevere and Other Poems*, which was published in 1858, Morris based many of the poems on Arthurian and medieval themes, but six were based on events drawn specifically from Jean Froissart's *Chronicles*[10]. These Froissartian poems—"Sir Peter Harpdon's End," "Concerning Geffray Teste Noire," "The Eve of Crécy," "The Haystack in the Floods," "The Judgment of God," and "Sir Giles' War Song"—convey a brutality and a familiarity with violence that contradicts the idealized nostalgia credited to Victorian medievalist poetry.[11] Even though Charlotte Oberg argues that there is a correlation between the "grisly details of battle" in the Froissartian poems and Morris's later prose romances, by the time he had published *House of the Wolfings* and his Chaucerian *Earthly Paradise*, he had found ways to integrate an abstracted form of what Oberg calls the "gore" of the Froissartian poems into his main body of work.[12] While he was still focused on Froissart, however, the "gore" and dead bodies had to be buried within his poems. In a previous article, I have written about how "Sir Peter Harpdon's End" questions the way in which romance memorializes and obscures violence;[13] each of Morris's other Froissartian poems touch on that same relationship by using the imagery of dead and/or concealed corpses as a metaphor for both the violence in the narrative and the difficulty of recovering the past. "Concerning Geffray Teste Noire" has a pair of dead bodies made available for autopsy, while "Haystack in the Floods," "The Judgment of God," "Father Giles' War Song," and "The Eve of Crécy" all attempt to overlay a romance narrative over an historical one to suppress the brutal violence they report.

"Concerning Geffray Teste Noire" and the Discovery of the Past

"Concerning Geffray Teste Noire" is one of the most historically specific of the Froissartian poems, and the only one that references Froissart by name.[14] A first person, narrative poem composed of rhyming quatrains, it is told from the perspective of a "John of Castel Neuf," one of the knights sent by the duke of

Berry to force the Gascon freebooter Geffray Teste Noire from his stronghold in
the castle of Ventadour.[15] Sir John begins the poem by telling a listener named
"Alleyne" a war story about an ambush that was intended to capture Teste
Noire. This is similar to many moments during and after the *Voyage en Béarn*
section of Book Three of the *Chronicles*. In this section, Froissart received his
information on events from a procession of knight-informants. Morris presents
John of Castel Neuf as one of these informants; he even tells his listener that
he may meet Froissart, "the Canon of Chimay," while "going to Ortaise" in
the region of Béarn.[16] Through his narrator, Morris quickly demonstrates his
familiarity with Froissart and shows a concern with the mechanics of his own
narrative's transmission and reception.

From this strongly Froissartian narrative of military ambush, the poem
quickly shifts into the Victorian genre of a murder mystery, as John discovers
the skeletal remains of two people buried in the undergrowth of the forest in
which the ambush has been laid. His discovery creates a framed narrative in
the poem that greatly troubled its initial readers,[17] but it is this second narrative
which establishes numerous tensions within the poem that contribute to its
aesthetic success. There is tension in the murder mystery itself, in the autopsy
of the bones that John has found and his desire to make them tell the story
of their violent deaths. There are also parallel tensions between John's desire
to understand a past event that is removed from his dangerously immediate
present and Morris's desire to correctly render the distant, fourteenth-century
past described in his poetic narrative. Finally, there is a tripartite tension in
the purported genre of the poem, in that it strives alternatively to be chivalric
romance, Victorian murder mystery, and historical record.

Each of these tensions is embodied in the fragmentary form of the poem.
In addition to containing abrupt changes of narrative perspective, the verse
itself can be difficult owing to the tentativeness of the speaker. Mark Girouard
ascribes similar "sudden openings and awkward hesitating rhythms" in "The
Defense of Guenevere" to Morris's difficulty in assimilating medieval sexual
mores to his own period.[18] While a debased sexual desire does enter into this
poem, the narrator's tentativeness is at first brought on merely by the discovery
of the mysterious skeletons. John stutters as he and Aldorvrand, a fellow knight,
examine the bones:

> "That must have reach'd the heart, I doubt—how now,
> What say you Aldorvrand—a woman? Why?"
> Under the coif a gold wreath on the brow,
> Yea, see the hair not gone to powder lie,
>
> "Golden, no doubt, once—yea, and very small—
> This for a knight; but for a dame, my lord,
> Loose-hung bones seem shapely still, and tall,—
> Didst ever see a woman's bones, my lord?"[19]

John's dialogue with Aldorvrand embodies a dark side to what Wolfgang Iser termed the hermeneutic of discovery. If interpretation—in this instance, through autopsy—is a voyage of discovery, then it can also involve the mystery and obfuscation of becoming lost. In terms of texts, the reader might not be able to make sense of what is being read if it defies his or her expectations too much. This is exactly what happens to John, as the corpse that is most clearly the knight is not wearing armor. It takes his fellow knight Aldorvrand to point out that the other body, which is wearing the mail shirt, is in fact that of a woman. Aldorvrand's question, "Didst ever see a woman's bones, my lord?" resonates with the chivalric context of battle and ambush in which the two knights find themselves. It suggests that both men's and women's bones—the bones of victims—could be a common sight in such a setting. Indeed, the shock of the question sends the poem into yet a third nested narrative, as John answers Aldorvrand's question: "Often, God help me!"[20]

John's answer has an exclamatory hint of trauma to it because it forces him to recall his experience in another, earlier episode in Froissart's *Chronicles*: the 1358 peasant uprising known as the Jacquerie. After admitting to having seen women's bones, he descends into a reverie about the event:

> I was a simple boy, fifteen years old,
> The Jacquerie froze up the blood of men
> With their fell deeds, not fit now to be told:
>
> God help again! We enter'd Beauvais town,
> Slaying them fast, whereto I help'd, mere boy
> As I was then; we gentles cut them down,
> These burners and defilers, with great joy.
>
> Reason for that, too, in the great church there
> These fiends had lit a fire, that soon went out,
> The church at Beauvais being so great and fair—
> My father, who was by me, gave a shout
>
> Between a beast's howl and a woman's scream,
> Then, panting, chuckled to me: "John, look! look!
> Count the dames' skeletons!"[21]

I quote the passage at length to show its brutal character, which was unlike anything seen in other nineteenth-century English medievalist verse. It is tempting to see in the passage a nascent socialist critique of the oppression of the upper class; "we gentles" slaughter the popular uprising of the Jacquerie merely for burning down "the church in Beauvais."[22] Certainly the image of John's father as being halfway between "beast" and "woman" is not very sympathetic and agrees well with that reading.

However, such a reading misrepresents Froissart's original narrative, and Morris's nested narratives, by suggesting that they were unified: all of the narratives, Froissart's and Morris's alike, were fragmentary, albeit for different reasons. Froissart portrays the Jacquerie as a serious threat to the stability of the country, and not a popular uprising; Froissart's narrative was politically reactionary in a way that was difficult for Morris to integrate into his own poem. Buried within the other two narratives, the Jacquerie narrative becomes Morris's own "skeleton," his own corpse for dissection. Froissart's account of the Jacquerie is a text that Morris simply does not know what to do with, precisely because the *Chronicles'* fully valorized presentation of chivalric violence, directed against the peasantry, contradicted received Victorian notions of the duty of knights to protect the weak and innocent. Morris's confusion over the Jacquerie narrative is demonstrated by the fact that John speaks of how the knights killed the peasants "with great joy," a passage which is reminiscent of Froissart's glowing description of the count of Foix and the Captal de Buch slaughtering the Jacques "like cattle."[23]

Morris was befuddled precisely by the right to licit violence that he found in Froissart's narratives. By the mid-nineteenth century, any distinction between licit and illicit violence had greatly eroded, so that Morris's narrator could hardly justify the killings of the Jacques to his listeners. This position was far removed from Froissart, who saw the Jacquerie as an exemplary case of violence being used to uphold social order. Rather than giving Froissart (or John of Castel Neuf) the benefit of the doubt, Morris aligns the Jacquerie episode with the old bones that John discovers: he questions his own ability to interpret the record of the past, to make the dead speak. This association is repeated in John's autopsy of the bodies, a gesture that Morris links to John's status as a knight and veteran. John goes so far as to ask himself:

> How could it be? Never before that day,
> However much a soldier I might be,
> Could I look on a skeleton and say
> I care not for it, shudder not—[24]

Morris associates a callousness towards violence as a mark of heroic masculinity: his question, "How could it be?" could just as well apply to his own fascination with Froissart's *Chronicles.*

Still, John's meditation on the bones before him takes a decidedly romantic turn as he begins to imagine the skeletal lady as she must have been in life. Using the romantic convention of the wounding pain of love, John speaks to the skeletal lady, saying, "Your face must hurt me always; pray you now, / Doth it not hurt you too?"[25] By dwelling on the violence of the past and trying to romanticize it, John has descended to the level of necrophilia. This horror is brought about precisely by the intrusion of romance into the historical mediation of the narrative. Silver has observed of the skeletal lady that, "While she blends the aesthetic and the sensuous . . . hers is the burden of a desirability that can only torment her worshippers."[26] The same could be said of Morris's enthrallment with the past. Translated back to Morris's relationship with Froissart's text, the implication seems to be that the social system that lionized the violence of chivalry—including the aristocratic violence perpetrated during the Jacquerie—is itself now dead, and any modern desire for that violence is taboo. The generic tension in the poem is created when Morris conveys this message through a convention of chivalric romance—the theme of death in love.

The poem ends on a final note of indeterminacy by bringing its subject matter back to death and the transmission of stories. John implores his listener to repeat his story to Froissart so that it can be recorded, saying of the death of Teste Noire:

> John Froissart knoweth he is dead by now,
> No doubt, but knoweth not this tale just past;
> Perchance then you can tell him what I show.[27]

But the poem does not end until John returns fully to the subject of his *own* death, relating that he has since put the two skeletons he recovered into his "new castle." John of "Castel Neuf" has thus internalized the "old bones." He has memorialized them in a chapel with a funeral effigy made by "This Jacque Picard, known through many lands, / [He] Wrought cunningly; he's dead now—I am old."[28] These are the final lines of the poem. After all of the frustration and uncertainty about the ability to read the past, to make the dead speak about the violence exercised on them, the speaker reluctantly implies that nothing can overcome the force of human mortality. Morris's frustration about the ability to read the past, especially *vis-à-vis* violence, is something that no critics I have encountered have yet commented on. Indeed, Harley S. Spatt, speaking of Morris's early work, has said that it "may be seen as a series of experiments testing men's aspiration to revive the past in memory....There was nothing terribly original in this focus."[29]

"Haystack in the Floods:" The Language of the Condemned

Morris's narrative structure in "Concerning Geffray Teste Noire" was, in fact, quite original, but he was less successful in most of his other Froissartian poems. Morris was unusual in that he seemed most anxious about his ability to transmit, through his own work, Froissart's fourteenth-century attitudes towards the "reality" of violence. In spite of this, almost all of the critical literature on Morris's Froissartian poems focuses on "The Haystack in the Floods," because the relationship between the two lovers of the poem, Robert and Jehan, resembles other Victorian "courtly love" poems of the time.[30] "Haystack in the Floods" does mimic some of the sense of tragedy in Swinburne's "Tristram of Lyonesse" or Tennyson's "Passing of Arthur."[31] Certainly, similar issues of transmission and mortality inhabit the tragic end of Tennyson's *Idylls*, which, John D. Rosenberg has maintained, illustrate how "the great world of Arthurian myth came into being solely to memorialize this primal scene of loss, the loss of a once perfect fellowship in a once perfect world."[32] Rosenberg compares the repetition of themes of loss in *In Memoriam* and *Idylls of the King* to Rossetti's repetition of faces in his paintings: "at bottom elegy and idyll are, if not the same poem, variations on the same theme—Tennyson's single overriding theme—the theme of loss; or, as he phrased it to himself in early boyhood, the 'Passion of the Past.'"[33] Whether it is conjoined with the Arthurian material or opposed to it, "Haystack in the Floods," along with "The Judgment of God," continues Morris's unique theme of gruesome death combined with uncertainty and fragmentation.

"Haystack in the Floods" is set in heroic couplets and tells the story of a Gascon knight, Robert, and his lover, Jehane, who are trying to escape from French territory into Gascony. They are apprehended by "that Judas, Godmar"—who is apparently a rival for Jehane's love—just before crossing a river into Gascony. Godmar gives Jehane one hour to choose between declaring her love for him or seeing Robert killed before her eyes. Even though Jehane seems quite certain about her choice, we are told that during the hour she "fell asleep: and while she slept, / And did not dream, the minutes crept."[34] Jehane is unable to make this act of violence intelligible to herself: she cannot even dream about it. When she gives her abbreviated and ambiguous answer to Godmar, "I will not," we learn that Robert himself is in a frustrated and incomplete state: unable to weep, "He seemed to watch the rain."[35]

In a variation on trying to make contact with the dead, Jehane tries to touch her condemned lover, but only his sleeve manages to brush her "poor grey lips."[36] This gesture of frustrated intimacy is followed by another of Morris's gruesome scenes, in which the omniscient narrator moves into Jehane's perspective, describing how she

> saw him bend
> Back Robert's head; she saw him send
> The thin steel down; the blow told well,
> Right backward the knight Robert feel,
> And moan'd as dogs do, being half dead,
> Unwitting, as I deem[37]

Not only does Godmar abrogate to himself the power of executioner—a power which by the fourteenth century was already legally well-defined—but he reduces Robert to merely animal expressions, bereaving him of language itself. Silver maintains that through Godmar's sadism, "Violence replaces sexuality," although she interprets that substitution in modern terms of the power balences of sexual relations.[38] In fact, the interaction between Godmar and Robert combines violence and sexuality by recognizing them both as two different types of physical intimacy. Godmar not only gives himself power over Robert's body, but also "authorizes" himself by becoming the reader of his own unfolding story. He depicts that story not as a chronicle but as a *chanson de geste*, saying near the end of the poem, "So, Jehane, the first fitte is read!"[39] Jehane herself is rendered speechless, and the poem ends, like "Concerning Geffray Teste Noire," on a laconic note: "This was the parting that they had / Beside the haystack in the floods."[40]

Far from being an adaptation of Froissartian events to Arthurian themes, "The Haystack in the Floods" is Morris's recognition that he cannot read the violence that is present in the literature of the fourteenth century. Freedman speaks of the difficulty that both Tennyson and Morris had in trying to "appropriate the Arthurian," particularly Malory's expression of chivalric violence.[41] Morris seems to have known, at times, that he could only write about medieval violence—and especially chivalric violence—in a limited way. The self-conscious way in which he fragments his relationship with the violence of the medieval past in "Haystack in the Floods" and "Concerning Geffary Teste Noire" is part of the aesthetic success of these poems.

"The Judgment of God," "The Eve of Crécy," and "Sir Giles' War Song": Failures of History, Failures of Poetics

If Morris was keenly aware of historical distance, he also occasionally failed to embody his struggle with medieval violence in the structure of his poems. In "The Judgment of God," he attempts to wed the historical Froissartian atmosphere with a romantic Arthurian one by telling the story of Lord Roger, a French knight who, having rescued his lover from being burned at the stake, must now defend her honor in trial by combat. The poem as a whole seems to have a less certain idea about chivalric relationships than "Concerning Geffray Teste Noire" or "Haystack in the Floods." In the first stanza, Roger's father instructs him how to win the battle through guile:

> "Swerve to the left, son Roger," he said,
> "When you catch his eyes through the helmet-slit,
> Swerve to the left, then out at his head,
> And the Lord God give you joy of it!"[42]

Charlotte Oberg saw irony in these lines, saying that, "because we see that the Hainault knights are no better [than the Parisians], we are brought to conclude that questions of honor and justice are truly irrelevant in this situation."[43] Morris himself seems to invite such an ironic reading in this poem, since his knight claims to "not fear death or anything," even though he anxiously wonders aloud whether or not, even if he wins, "Is not that wrong turn'd right at last / Through all these years, and I wash'd clean?"[44] What sin needs to be "washed clean" remains uncertain, although the reader can guess that it was adultery. Indeed, this poem's ambiguities appear as idiosyncrasy and uncertainty rather than an aesthetic component of the poem's structure.[45] In having the knight simply mourn his past, Morris misses the opportunity to reflect on his own struggles with the violent "sins" found in Froissart's *Chronicles*. Likewise, the knight observes that even if he wins, the "hate" of his enemies[46] "Will grow to more than this mere grin."[47] Both the chivalric commentaries and Froissart's *Chronicles* frequently mention the role that chivalric culture played in mediating conflicts between knights so that they could not proliferate in the way Morris imagines here. Morris's unmodified interjection of the Arthurian narrative into this poem demonstrates his inability to view chivalry as such a mediating institution.

In a similar manner, "The Eve of Crécy" and "Sir Giles' War Song" try to remove any uncertainty about the speaker's stance towards the violence of the war, and come across as quite uncomplicated, and aesthetically unsatisfactory, paeans to warfare. "The Eve of Crécy" is a ballad sung by a French knight on the eve of the famous battle in honor of his lady, Margaret. Oberg observes that "The Eve of Crécy" is "deceptive in its overt simplicity," and that "its real meaning turns on the paradox by which death and dishonor come through what should have insured life by bringing fame, riches, and love."[48] In this simple irony lies its failure: Morris focuses on the courtly relationship only, ignoring the military honor that plays a much more significant role in Froissart's narratives. The irony in "Sir Giles' War-Song" is less simple, as it is about the capture of the French constable Olivier de Clisson, who figured significantly in numerous accounts of French chivalry, including Froissart's. Sir Giles' claim that the "clink of arms is good to hear" is backed up by the excitement with which he reports the capture of Clisson at the end: "I pulled him through the bars to ME, / *Sir Giles, le bon des barrières.*" In this short lyric, Morris undercuts his understanding of Sir Giles' love of battle at the beginning with the brutal abruptness of the ending. Morris struggled with his inability to recognize and reproduce an authentic representation of the violence of the past in each of his Froissartian poems, and they vary aesthetically based on the extent to which he was able to incorporate that struggle into their poetic and narrative structures.

Conclusion

A picture thus emerges of William Morris as an artist who struggled with how to depict violence: both the violence of history and the violence of his own age, which he abhorred.[49] He struggled in particular with the fact that Froissart's *Chronicles* neither apologized for nor hid their violence. Morris's complete turn from Froissart to Chaucer as his source for fourteenth-century inspiration signaled his choice of one historical narrative over another, a choice that has been widely replicated in both popular and scholarly medievalism since the nineteenth century. It is a significant refusal in that it could have been integrated into the overall ideology of Victorian medievalist nostalgia. It could have viewed the Middle Ages, and particularly *chivalry*, as the last moment before the law, of both bourgeois society and the State, refused, in the words of Benjamin, "to admit the natural ends of such individuals in all those cases in which such ends could…be usefully pursued by violence."[50] In spite of this, Morris and his contemporaries could not envision a society in which the individual—even a politically enfranchised individual—had that much access to violent means.

EASTERN KENTUCKY UNIVERSITY

NOTES

1   Early biographies of Morris include J.W. Mackail, *The Life of William Morris*, 2 vols. (London and New York: Longmans, Green & Co., 1899); E.P. Thompson, *William Morris: Romantic to Revolutionary*. More recent biographies of note include John Burdick, *William Morris: Redesigning the World* (New York: Todtri Prod. Ltd., 1997); Charlotte H. Oberg, *A Pagan Prophet: William Morris* (Charlottesville, VA: UP of Virginia, 1978).

2   Thompson, E.P. *The Communism of William Morris: A Lecture by Edward Thompson given on the 4th May 1959 in the Hall of the Art Workers' Guild, London* (London: William Morris Society, 1965), 10.

3   May Morris, *William Morris: Artist, Writer, Socialist*, vol. 1 (Oxford: Oxford UP, 1936), 148; qtd. in Jennifer Harris, "William Morris and the Middle Ages," in *William Morris and the Middle Ages: A Collection of Essays, Together with a Catalogue of Works Exhibited at the Whitworth Art Gallery, 28 September-8 December 1984* (Manchester: Manchester UP, 1984), 2.

4   Quoted in D.H. Madden *A Chapter of Medieval History: The Fathers of the Literature of Field Sport and Horses* (London: John Murray, 1924), 7.

5   C.S. Lewis, *The Allegory of Love; A Study in Medieval Tradition* (London: Oxford UP, 1936), 1.

6   Paul de Man, "Shelley Disfigured," in *Deconstruction and Criticism*, ed. Harold Bloom (New York: Seabury, Continuum, 1979), 68.

7   Gabrielle M. Spiegel, *The Past as Text: The Theory and Practice of Medieval Historiography* (Baltimore, MD: Johns Hopkins UP, 1997), 4.

8   Stephen Greenblatt, "Presidential Address 2002: 'Stay, Illusion'—On Receiving Messages from the Dead," *PMLA* 118 (2002): 417-26. 420-421.

9   Jonathan Freedman, "Ideological Battleground: Tennyson, Morris, and the Pastness of the Past," *The Passing of Arthur: New Essays in Arthurian Tradition*, ed. Christopher Baswell and William Sharpe (New York and London: Garland, 1988), 235.

10   On whether or not "Father John's War Song" qualifies as a Froissartian Poem, see Peter Faulkner, introduction to *William Morris: Early Romances in Prose and Verse* (London: J.M. Dent & Sons, 1973), xiv-xv.

11   Carole Silver, *The Romance of William Morris* (Athens, OH: Ohio UP, 1982), 33. William Stafford, "'This Once Happy Country': Nostalgia for Pre-Modern Society," *The Imagined Past: History and Nostalgia*, ed. Christopher Shaw and Malcolm Chase (Manchester and New York: Manchester UP, 1989), 33-46, 36-39; Mark Girouard, *The Return to Camelot: Chivalry and the English Gentleman* (New Haven, CT: Yale UP, 1981), 188.

12   Charlotte H. Oberg, *A Pagan Prophet: William Morris* (Charlottesville, VA: UP of Virginia, 1978), 103.

13   Gerald Nachtwey, "Froissart's *Chronicles*, Fourteenth-Century Chivalry, and the Murder of Pierre Arnaut." *Medieval Perspectives* 20 (2005): 56-78.

14   William Morris, "Concerning Geffray Teste Noire," in *Early Romances in Prose and Verse*, ed. Peter Faulkner (London: J.M. Dent & Sons, Ltd., 1973), 77. Note that the spelling of Geffray Teste Noire's name varies widely. In referring to the Morris poem I retain his spelling; in referring to Froissart's account of the man, I will use the spelling of the nineteenth-century translator Thomas Johnes, which is "Geoffry Tête-Noire."

15   The story is told in Book Two of Froissart's *Chronicles*.

16   Morris, "Geffray Teste Noire," 72.

17   Faulkner, *Early Romances in Prose and Verse*, 292.

18   Girouard, *Return to Camelot,* 180.
19   Morris, "Geffray Teste Noire," 74.
20   Ibid.
21   Ibid., 75.
22   Such a reading is suggested in Florence S. Boos, "Alternative Victorian Futures: 'Historicism,' *Past and Present* and *A Dream of John Ball,*" in *History and Community: Essays in Victorian Medievalism,* ed. Florence S. Boos (New York and London: Garland, 1992), 35.
23   Jean Froissart, *Froissart: Chronicles,* trans. and ed. Geoffrey Brereton, (London: Penguin, 1978), 154. Referred to hereafter as "Brereton."
24   Morris, "Geffray Teste Noire," 76.
25   Ibid., 76.
26   Silver, *Romance of William Morris,* 39.
27   Morris, "Geffray Teste Noire," 76.
28   Ibid., 77.
29   Hartley S. Spatt, "William Morris and the Uses of the Past," *Victorian Poetry* 13 (1975): 4.
30   John Hollow. "William Morris' 'The Haystack in the Floods'." *Victorian Poetry* 7 (1969): 353-355; Dougald B. MacEachen, "Trial by Water in William Morris' 'The Haystack in the Floods'," Victorian *Poetry* 6 (1968): 73-75; Dianne F. Sadoff, "Erotic Murders: Structural and Rhetorical Irony in William Morris' Froissart Poems." *Victorian Poetry* 13 (1975): 11-26.
31   Antony H. Harrison, "Swinburne's Tristram of Lyonesse: Visionary and Courtly Epic," in *Tristan and Isolde: A Casebook,* ed. John Tasker Grimbert (New York: Garland, 1995), 301-323; Joseph E. Riehl, "Swinburne's Doublings: Tristram of Lyonesse, The Sisters, and The Tale of Balan," *Victorian Poetry* 28.3-4 (1990): 1-17; Nicolas Tredell, "Tristram of Lyonesse: Dangerous Voyage," *Victorian Poetry* 20.2 (1982): 97-111. 1982; Freedman, "Ideological Battleground," 235-248.
32   John D. Rosenberg, "Tennyson and the Passing of Arthur," *The Passing of Arthur: New Essays in Arthurian Tradition,* ed. Christopher Baswell and William Sharpe (New York and London: Garland, 1988), 227.
33   Rosenberg, "Tennyson and the Passing of Arthur," 230.
34   William Morris, "The Haystack in the Floods," in *Early Romances of William Morris,* ed. Peter Faulkner (London: J.M. Dent & Sons, Ltd., 1973), 121.
35   Morris, "Haystack in the Floods," 121.
36   Ibid.
37   Ibid., 121-122.
38   Silver, *Romance of William Morris,* 35.
39   Morris, "Haystack in the Floods," 122.
40   Ibid.
41   Freedman, "Ideological Battleground," 238.
42   William Morris, "The Judgment of God," in *Early Romances of William Morris,* ed. Peter Faulkner (London: J.M. Dent & Sons, 1973), 91.
43   Oberg, *Pagan Prophet,* 156.
44   Morris, "Judgment of God," 92.
45   Peter Faulkner, *William Morris: Early Romances in Prose and Verse,* 294. Hollow attributes the vagueness to Morris' struggle with religious belief in John Hollow, "William Morris and the Judgment of God," *PMLA* 86.3 (1971): 447.
46
47   Morris, "Judgment of God," 93.

48   Oberg, *Pagan Prophet*, 155.
49   For Morris' attitudes about the Eastern Question Society latter in his life see: William Morris, *The Collected Letters of William Morris*, Vol. 2, ed. Norman Kelvin (New Jersey: Princeton UP, 1987), 425.
50   Benjamin, "Critique of Violence," in *Reflections: Essays, Aphorisms, Autobiographical Writings*. trans. Edmund Jephcott (New York and London: Harcourt Brace Jovanovich, 1978), 280.

Dante as Surfer Medievalism: Sandow Birk's Commedia Illustrations

Karl Fugelso

In the summer of 2001, Sandow Birk and another avid surfer, Marcus Sanders, were sharing a beer in a Long Beach bar when they decided to update the *Divine Comedy*.[1] Birk had already skimmed Dante's text and had been toying with the idea of illustrating it, but:

> Most people I'd talk to about the project[, . . .] everyone sort of knew about [the *Commedia*], but almost no one had really read it. You'd go down to Borders [bookstore] and see the five versions they have….[but] they're really not that easy to read. It was sort of [through] the frustration of slogging through them that we came up with the idea that maybe [Sanders and I could] just rewrite it ourselves.[2]

So Birk fought his way through one of those translations, began sketching contemporary urban landscapes refracted through Gustave Doré's mid-nineteenth-century engravings of the *Commedia*, and sent the drawings to Sanders, who was editor of the Surfline web site and had contributed to *Surfing* magazine.[3] Sanders then got "stoked" by these "super-cool" illustrations, blended their approach with a translation or two from Borders, and helped Birk coordinate the result with two-hundred lithographs derived from the drawings.[4] Finally, they shipped each cantica one-by-one to Trillium Press, which initially released them as limited-edition *livres d'artiste* and later sold them to Chronicle Books for a three-volume edition found in many Borders.[5]

To lend the edition authority, and perhaps to counter the lack of *gravitas* in such lines as "For God's sake, just lead me the fuck out of this depressing darkness," Chronicle recruited four established scholars to inaugurate each volume with two brief essays praising Birk and Sandow for faithfulness to the spirit of Dante and for keeping the *Commedia* relevant to early twenty-first-century American readers.[6] After a highly flattering preface by the *LA Weekly* art critic Doug Harvey, Michael F. Meister, an assistant academic vice-president and professor of religious studies at Saint Mary's College of California, introduces the first volume with a claim that Milton's famous description of hell as "darkness visible" captures "the astuteness of [Birk and Sandow's] new rendering of the *Inferno*, accompanied by extraordinary illustrations that themselves translate the darkness of Dante's Hell and make it visible to us in all its loathsome horror."[7] In the preface for *Purgatorio*—just before an introduction by Professor Meister insisting, "[t]he visual breadth of Birk's illustrations continues to breathe life into Dante's epic creation, and the lively wording of Sanders and Birk's text enables it to address us where we live"[8]—independent curator, art critic, and writer Marcia Tanner describes Birk's (and presumably Sandow's) interpretation as "a complex, provocative, multilayered work, rich with internal contradictions, profound ironies, and contemporary resonance."[9] And in the preface for *Paradiso*, just before another paean by Meister and a foreword reprinting Mary

Campbell's 1999 description of the *cantica*, the eminent Boston University *dantista* Peter Hawkins praises Birk's "extraordinarily layered" work for its irony, wit, and boldness in making the *Commedia* more accessible.[10]

Hawkins and the other promoters were then echoed by many critics, as the latter largely welcomed Birk and Sandow's work. In a review for *Art Scene*, Ray Zone hailed the *Inferno* illustrations as "an auspicious beginning" filled with "great wit in small details and, as with all of Birk's *oeuvre*, a fine and dry satire quietly evident."[11] In *Orange County Weekly*, Rebecca Schoenkopf called the *Commedia* prints "wonderful" and judged them a worthy complement to Birk's *Commedia* paintings, as the glories of the latter "enslave [our] interest."[12] In interviewing Birk for *LA Weekly* shortly before the *Inferno* was due to be published and exhibited on March 1, 2003, Robert Lloyd claims, in what appears to be a deliberate understatement, that Birk's illustrations are "good," with many "clever steals and references."[13] And, as we can read on the back cover of the *Purgatorio*, *Bookpage* found Birk and Sandow's *Inferno* "funny and deeply affecting"; *The San Francisco Chronicle* extolled it as "a triumphant cathedral that will bring new readers to Dante" and claimed that "for all its visual splendor[,] for all its deadpan wit," it "is at bottom a work of profound satiric fury"; and *The Week* called it "a triumph of nerve and wit."

In fact, although the illustrated details that preface each canto are rather simple and direct, many of the main lithographs, which appear one per canto, do indeed have cute twists on Dante's text. In the illustration for *Inferno* 1, Birk portrays a "Shell" sign with a burned-out "S". A highly appropriate "Sizzler" sign and highly inappropriate "In-n-out" sign are particularly prominent in *Inferno* 6, behind the gluttons mired in the third circle of hell. Virgil and Dante can get falafel-to-go on the near shore of the Styx in *Inferno* 7. The heretics in *Inferno* 9 boil in overheated examples of a California icon—jacuzzis. Farinata and Cavalcante protrude in *Inferno* 10 from a tomb in which they are eternally parked beneath a sign stating, "Don't even think of parking here." The Minotaur of *Inferno* 12 appears on a Greek-food stand. In *Inferno* 17, Geryon approaches a truly violent act against both nature and art—a statue of Bob's Big Boy. Virgil and Dante gaze at the false counselors of *Inferno* 20 from in front of a Subway sandwich shop. A Holiday Inn welcomes pilgrims in *Inferno* 22, as the flight of the quarreling devils is underscored by a JetBlue billboard at upper left, and as we are thanked at right for disposing of our trash properly. The coffee shop behind the thieves in *Inferno* 24 is evidently run by El Diablito. The one-legged, kneeling Sower of Discord at right in *Inferno* 29 wears a tee-shirt declaring "United We Stand." In *Inferno* 33, traitors frozen up to their neck or face appear beneath a parking sign stating "Head In Only." And so forth.

Yet, as fun as these puns may be, they are not particularly profound, and they concomitantly play into one of three main charges that Birk's early supporters seem to anticipate.[14] Amid some backhanded compliments and faint praise, the paid promoters frequently imply, and occasionally admit, that many viewers may find the lithographs shallow, imitative, and/or too irreverent. In the preface to the *Inferno*, Harvey insists that Birk's "relentless identification of our contemporary environment [. . .] with what many consider the most vivid visualization of Hell ever realized is at once subversively funny and deeply disconcerting,"[15] and he notes that Birk's "foremost connection" to the *Commedia* is through Doré's engravings.[16] In the introduction to the *Inferno*, Meister claims that the "'dialect'" of Birk and Sanders is "brassy and raw at times, but the sagacity of this edition is that the entire text is a transparency laid against the backdrop of Birk's images,"[17] and he goes on to argue that:

> This new version of the *Inferno* complements Birk's numerous illustrations
> with its own vernacular—sometimes raw and obscene, and definitely fitting
> for the streets....In avoiding the formality of some translations, they have
> produced a hellish idiom that enables the pilgrim and the reader to both
> face and make sense of what they experience at every level on their trek
> downward.[18]

In the preface to *Purgatorio*, Tanner observes that Birk and Sandow "retool Dante's extended similes, using imagery contemporary readers can relate to, and these gritty, witty analogies are among their most vivid and original passages. But they don't pretend it is a definitive text,"[19] and she claims, "Birk's desolate cityscapes and vignettes of urban detritus entirely resemble 'the appearance of the mundane world'—maybe a little too closely for comfort."[20] In the preface to *Paradiso*, Hawkins opens with the question "What Would Dante Think?"[21] and moves on to note "what distinguishe[s] Sandow Birk from [Sandro Botticelli and other eminent *Commedia* illustrators] [i]s his brash irreverence not so much for the *Inferno* itself but for the sage and serious Dante who had been constructed over the centuries"[22]; "at times the text reads like a streamlined, poor man's version of translators John Ciardi and Robert Pinsky"[23]; "Italianists and keepers of the flame are sure to be outraged"[24]; "This kind of living language can have a very short shelf life, [. . .] and therefore appear embarrassingly out of touch to next year's 'futura gente'";[25] and "the point [of reading Birk and Sandow's interpretation] should not be to focus on what the adaptation 'got wrong' about Dante, but rather to pay attention to what this new world of image and text has to reveal."[26] And in the introduction to *Paradiso*, Meister repeatedly praises Birk and Sandow for being "intrepid and venturesome" in adapting Dante's work to "the unabashed argot of a twenty-first century world."[27]

Not surprisingly, Meister and the other essayists were often echoed by the reviewers. While praising Birk's paintings of the *Inferno* as an excellent complement to his drawings, Schoenkopf winds up classifying the latter as "a little bit boring and still not as imaginative as [some of Birk's earlier work]."[28] In a *Los Angeles Times Sunday Magazine* preview of an exhibition featuring some of the drawings, Richard E. Cheverton notes that the "eagerly anticipated" show and "entirely incredible" book sprang from a "naïve" conversation in what seems like "the setup for a joke with a sagging punch line: Two surfers get together in a bar and, having nothing better to do, decide to illustrate and rewrite Dante Alighieri's The *Divine Comedy*."[29] In interviewing Birk, Lloyd claims the foundation of Birk's art is "cool—not the cool of Miles Davis, but 'cool' as a seventh-grader might say it."[30] Moreover, after noting that Birk's illustrations are "closely modeled" on Doré's, Lloyd claims Birk's "magpie/mockingbird aesthetic [. . .] can only work if the product outstrips the concept."[31]

Lloyd goes on to insist that they do, but other viewers may not agree, for Birk relies so heavily on Doré for composition, shading, and virtually all other artistic aspects of the lithographs that the latter could be seen as closer to plagiarism than to (other forms of) commentary.[32] In Birk's illustration of *Inferno* 2, for example, the location of almost every star in the sky is precisely replicated, apart from those that are eclipsed by the change in type, if not location, of shrubbery. And though Birk's foliage in this illustration is indeed more southern Californian than Doré's, the contours of the landscape here and in almost every one of Birk's other *Inferno* illustrations are largely identical to those of Doré's landscapes. In fact, it sometimes seems that, in terms of scope and scale of setting, there would be no difference between the two series of illustrations if not for Birk's adaptation of fourteen scenes to a more vertical format than that employed by Doré, for those shifts require Birk to eliminate much of Doré's peripheral material and to concomitantly give the lithographs a more intimate, less panoramic feel.

Of course, in terms of style and technique, there are many minor differences between Birk and Doré, as there are between any two artists. However, in this case those departures often seem to spring less from choice than from a limit in Birk's ability. As can be seen in the scratchy, broken lines of his terrain in the illustration for *Inferno* 2, he seems to have far less manual dexterity than did either Doré or Doré's engravers. And even in Birk's sky, where the uncommon straightness of his lines suggests he used a ruler, the thickness and space between his strokes varies widely, sometimes vanishing altogether at points that do not match the shading of Doré's sky and do not otherwise make sense relative to the perspective of Birk's sky. Nor does Birk otherwise come close at any point in his lithographs to the celebrated subtleties of Doré's shading. Even apart from the innovative system of washes employed by Doré and his printer, their engravings derive such a wide range of tonal gradations from the thickness, proximity, and direction of their lines that they make Birk's roughly six stages of shading look rather clumsy and far less illusionistic.[33]

All this is not to rule out the possibility that Birk sometimes intended a sketchy appearance for his lithographs. In fact, apart from his sky in *Inferno* 2 and in a few of the other prints, he rarely seems even to aim for Doré's renowned control of line and shading. Instead, he often leans more towards twentieth-century illustrators such as Renato Guttuso, whose *Commedia* sketches from the 1950s displace mimetic precision with expressiveness via slight abstraction, or at least via overtly careless departures from the strictest ideals of academic realism.[34] For example, the hooks at the end of some lines shading Birk's guard rail in *Inferno* 2 do not follow Doré's ideals or (other) traditional academic principles of ocular realism, but they do record the hand of an artist who is evidently working quickly to record a fleeting mental image and/or emotion. And the short, sometimes detached, sometimes artificially tangled lines of Birk's turf in *Inferno* 2 may not realistically simulate grass, but they do follow Western conventions for the sketchy suggestion of grass, and some critics may even prefer them over more detailed and precise counterparts, such as those in Doré's engraving of this canto.

However, many of Birk's sketchy lines appear amid, and sometimes contribute to, other abstractions that are so inconsistent as to imply that they are lapses rather than choices. For instance, the words on the banner wrapped around Virgil in the illustration of *Inferno* 11 do not perfectly follow the contours of his form, much less respect the wrinkles in the banner, yet those words are almost paradigms of perspectival consistency relative to the phrase "*Papo anastacio*" on the refrigerator at right.[35] The letters in these words angle down to the right, in accord with the surface on which they are supposedly painted, but they do not adhere to the recession of the refrigerator into space. Instead, they cling to the surface of the image and depart from the illusionistic setting immediately around them.

A similar lack of illusionism can be seen in some of Birk's figures. Whereas the muscles and bones of Doré's figures generally seem in location and proportion, Birk's figures often suffer from superfluous and/or misshapen lumps, dips, and grooves. For example, though the muscles of Doré's gluttons are extraordinarily defined for sinners who habitually overeat, they do not have, or wrap around, anatomically incorrect bulges such as those in the wrists and triceps of Birk's gluttons. And the faces of Birk's figures, most notably Virgil and Dante, rarely correspond to the configurations we might expect for the emotions that Birk seems to be trying to express. Perhaps owing to the speed embodied by his sketchy style, and by the fact he finished illustrating all three cantiche within four years, he does not match Doré (and many other *Commedia* artists) in the clarity and consistency for which he, and they, appear to be striving.

Perhaps the biggest questions about the merits of Birk's lithographs revolve around his iconography. His program as a whole could be seen as a shallow replacement of the protagonist's original contexts with Birk's own, but even this strategy of refracting the three realms of Dante's afterlife through twenty-first-century cities is rarely, if ever, exploited to its fullest potential. In choosing only one of the multiple scenes Doré executes for each canto, Birk almost always favors the most renowned and/or dramatic image over that, or those, offering greater commentary on the *Commedia* and sometimes even on contemporary cities. For example, in the first canto of the *Inferno*, he draws on Doré's famous scene of the Pilgrim entering the wilderness, rather than, say, Doré's less well-known, but more sublime, image of the Pilgrim confronting the lion across a vast valley that would nicely adapt to the canyons of almost any twenty-first-century city. Furthermore, Birk often adapts his pictorial model around a single theme, such as the easy substitution of fat victims of modern consumer culture for Doré's steroid gluttons, or the replacement of the fiery terrain beneath the sodomite Brunetto Latini in *Inferno* 15 with a flaming construction site. Birk fails to acknowledge the complexities of modern urban living, much less of modern American life, and, as in the illustration of the gluttons, he often does not push past the most clichéd stereotypes of that lifestyle's numerous dangers. He does not question why modern consumer-culture has such a firm grip on so many of us, why even, or particularly, the most affluent among us kill ourselves with habits that would seem more likely to spring from the ignorance and despair that accompany poverty, why we cannot seem to extirpate the roots of our (un)happiness.

This brings us back to the question with which this paper implicitly began: why bother with Birk's illustrations? Although they may not say much about the *Commedia* relative to the original contexts of its production, and though they may not enlighten us much about modern urban living, or at least not as much as Birk and some of his supporters seem to think, their very shortcomings in these areas are themselves informative. In their comparative shallowness, they reveal a great deal about the contexts in which they were produced. They are a window onto the values and abilities of an artist whom many critics treat as a leader of the West Coast art scene and who, to judge from the tremendous popularity of his work, is in touch with the tastes and values of a much larger public.[36] Moreover, as widely circulated examples of superficial medievalism that aspires to much more, they paradoxically foreground a profound issue—namely, the range of subjects that we medievalists should address. We have not yet reached the point where our conferences need to limit the number of proposals they accept, but that may not always be the case, and many of our publications, such as *Studies in Medievalism*, have already had to make choices based on criteria other than the professionalism with which papers are presented. They have had to determine whether subjects are deep enough in and of themselves to sustain the interest of our typically wide-ranging audiences, whether a topic even allows, much less invites, its author to broach issues that have relevance to anyone other than specialists in, say, a particular text or painting.

Of course, as I hope is the case with this paper, even a comparatively shallow subject may, in its very shallowness, be a worthwhile focus of discussion. But I believe that this value declines in direct proportion to the number of presentations devoted to the shallowness of their topics and quickly reaches a level where at least that aspect of those subjects no longer merits our time and attention. Beyond that point we must decide what we can cover with our limited resources, who should make such decisions, who constitutes our ideal audience, and, ultimately, where we wish our field to go.

TOWSON UNIVERSITY

NOTES

1   As noted by Richard E. Cheverton in "L.A.'s 'Inferno'," a preview of "Dante's Inferno" at the Koplin Del Rio Gallery, West Hollywood, March 1-April 5, 2003, *Los*

Angeles Times Sunday Magazine (February 16, 2003), accessed _____ at <http://articles. latimes.com/2003/feb/16/magazine/tm-birk07>.

2   As quoted in Cheverton, "L.A.'s 'Inferno'," accessed _____ at <http://articles.latimes. com/2003/feb/16/magazine/tm-birk07>.

3   Birk began each illustration with a drafting pen and 000 nib on textured film, then finished it with black pencil and, to etch white lines back into the dense surface of the film, scalpels and razor blades, according to Ray Zone in a review for *Art Scene* of the Koplin Del Rio Gallery previewed by Cheverton (see note 1, above), accessed at <http://artscenecal.com/ArticlesFile/Archive/Articles2003/Articles0303/SBirkB.html>. Note that, although many of Birk's promoters and other critics have conflated his hell with Los Angeles (as well as his purgatory with San Francisco and his paradise with New York City), Birk claimed in an interview with Robert Lloyd of *LA Weekly* shortly after the Koplin Del Rio show opened ("Sandow's Inferno: Out of L.A. and into the Fire" [March 6, 2003], accessed _____ at <http:///www.laweekly.com/2003-03-06/news/ sandow-s-inferno/>), that one of his big fears was that "people would leap to the conclusion that 'L.A. is hell,' which is just so cliché and simple. I love L.A., and I don't think L.A.'s hell at all." In that same interview, Birk said in reference to a painting that sums up in many ways his view of hell, "It's kind of a fictional view of urban America, as the setting for a further stroll through hell, [. . .] and it has downtown L.A. back here, and the Hollywood sign, and sort of these freeways, and this is the entrance to hell through the parking lot, and then this here's the World Trade Center, the ruins of it, and that's the Golden Gate Bridge. So it's mostly L.A., but it's not specifically L.A." For the background on Sanders, see Cheverton, "L.A.'s 'Inferno'," accessed _____ at <http:// articles.latimes.com/2003/feb/16/magazine/tm-birk07>.

4   For these quotes, and for information on Birk and Sandow's process, see Cheverton, "L.A.'s 'Inferno'," accessed _____ at <http://articles.latimes.com/2003/feb/16/magazine/ tm-birk07>.

5   The Trillium editions were released from 2003 to 2005 and were limited to 100 copies at $3,000.00 each. The Chronicle editions were released almost simultaneously from 2003 to 2005 in softbacks costing $22.95 per volume

6   For the quote, see line 124 in the first canto of Birk and Sandow's *Inferno*.

7   Michael F. Meister, "Introduction" to Birk and Sandow's *Inferno*, xi. For Doug Harvey's preface, "Sandow Birk's Fast-Food Inferno," see pages vi to ix of that volume.

8   Michael F. Meister, "Introduction" to Birk and Sandow's *Purgatorio*, xiii.

9   Marcia Tanner, "Preface" to Birk and Sandow's *Purgatorio*, x

10   For the quote, see Peter Hawkins' preface, "Modern Uso," in Birk and Sandow's *Paradiso*, vi. Mary Campbell's foreword, "Wrath, Order, Paradise," appears on pages xv-xxiii of that volume and was reprinted from *The Poets' Dante*, ed. Peter S. Hawkins and Rachel Jacoff (New York: Farrar, Straus & Giroux, 2001), 383-94. Michael F. Meister's introduction appears on pages xxv-xxxi of Birk and Sandow's *Paradiso*.

11   Ray Zone, "Sandow Birk," accessed _____ at <http://artscenecal.com/ArticlesFile/ Archive/Articles2003/Articles0303/SBirkB.html>.

12   Rebecca Schoenkopf, "Sandow Birk Goes to Hell," *Orange County Weekly* (February 16, 2006), accessed _____ at <http://www.ocweekly.com/component/content2/view/ sandow-birk-goes-to-hell_2006-02-16/>.

13   Lloyd, "Sandow's Inferno: Out of L.A. and into the Fire," accessed _____ at <http:/// www.laweekly.com/2003-03-06/news/sandow-s-inferno/>.

14   It should be noted that shortly after Birk and Sandow completed the *Inferno*, Birk told Lloyd in the interview for *LA Weekly* ("Sandow's Inferno: Out of L.A. and into

the Fire," accessed _____ at <http:///www.laweekly.com/2003-03-06/news/sandow-s-inferno/>), "We're really proud of it [. . .] I wouldn't be surprised if it gets blasted by some scholar who's offended, like, 'Who the fuck are these kids who think they can mess with this thing?' But we're not saying read ours *instead of*; read ours *also*. Because it's more fun. And it's easier. And it has good pictures." In "L.A.'s 'Inferno'" (accessed _____ at <http://articles.latimes.com/2003/feb/16/magazine/tm-birk07>), Birk is also reported by Cheverton to have said, "We're really, really faithful to the text—it's sort of sacred. [. . .] Even the way we mess around with it, like putting slang words in there, is probably sacrilegious to high scholars and stuff. [. . .] We weren't trying to make fun of it or anything. We were trying to be serious, yet, from our sort of naïve viewpoint, just make it more accessible." And Tanner reports in her preface to Sandow and Birk's *Purgatorio* (vii), that Birk sent her an e-mail on August 15, 2003 in which he said "We have no presumption that our version is as scholarly or poetic as existing translations, [. . .] We're not Dante scholars in any sense, and we always imagined that no one would read only our version. Rather, we want people to read Dante and *also* our version" (Birk's italics, apparently).

15 Doug Harvey, "Preface: Sandow Birk's Fast-Food Inferno," ix.
16 Doug Harvey, "Preface: Sandow Birk's Fast-Food Inferno," vi.
17 Michael F. Meister, "Introduction" to Birk and Sandow's *Inferno*, xii-xiii.
18 Michael F. Meister, "Introduction" to Birk and Sandow's *Inferno*, xiv.
19 Marcia Tanner, "Preface" to Birk and Sandow's *Purgatorio*, vii.
20 Marcia Tanner, "Preface" to Birk and Sandow's *Purgatorio*, vii.
21 Peter S. Hawkins, "'Modern Uso'," vi.
22 Peter S. Hawkins, "'Modern Uso'," vii.
23 Peter S. Hawkins, "'Modern Uso'," viii.
24 Peter S. Hawkins, "'Modern Uso'," viii.
25 Peter S. Hawkins, "'Modern Uso'," ix.
26 Peter S. Hawkins, "'Modern Uso'," xiv.
27 Michael F. Meister, "Introduction" to Sandow and Birk's *Paradiso*, xxxi.
28 Schoenkopf, "Sandow Birk Goes to Hell," accessed _____ at <http://www.ocweekly.com/component/content2/view/sandow-birk-goes-to-hell_2006-02-16/>.
29 Cheverton, "L.A.'s 'Inferno'," accessed _____ at <http://articles.latimes.com/2003/feb/16/magazine/tm-birk07>.
30 Lloyd, "Sandow's Inferno: Out of L.A. and into the Fire," accessed _____ at <http:///www.laweekly.com/2003-03-06/news/sandow-s-inferno/>.
31 Lloyd, "Sandow's Inferno: Out of L.A. and into the Fire," accessed _____ at <http:///www.laweekly.com/2003-03-06/news/sandow-s-inferno/>.
32 According to Cheverton, Birk claimed "I'd simply look at [Doré's (work)] and update it." And on pages vii-viii in the preface to Birk and Sandow's *Purgatorio*, Marcia Tanner claims that in an e-mail August 28, 2003, Birk said, "Doré's goal, and strength, to me, is that he took this dreamy poem and depicted it in concrete settings, making the 'vision' of Hell and Purgatory imaginable as real places that one could go to and walk around [. . .] Dante's poem does that too, but Doré really created the visual idea of what the place would like. Now that he's done that, I don't have to. I can spin off his 'accurate' depictions and make my own comments on the world."
33 For more on the innovative shading in Doré's engravings, see Claude Bouret, "Doré, ses gravures et ses graveurs," in *Gustave Doré, 1832-1882* (Strasbourg: Musée d'Art Moderne, Cabinet des Estampes, 1983), 207-13.
34 For a broad introduction to Guttuso's life and career, begin with Giorgio Barberis and Marzio Dall'Acqua, *Renato Guttuso (1911-1987)* (Cherasco: Edizioni Città di

Cherasco, 2001). For discussion of his *Commedia* illustrations in particular, see *Il Dante di Guttuso: Cinquantasei tavole dantesche disegnate da Renato Guttuso* (Milan: Mondadori, 1970); Giuseppe Ungaretti, *Renato Guttuso: Zeichnungen 1930-1970* (Berlin and Vienna: Propyläen-Verlag, 1970); *Guttuso e Dante: mostra patrocinata dalla Regione Abruzzo: Casa di Dante in Abruzzo Castello Gizzi, Torre de'Passeri (Pescara), settembre-ottobre, 1982* (Milan: I.D.E.A. Studio, 1982); *Renato Guttuso: disegni danteschi* (Rome: Galleria d'arte il gabbiano via della frezza, n.d.); and Karl Fugelso, "*Commedia* Images in the Neo-Gothic Age(s)," *Studies in Medievalism* 14 (2005), 175-99, esp. 182-84. For widely available reproductions of Guttuso's works, see Eugene Paul Nassar, *Illustrations to Dante's "Inferno"* (London and Toronto: Associated University Presses, 1994); and Charles H. Taylor and Patricia Finley, *Images of the Journey in Dante's "Divine Comedy"* (New Haven and London: Yale University Press, 1997).

35   Note that "Anastacio Papa," the corresponding inscription in Doré's engraving of *Inferno* 11, recedes into space with the tomb slab on which it is supposedly inscribed.

36   For evidence of Birk's stature among artists on the West Coast, particularly in Los Angeles, see, among others, Zone, Cheverton, Lloyd, and especially Schoenkopf.